P9-DMY-032
SOUTH CAROLINA

On-the-Road Histories

SOUTH CAROLINA

Kenneth Townsend

First published in 2009 by

INTERLINK BOOKS
An imprint of Interlink Publishing Group, Inc.
46 Crosby Street, Northampton, MA 01060
www.interlinkbooks.com

Library of Congress Cataloging-in-Publication Data
Townsend, Kenneth William, 1951–
South Carolina / by Kenneth Townsend.
p. cm. — (On-the-road histories)
Includes index.
ISBN-13: 978-1-56656-667-4 (pbk.)
ISBN-10: 1-56656-667-3 (pbk.)
1. South Carolina—History. 2. South Carolina—Description and travel.
3. South Carolina—History, Local. I. Title. II. Series.
F269.T68 2006
975.7—dc22
2006014577

Printed and bound in Korea

Color images were provided by www.dreamstime.com, copyrighted by the individual photographers listed, unless otherwise noted in the text. Historical, black & white images were kindly provided by the Library of Congress: www.loc.gov.

Raven Cliff Falls, located in Caesars Head State Park, South Carolina © Lyle Fink

Contents

Picturesque St. Michael's Church in Charleston, built in 1761.
Image © David Davis

Landrum
Chesnee
Campobello
Blacksburg
Clover
Gaffney
Cleveland
Inman
Boiling Springs
Cowpens
Smyrna
Slater
Travelers Rest
Wellford
York
India Hook
Greer
Spartanburg
Pacolet Mills
Sharon
Salem
Pickens
Sans Souci
Greenville
Reidville
Roebuck
McConnells
Easley
Welcome
Pauline
Jonesville
Lowrys
Walhalla
Mauldin
Norris
Lockhart
Lando
Golden Grove
Simpsonville
Woodruff
Buffalo
Union
Chester
Seneca
Clemson
Fountain Inn
West Pelzer
Enoree
Cross Anchor
Gray Court
Cornwell
Carlisle
Townville
Northlake
Anderson
Belton
Princeton
Laurens
Whitmire
Shelton
White Oak
Clinton
Gluck
Honea Path
Joanna
Winnsboro
Ware Shoals
Kinards
Starr
Waterloo
Monticello
Due West
Rion
Cross Hill
Iva
Hodges
Newberry
Pomaria
Lowndesville
Silverstreet
Prosperity
Abbeville
Greenwood
Chappells
Richtex
Chapin
Verdery
Calhoun Falls
Epworth
Irmo
Kirksey
Mount Carmel
Saluda
West Columbia
Troy
Lexington
Cayce
McCormick
Summit
Red Bank
Batesburg
Pineridge
Plum Branch
Johnston
Monetta
Gaston
Parksville
Edgefield
Pelion
Trenton
Swansea
Modoc
South Carolina
Eureka
Wagener
Meriwether
Perry
North
Graniteville
Aiken
North Augusta
Burnettown
Windsor
Springfield
Neeses
New Ellenton
Williston
Cope
Blackville
Jackson
Bamberg
Hilda
Snelling
Barnwell
Govan
Kline
Ulmer
Millett
Martin
Allendale
Fairfax
Miley
Gifford
Hampton
Estill
Scotia
Garnett
Coosawhatchie
Tillman
Hardeeville
S o u t h
★ State Capitals
County Seat
Cities 500,000+
Cities 100,000-499,999
Cities 50,000-99,999
Cities 10,000-49,999
Cities 0-9,999

arolina

Interstate Highways
U.S. Highways
State Roads
Major Rivers
Intermediate Rivers
Lakes

0 10 Miles 25 Miles 50 Miles
0 10 KM 25 KM 50 KM

Inhabitants Before European Discovery

Origins of the First Americans

Several theories attempt to explain the origin of the peoples who have become known generically as Native Americans, or American Indians. The most widely accepted theory posits that hunter-gatherer peoples of East Asia (eastern China and Russia) pursued large herds of fur-bearing animals northeast across the continent and during the Ice Age moved into present-day Alaska by way of a land bridge that has since been swallowed by the seas and is today the Bering Strait. No one is quite certain when the migration occurred; estimates place it between 20,000 and 30,000 years ago. According to the theory, once in Alaska these peoples fanned over North America, principally spreading along the Pacific Coast into southern California. Those who remained in North America then swept through the Southwest and moved eastward toward the Atlantic Ocean, then northward and ultimately west to the edge of the Great Plains. As the migration unfolded, these peoples relinquished the hunt and, between 5,000 and 8,000 years ago, established sedentary, farming villages.

Within the last 30 years, numerous anthropologists and ethnologists have suggested that America's native peoples may have also migrated directly across the Pacific and Atlantic Oceans. They propose that migrations originated in Southeast Asia, with families and entire communities moving eastward from island to island over the course of thousands of years, eventually reaching the western coast of the Americas about 10,000 years ago. Similar passages crossed the South Atlantic, perhaps from the more southerly regions of Africa, making landfall in the continents maybe 8,000 years ago.

These theories are rooted in archaeological evidence, and scholars today generally conclude that each of these migration patterns occurred simultaneously. There is, however, a third explanation for the origin of native peoples in the Americas. Many American Indians in both continents hold tightly to the cultural values and spirituality of their ancestors and are consequently termed "traditionalists." Traditionalists contend that American Indians did not migrate into the Western Hemisphere; instead, native peoples were always present on this land, placed here by the force that created all life. Stories of human origin on ancestral lands are found among all cultural groupings of native peoples, and each story places human beginnings in those lands. Most are richly detailed, some are quite simple, and often they include periods of creation followed by earthly destruction and the renewal of life.

Native American Cultures in South Carolina

The earliest evidence of human activity in present-day South Carolina dates to about 13,000BCE. These people were principally hunters of the bison that still ranged the eastern regions of North America, which suggests they were still somewhat nomadic. They supplemented their diet by gathering berries, nuts, roots, and leaves from the increasingly lush environment that was developing as the earth began a warming trend. It appears that they hunted in groups using clubs, but by 10,000BCE many apparently had crafted crude spears. Archaeologists also believe small scraping instruments were fashioned from shell and stone; in the early 1980s fossilized bones were discovered at Edisto Island, south of Charleston, that bore gashes probably caused by scraping meat from killed animals.

As the climate warmed, plant life increased, offering a wider bounty of foods to sustain native peoples. The harvesting of fish, crabs, and shrimp in rivers and along coastal waters added to the increasing supply of readily available foods. By 1000BCE, bands of native peoples adopted simple farming, and this more than anything else directly led to the founding of permanent villages in which agriculture provided the bulk of food, supplemented now by hunting and fishing. As sedentary life evolved, native peoples crafted elaborate, well-fashioned pottery, constructed sturdy houses, erected palisades around their villages for security, and adopted bows and arrows as the preferred tools for hunting and community defense.

At about the same time, newcomers entered the woodlands of what is now South Carolina—people generally identified as "Mississippians." Probably migrating from the present Midwest, they were likely attracted to the region because of its warmer climate and agricultural potential. They quickly established permanent agrarian-based villages and cultivated corn, squash, and a variety of beans. Those who already lived in the Carolinas considered the Mississippians invaders and regularly attacked the unwelcome communities. In response, Mississippians also built palisades around their villages, structures that were eventually constructed by most native communities throughout the eastern half of America as populations soared.

Scholars describe Mississippians as "mound builders." In the center of their communities stood massive earthen structures, some reaching 100 feet high and flattened on top. Mounds frequently included underground rooms, and occasionally they served as enclosed graveyards. Archaeologists believe these were primarily religious structures, with community ceremonies centered on top or inside the mound. One of the larger and presumably more powerful Mississippian villages stood on the bank of the Wateree River in present-day Kershaw County.

Debate persists regarding the extent of the indigenous population in North and South America at the time of Christopher Columbus's first voyage to the New World. Widely accepted in the late nineteenth century was a pre-Columbus hemispheric population of 10 to 15 million, of which about 850,000 were thought to live within the current boundaries of the United States. The evolution of specialized academic disciplines such as anthropology and ethnology in the early twentieth century, however, brought reassessment. Specifically, scholars realized that European fishermen and explorers carried with them to the Americas Old World diseases and epidemics that ultimately ravaged the indigenous population long before European settlement began in North and South America. For example, it is virtually uncontested by academics today that in the early seventeenth century the Native Americans of present-day Massachusetts suffered a 50 percent reduction in population due to European germs in the decade before the English built a permanent settlement there. Given this altered view, population figures for Indians of the Americas have been elevated substantially. In the late 1960s, Alvin M. Josephy, Jr., one of the foremost scholars of the Indian heritage in the Americas, estimated a total native population of 70 million in 1492, with about 5 million of those residing inside the present-day United States. Writing nearly 30 years later, historian David Stannard placed the total pre-Columbian population closer to 100 million and pointed to other scholars who were at that time revising the population figure upward toward 145 million, with 18 million of those natives living north of Mexico in 1492.

Equally uncertain is the extent of the Native American population in South Carolina as Europeans moved into the Americas. One anthropologist has suggested that at the time of first encounter with Europeans in the 1520s about 1,800 native people lived along the South Carolina coast, a region roughly 100 miles long and 80 miles wide. The general warmth of the region and abundant rainfall made that stretch of land most conducive to agriculture; the many rivers and swamps, along with the ocean nearby, offered a true bounty of fish, and forested inland sections were filled with small game. The sheer abundance of food alone would have likely permitted substantial family growth and therefore a much higher population along the coast. Walter Edgar, presently the eminent historian of South Carolina, does not directly refute the shallow population estimate of coastal natives, but he does support a statewide Indian population figure of 15,000 in the year 1600 and a range of 17,000 to 30,000 100 years earlier. The higher end of Edgar's estimate more closely matches that of renowned anthropologist James Mooney, who estimates 24,600 native inhabitants among the largest South Carolina tribes and approximately 5,000 other Indians comprising all remaining groups in 1600.

The natives of present-day South Carolina grouped themselves by language: Algonkian, Siouan, Iroquoian, and Muskogean. The Cherokee (Iroquoian) resided in the westernmost section of South Carolina and spread themselves throughout the mountainous region of Georgia, North Carolina, and Tennessee. The Catawba (Siouan) dwelled in the Carolina foothills in present-day York and Lancaster Counties, and other Siouan-speaking communities such as the Yamasee dwelt in coastal areas north of Charleston. Algonkian-speaking natives such as the Savannah lived along the river that today bears their name in central South Carolina, and the Muskogean resided in the area of Beaufort. A modern traveler should note, however, that speakers of the Siouan language were ethnically and culturally distinct from the Sioux, or Lakota, of the American West, although many coastal Siouan descendants today dress in the attire of the more popular Sioux.

By the time of first contact with Europeans, the Woodlands culture of the Carolinas was well developed. Across South Carolina, agriculture sustained Indian communities. A variety of crops were planted, harvested, and preserved for winter use. Some peoples grew tobacco, primarily for spiritual and medicinal purposes. Deer, rabbits, squirrels, turkeys, and occasionally bears added to their diet, hunting typically being the men's chore. The bow and arrow served as the principal hunting tool, although many peoples, including the Cherokee, Catawba, Yamasee, and Chicora, often hunted birds and squirrels with blowguns, weapons that were generally five feet long with small, eight-inch darts. It is important to note that Indians wasted little of the animals they killed. They fashioned deer hides and bearskins into winter clothing, bedding, and home insulation. Bones were crafted into arrowheads and arrow shafts, sometimes used as buttons on garments, and often as small tools. Deer hooves were cleaned, crushed into powder, and commonly employed as a food thickener. Some parents placed pebbles into a cleaned hoof, covered it with hide, and attached a small stick to it to create a baby rattle. Antlers were used as digging and farming implements; muscle tissue was separated into thin ribbons to be used as sewing thread; brains rubbed over deer hide softened the material for loincloths; and ribs sometimes became runners on snow sleds.

Fishing was also important. In the rivers, Indians frequently constructed corrals, or pens, in which fish were

The Catawba Nation

A Siouan language–speaking native people, the Catawba, have lived in the area of present-day York and Lancaster Counties along the border separating North and South Carolina for at least 400 years, probably migrating to the area from the Ohio River Valley. At the time of first encounter with Europeans, they identified themselves as Iyeye, or Nieye, meaning "The People." Spanish records list these Indians as Esaw, and occasionally Isaw. Since the early eighteenth century, the Iyeye Nation has operated under the name "Catawba," meaning "river people."

The Iyeye dwelled along the Catawba River, which ranges from the North Carolina mountains deep into the South Carolina midlands region. Their western boundary extended to the lands of the Cherokee, the Catawbas' historic enemy. Estimates by anthropologists James Mooney and Barry Pritzker place the total Catawba population between 5,000 and 6,000 respectively in the early seventeenth century, most likely making them one of the largest Siouan tribes east of the Mississippi River and one of the three largest Indian nations completely within what is now South Carolina. Their homes were most often circular, bark-covered huts in communities enclosed by a protective palisade, and they were principally an agrarian people, although small game and fish supplemented their diet. In the center of their villages was a common ground where spiritual or community functions were held.

Throughout much of the colonial period, the Catawba engaged in a lucrative fur trade with British exporters and, to protect their commercial interests, allied themselves with the British and Yamasee Indians in war against the Tuscarora Nation along the Carolina coast. Angered by what they perceived as an unfair alteration in their trade relationship with the British, the Catawba joined with the Yamasee in war against the English, this war ultimately destroying the Yamasee. With the end of hostilities, surviving Catawbas were forced onto a small reservation established by the South Carolina colonial government and into a dependency relationship with the British to ensure their own survival. European diseases, however, swept through the reservation and substantially reduced their total population. By 1725, the Catawba numbered only 1,400. During the American Revolution the Catawba allied themselves with patriot forces, still angered at earlier British mistreatment and hopeful that their support would net them positive gains with victory. Promises of humane treatment and favorable treaties were forgotten by the newly founded United States government and by the South Carolina state assembly as war with Great Britain ended, and many Catawbas chose to vacate their ancestral homes. Some traveled into tidewater Virginia, intermarried with Pamunkey

Indians and there enjoyed a slightly better reservation existence. A few others ventured west, taking residency in Cherokee villages. Disease, warfare, and migration from South Carolina took their toll on the Catawba people; in 1825 the United States Bureau of the Census cited a mere 118 Catawbas in South Carolina.

Beginning in the 1930s, the fragile, surviving Catawba Nation commenced efforts toward tribal regeneration, a move common among American Indians nationally and encouraged by United States Commissioner of Indian Affairs John Collier as part of his "Indian New Deal" program. The Catawba worked to recover long-lost artistic skills and renew traditional Catawba culture. In the 1980s, the revitalized Catawba Nation initiated suits in federal courts to reclaim lands lost to non-Indians over the previous three centuries, including an effort to exert tribal ownership of all lands then part of the prosperous Carowinds Amusement Park that straddled the North and South Carolina state border near Charlotte, North Carolina. Concurrently, the Catawba Indian Nation petitioned the United States Bureau of Indian Affairs for status as a federally recognized Indian nation, receiving that designation finally in 1993. Today, the tribe's 5,000 members occupy a 640-acre reservation between Rock Hill and Fort Mill, and a museum with regularly scheduled programs is open to visitors. The reservation is located off South Carolina Highway 21/5, south of Fort Mill. For information, contact the Catawba Indian Nation at P.O. Box 188, Catawba, South Carolina or phone (803) 366-4792. Additional information is available at www.catawbaindiannation.com.

Must-See Sites: Catawba Cultural Preservation Center

Situated on SC Hwy 5 between Lancaster and Rock Hill, the Catawba Cultural Preservation Center preserves the cultural heritage of the Catawba Indian Nation. The museum exhibits tribal artifacts, provides a visual history of the Catawba people, and throughout the year sponsors demonstrations and activities to educate visitors on the culture and history of the Catawba. A gift shop is on the premises. The center is located at 1536 Tom Stevens Road, Catawba, South Carolina. Call (803) 328-2427.

able to reproduce and be readily accessed when desired. Others temporarily dammed sections of streams from which they harvested fish floundering in shallow rapids. Many Indians ventured into the ocean in dugout canoes, sometimes staying at sea for days and spearing fish that passed their boats. As with small game, Native Americans used every part of the fish they caught. The meat was a source of food, bones were made into sewing needles, and the remainder served as fertilizer for crops.

South Carolina's native peoples more often than not lived in "longhouses," structures that were typically 10 feet wide and ranged from 25 to 55 feet in length. Thin tree trunks lashed together formed the house frame, and twigs and a mud plaster filled the gaps. In the warmer, coastal sections of South Carolina, mats of woven reeds were fitted over the house framing and often were raised or lowered to control airflow. Longhouses accommodated as many as twenty family members, separate rooms sectioned by hanging animal hides or handmade blankets. Smaller families required less space and, consequently, opted for smaller, circular-shaped structures. Unless the villages were situated on islands or peninsulas, they were typically encircled by palisades as defense against raids by other groups or as security against potentially dangerous animals. During summer months, those living near the coast and in relative peace with their neighbors took temporary residence along the water's edge in structures that usually had a thatched roof, no walls, and were elevated slightly off the ground for better air circulation. By the 1700s, both the Catawba and the Cherokee constructed wood-frame houses, the Cherokee covering their roofs with wooden shingles.

Individual villages in present-day South Carolina generally numbered no more than 250 residents, although summer communities on the coast might bring two or three small villages together until the cool autumn breezes returned the inhabitants to their inland communities. Most villages were organized neatly, with the housing area, herb gardens, and storage buildings all sectioned separately and surrounding a central commons used for community activities.

Marital relationships varied widely among native peoples of South Carolina, as they did throughout the eastern woodlands region. Monogamy was strictly enforced in many communities while in others polygamy was accepted. Some peoples permitted a rather high degree of sexual promiscuity before marriage, but only a few allowed a man to be promiscuous without his wife's consent following marriage. Ethnohistorian Barry Pritzker has noted that among the Cherokee, for example, men and women, both married and single, were allowed nearly unlimited sexual freedom. In sharp contrast, the Catawba punished adulterous men but seldom denounced female adultery. The Cherokee, Catawba, and most Indian nations across South Carolina permitted divorce initiated by either partner. Given that these nations were matrilineal and women owned the homes in which the family dwelled, men rejected by their wives generally returned to their mother's home. After the death of a husband, widows were encouraged to remarry quickly, preferably to the brother of her deceased husband. Still others demanded and enforced a prescribed period of mourning before another marriage was allowed.

Pritzker also notes that the Cherokee valued harmony within the home and larger community highly. Toward that end, children were treated gently and were rarely punished. Learning from one's misdeeds was expected. At most, Cherokees relied on community scorn and family ostracism to counter the most offensive behavior.

Warfare among the peoples of the Eastern Woodlands cultural region, including those in present-day South Carolina, was rather common. The Catawba, or "River People," lived in a near perpetual state of conflict with the neighboring Cherokee, the two often competing for control of the hunting territory that separated their areas of residency. On occasion, Catawba war parties traveled deep into Tennessee and Kentucky waging war against the Shawnee, and, as Pritzker notes, on several documented occasions they battled bands of Iroquois in western New York. As they most likely migrated into the South Carolina upcountry from the Ohio River Valley, forced out of that region by stronger Indian nations and lured into the South by a warmer climate, it is generally assumed that the Catawbas' long-distance raids were acts of vengeance and retribution to settle old scores.

Warfare became more frequent and intense among South Carolina's Indians in the eighteenth century, as

English merchants along the coast and neighboring tribal nations built mutually lucrative trade arrangements with one another. Throughout the seventeenth century and well into the eighteenth century, European demand for fur rose substantially as the continent's population swelled. Beaver pelts were ideal for the manufacture of broad-brimmed hats, and "small furs" such as otter and fox were used to trim gowns and outer garments. Leather was in ever-increasing demand for breeches, book covers, saddlebags, and a host of other uses. The sheer abundance of beavers, deer, and other furbearing animals across the Americas made the colonies Europe's principal supplier of fur.

South Carolina's native peoples scored lucrative fur trade arrangements with British settlers soon after the founding of Charles Town. From hunting expeditions that ranged southward into Florida and westward into Alabama, Yamasee hunters brought beaver skins and deer hides to coastal merchants, receiving in exchange an array of European manufactured goods. The Catawba in the foothill region and the Cherokee in the mountains regularly supplied furs and hides to English traders who ventured into the western territory.

English-produced metal tools proved much more durable than those made of bone, clay, stone, and wood. Hatchets, awls, chisels, knives, fishhooks, hoes, and kettles were all in demand among Native Americans. European fabrics were lighter than animal hides, faster to dry, more colorful, and easier to fashion into garments. Although the Indians' bow and arrow delivered a higher rate of fire in battle, European guns were desired for the greater internal damage musket balls caused enemy warriors, for the fear they engendered in enemy hearts, and for the status they provided their owners. Alcohol, or "water that burns," was often sought by Indians for its intoxicating effect and for the sense of invincibility it inspired. Numerous novelty items were also popular, among them mirrors and jewelry. Said one Indian hunter, "The beaver does everything perfectly well; it makes kettles, hatchets, swords, knives, bread—in short, it makes everything." The same could have been said about the deer.

The volume of deerskins passing through the port at Charles Town dwarfed the number of beaver pelts,

Must-See Sites: Fripp Island

Fripp Island was a principal hunting area of the Yamasee Indians until they were driven from South Carolina and the island was granted to English sea captain Johannes Fripp for his naval exploits against French and Spanish shipping along the southern coastline. Today, Fripp Island is a luxury resort located nineteen miles east of Beaufort and featuring nearly four miles of pristine beach, three championship golf courses, a water park, tennis courts, and a marina. The island remains a protected wildlife preserve; deer are plentiful and have grazing rights wherever they happen to be. For more information, see www.frippislandresort.com.

averaging roughly 54,000 annually between 1700 and 1715 and topping 150,000 annually for the years 1740 to 1760. The Yamasee and their Creek cousins together sent more than 80,000 skins through Charles Town in 1720 alone, and Cherokee hunters supplied more than one million deerskins in the twenty years between 1739 and 1759.

The wealth generated for Native Americans and the fundamental alteration European goods brought to their standard of living compelled hunters to range deep into the lands of traditional enemies. The Yamasee challenged the Tuscarora to the north and ventured into the midlands region of South Carolina; the Catawba and Cherokee traveled far into each other's guarded hunting areas, and smaller tribal groups often slipped into their neighbors' forests for the valued skins. Each foray risked retribution, and frequently the retaliatory raids mushroomed into full-scale war. Indeed, throughout the first half of the eighteenth century, South Carolina's native peoples from the coast to the mountains endured near perpetual war—warfare resulting from competition for trade with English merchants.

The fur trade also affected native cultural traditions and tribal structures. The Indians' preference for European

Must-See Sites: Edisto Island

For nearly 4,000 years, Edisto Indians occupied the island that today bears their name. Surrounded by the mounting tide of English settlement, the island's natives were pressured to sell their land in 1674 to one of the colony's Lords Proprietors, Lord Anthony Ashley Cooper, earl of Shaftsbury. English planters who settled on Edisto Island profited from rice, indigo, and cotton production and built beautiful estates. Several magnificent eighteenth- and nineteenth-century plantations homes are open to tourists each October. Evidence of the Edisto survives on the island, most visibly at the Spanish Mount Shell Mound, the tribe's refuse heap of clam and oyster shells, fish and animal bones, and sea shells. Edisto Island is a popular resort today, and tourists may stroll through surrounding marshes, walk along the relatively undeveloped shoreline, visit Edisto Beach State Park, which preserves the island's original natural setting, and get an up-close view of the island's local snakes and alligators at the Serpentarium. Accommodations for travelers range from a quaint campground to comfortable rental cottages. For more information, see www.edistobeach.com.

goods over those they had traditionally produced themselves compelled them to over hunt their lands and in doing so nearly deplete the deer and beaver populations across South Carolina by the early eighteenth century. As these animals' numbers declined, native peoples faced an increasingly harsh reality. Without the furs and pelts, trade with the English declined. Moreover, their traditional source of food, clothing, shelter, and tools was now gone. In consequence, communities found themselves with limited options for survival. They could migrate from South Carolina to new hunting areas elsewhere and once again be self-sufficient. A few nations chose this option, considering migration the preferred alternative to physical or cultural extinction, but this was considered a most extreme prospect.

Native peoples were spiritually tied to their lands; it was the land that defined their cultural values, their world view, their connection to their Creator, and their very identity. A second possibility was to provide the English settlers with another valued trade item—slaves. The Yamasee raided villages throughout the Lowcountry in the early eighteenth century, taking prisoners to sell to English merchants in Charles Town, who in turn sold Indian captives to planters in the Caribbean. This allowed the Yamasee to continue their profitable arrangement with the English, but it also incurred the wrath of nations throughout the region and led to a series of wars that ultimately devastated the Yamasee themselves. A third possibility for native peoples was to break free of their dependency on English goods, reassert their historic identity, and revitalize their traditional culture. In so doing, however, they made themselves vulnerable to both the encroaching English settlements and the neighboring peoples that continued their trade for guns and tools. Other, smaller nations felt compelled to abandon their independence and their identity for the security found in larger, stronger communities. The Sugaree, Esaw, Cheraw, and Pee Dee, for example, all joined with the more powerful Catawba. The South Carolina branch of the Tuscarora was so ravaged by warfare that it retreated into the coastal region of North Carolina and ultimately relocated from there to New York. Both the Yamasee and Catawba eventually waged losing wars against the English, many of the Yamasee themselves apprehended and sold into slavery and the Catawba nearly exterminated by mid-century. The only other considered option for Indians was to acculturate themselves to European norms and eventually assimilate with the new dominant culture. But this proved futile as English settlers remained unreceptive to the notion that native peoples could ever fully escape their "primitive" trappings, embrace Christianity completely, and genuinely adopt European values and customs.

European disease further complicated the Indians' continued existence in South Carolina. With the exception of coastal communities, Indians in present-day South Carolina encountered few Europeans in the 200 years following Columbus's first contact with the New World.

Indian Origin of South Carolina Place Names

Cities and Towns

Name of City or Town	*Indian Nation*	*County Location*
Awendaw	Sewee	Charleston
Cheraw	Cheraw	Chesterfield
Cherokee Falls	Cherokee	Cherokee
Congaree	Congaree	Richland
Elloree	Santee	Orangeburg
Eutaw Springs	Etiwan	Orangeburg
Eutawville	Etiwan	Orangeburg
Oswego	Iroquois (NY)	Sumter
Pocotaligo	Yamasee	Hampton
Pontiac	Ottawa (MN)	Richland
Saluda	Saluda	Saluda
Santee	Santee	Orangeburg
Santee Circle	Santee	Berkeley
Seneca	Cherokee, Seneca	Oconee
South Congaree	Congaree	Lexington
Tamassee	Cherokee	Oconee
Taxahaw	Waxhaw	Lancaster
Tokeena	Cherokee	Oconee
Wysackey	?	Lee
Yemassee	Yamasee	Beaufort

Counties

County Name	*Indian Nation*
Cherokee	Cherokee
Oconee	Oconee
Saluda	Saluda

Rivers

Name of River	*Indian Nation*	*County*
Ashepoo	Ashepoo	Colleton
Catawba	Catawba	York, Lancaster, Chesterfield
Chattooga	Cherokee	Oconee
Combahee	Combahee	Hampton, Colleton, Beaufort
Congaree	Congaree	Lexington, Richland
Coosaw	Coosa	Beaufort
Coosawatchie	Coosa	Allendale, Hampton, Jasper
Edisto	Edisto	Aiken through Charleston

Kadapau	?	Chesterfield, Darlington
Pee Dee	Pee Dee	Marlboro, Darlington, Marion, Horry, Georgetown
Salkehatchie	?	Barnwell, Allendale, Colleton, Hampton
Saluda	Saluda	Greenville, Pickens, Abbeville, Newberry, Saluda
Stono	Stono	Charleston
Tugaloo	Cherokee	Oconee
Wando	Wando	Berkeley, Charleston
Wateree	Wateree	Kershaw, Richland, Sumter
Waccamaw	Waccamaw	Horry, Georgetown

Lakes, Islands, and Bays

Name	*Indian Nation*	*County*
Lake Conestee	Cherokee	Greenville
Lake Keowee	Cherokee	Oconee, Pickens
Edisto Island	Edisto	Charleston
Kiawah Island	Kiawah	Charleston
Winyah Bay	Winyah	Georgetown

Recommended Websites

www.cherokeesofsouthcarolina.com
Useful site that traces Cherokee history and the Cherokee presence in South Carolina today.

www.catawbaindiannation.com
The home page for the federally recognized Catawba Indian Nation.

www.sciway.net/hist/Indians
Information from the South Carolina state database regarding Indian nations within the state. Indian groups may be searched individually at this site, and for each a brief history is provided along with the origin of tribal names, population figures, and cultural patterns.

www.accessgenealogy.com/native/southcarolina/index
This site is more extensive and detailed than that offered by Sciway, also including links to federal and state Indian records, census reports, biographies, myths and legends, and reservations.

www.500nations.com/South_Carolina_Tribes.asp
A collection of links to individual South Carolina Indian group headquarters, recognized and non-recognized.

Hernando de Soto's expedition in 1540 passed quickly through central South Carolina as it moved into North Carolina and westward into Tennessee before slipping south to the Gulf Coast. The Spanish, French, and English settlements that were established later that century or early in the next purposely hugged the Atlantic shore and typically isolated themselves from native communities. Inadequately led, poorly equipped, undermanned, and generally uncertain just how powerful Indians of the region might be, settlers rarely ventured inland. Unlike the permanent colonies planted in New England, the Caribbean, and Mexico, those founded on the Carolina coast in the sixteenth and seventeenth centuries generally survived for no more than a few years at best. The Europeans' brief tenure on the land and their self-imposed isolation from native communities limited the spread of disease to Indian communities.

Not only was European contact with native peoples minimal, the actual number of settlers in South Carolina remained small until the early 1700s. Only a few hundred Spaniards and Frenchmen called the Lowcountry home before the English arrival, and even the founding of Charles Town by the English in the 1680s produced a minimal European population. In contrast, flotillas of European fisherman and explorers frequently ranged the New England coast in the sixteenth century, and Puritans flooded the region and built a population of nearly 50,000 residents by 1660. Thousands of Spaniards rooted themselves in the Caribbean, and the islands' European population hit nearly 100,000 by 1600. A significant Spanish population also spread across Central and South America, ultimately spilling into the present-day US southwest. With these large populations came European disease and death to native peoples.

Not only were there fewer Europeans in what is now South Carolina before the eighteenth century, native communities were significantly smaller and certainly more dispersed than those of New England, the Gulf Coast, the Caribbean, Mexico, or Central America. Indians who contracted smallpox, typhus, or other diseases would have most likely infected only their own families and communities. Disease was unlikely to spread widely or affect large native populations.

This is not to suggest that Indians in South Carolina were unaffected by European disease. In de Soto's brief journey through South Carolina, he encountered several villages that had suffered tremendous loss of life from what he believed to be disease. Incidental trade with Spaniards at Port Royal may have introduced European germs to some Indians, a perspective argued by historians Walter Edgar and Douglas Summers Brown. Not mentioned by Edgar or Brown, however, is the likelihood of war parties that ranged tremendous distances. Catawba ventures into the Ohio Valley and upstate New York certainly brought them into contact with native communities likely touched by European diseases; Yamasee forays southward from Charleston most probably brought them into contact with infected Indians who traded with Spanish settlements, and Tuscarora advances throughout coastal North Carolina conceivably exposed them to diseases originating among English settlers at Roanoke Island and perhaps Jamestown. Disease, however, was not necessarily a European product. Writes Brown University anthropologist Shepard Krech, "America was not a disease-free paradise before Europeans landed on its shores." He cites a variety of diseases that were particularly vicious among sedentary, agriculturally based communities especially on America's mid- and southern Atlantic coast, and he points to the low protein afforded by the Indian food staple maize, which made them more susceptible to infection. Without question, he adds, European diseases proved far more virulent and devastating to Indian populations, but Native Americans nonetheless had their own deadly diseases.

Regardless of its source, scholars agree that disease rather than warfare accounted for the startling depopulation of Native Americans, although a firm estimate of the death rate remains impossible to determine across the continent or in South Carolina alone. Walter Edgar's native population estimate for the year 1500 is set conservatively at 17,000 and liberally at 30,000, a rather wide range indeed. For the year 1600, however, he seems quite secure in fixing the Indian population in South Carolina at 15,000. Depopulation over those 100 years, then, amounted to between 2,000 to 15,000 people.

Estimated Population of the Largest Indian Nations in South Carolina, 1600

(Estimates by James Mooney)

Catawba	5,000
Pee Dee	7,000
Waxhaw	5,000
Cusabo	1,200
Edisto	1,000
Santee	1,000
Wateree	1,000
Winyah	900
Waccamaw	900
Sewee	800
Congaree	800
Total	24,600

After 1700, conditions changed radically in what is now South Carolina. The European population rose substantially and rapidly. Settlers from the North Carolina coast inched south while Englishmen sailed directly from England or routed themselves into South Carolina through Barbados and other islands to the south. European trade with Indians developed quickly, with Englishmen traveling deep into interior lands in the early eighteenth century and many of them settling among Native Americans. Indeed, trade proved so profitable for Indians that they themselves encouraged expansion of the business and, in so doing, inadvertently exposed their villages more completely to European diseases. The actual death rate from infectious disease among South Carolina's Native Americans remains impossible to determine, but colonial records regularly cite widespread illness among native peoples and reference numerous Indian communities ravaged by one or more diseases, a reality also noted by traders across the region. Anthropologist Barry Pritzker claims that the Catawba

Indians of South Carolina Today

Federally Recognized Indian Nations (Location & Year of Recognition)
The Catawba Nation (Rock Hill, 1993)

State Recognized Indian Nations (Location & Year of Recognition)
Chaloklowa Chickasaw Indian People (Hemingway, 2005)
Cherokee Tribe of South Carolina (Columbia, 2005)
Pee Dee Indian Nation of Upper South Carolina (Little Rock, 2005)
Pee Dee Indian Tribe (McColl, 2005)
Santee Indian Nation (Pauline, 2006)
Waccamaw Indian People (Conway, 2005)
Wassamasaw Tribe (Moncks Corner, 2005)

Groupings Identifying Themselves as Indian Nations, Not Recognized (Location)
Beaver Creek Indian People (Salley)
Chicora Indian Tribe (Conway)
Chicora Siouan Indian People (Andrews)
Croatan Indian Tribe of Orangeburg (Cordova)
Edisto Indian Organization (Edisto Beach)
Free Cherokee (Chesnee)
Piedmont American Indian Association (Gray Court)

According to the 2000 United States Federal Census, there were 13,718 South Carolinians claiming an American Indian identity.

Nation alone suffered near extinction from smallpox by the mid-eighteenth century, its population declining from about 6,000 in 1600 to a mere 500 in 1750.

The effect of European settlement in South Carolina on native peoples proved nearly disastrous. Death, warfare, enslavement, and relocation reduced significantly the number of Indians who dwelled between the Atlantic

Must-See Sites: South Carolina Indian Affairs Commission Unity Powwow

Native American residents of the Palmetto State gather in Columbia each May to celebrate their heritage and to plan cooperative programs that serve the native population. Moreover, the powwow reminds all South Carolinians of the ethnic diversity present in the state today and throughout South Carolina's rich history. At the powwow, traditionally an all-day affair, Indians wear traditional garments, perform traditional dances, entertain observers with storytelling and music, and encourage spectators to participate in games. Exhibits on display highlight native cultures, and vendors sell Indian-made goods. For more information, contact www.southcarolinaindianaffairs.com.

Ocean and Appalachian Mountains. Surviving Native Americans found their cultural traditions and community structures compromised by British values, customs, religion, and economic pursuits. In their altered forms, some Indian communities continued to exist but did so by residing in remote, isolated stretches of wilderness not desired by the English, and later American, settlers. More often than not, they ultimately confronted the choice to relocate westward or to acculturate themselves to non-Indian norms in order to survive as a people.

A small native population remained in South Carolina throughout the nineteenth century, but in the 1930s America's federal government abruptly changed the course of its Indian policy and actually encouraged native peoples nationwide to increase their numbers and revitalize much of their traditional cultures. The Indian Reorganization Act (1934) along with a myriad federal programs championed by President Franklin D. Roosevelt collectively gave rise to the "Indian New Deal" and, by the eve of World War II, renewed tribal identity and structures. Beginning in the

1960s, Washington further permitted Indian communities to petition state and federal agencies for official recognition as nations. Although the procedure for tribal recognition is quite long and demanding, every Indian community within South Carolina has, over the last four decades, commenced the effort to secure legal tribal standing. To date, only one nation, the Catawba, has secured federal recognition, but seven others have attained state recognition. The 2000 federal census lists 13,718 American Indians in residence in South Carolina, about 1,300 of whom use principally their native Indian language.

2

Discovery and Early Settlement

Spanish and French Exploration and Settlements

By the 1520s, Spain was firmly entrenched in the Americas, with colonies stretching from the Caribbean islands well into present-day Mexico. Passion for gold and other forms of material wealth was intended to enrich the young nation and in so doing transform Spain into a superpower within Europe. Explorers, conquistadors, and settlers pushed ever farther into the newfound continents in search of the precious metal, and eventually extended the empire southward throughout most of South America and north into California and across the Great Plains. Their mission included the spread of Catholicism to the native populations, an avowed goal that wrapped their more earthly pursuits with the mantle of divine blessing. Spaniards in the Americas exploited every opportunity to expand the reach of Crown and Church.

In early summer 1520, Francisco Gordillo captained a vessel westward from Hispaniola, skirting Cuba and turning north along the Atlantic shore of present-day Florida, Georgia, and the Carolinas. In August, Gordillo's tiny ship reportedly anchored somewhere just above the Savannah River—today's Beaufort, Port Royal, St. Elena, and Hilton Head area. While some historians question the credibility of this alleged "first landing of Europeans in South Carolina," few doubt the veracity of Gordillo's arrival on the South Carolina coast some ten months later and his encounter farther north, near New York, with another Spanish explorer, Pedro de Quexos.

Like Gordillo, Quexos was scouting the North American shore, determining its length and seeking any resource that might contribute to Spain's growing wealth. In their conversations, the two captains hit upon the idea to transform their respective expeditions from exploratory missions to a slave-catching enterprise. Throughout the Caribbean, Spain enslaved Native Americans for mining operations and agricultural work. Indians there had fallen victim by the thousands to European diseases, however, causing a significant decline in available labor. Quexos and Gordillo recognized the financial windfall that awaited anyone who could supply Spain's established colonies with labor. Their plan conceived, it was now a matter of implementing their grand design.

On June 21, 1521 the two captains dropped anchor along the present-day South Carolina coast near the opening of a river they named for St. John the Baptist; soon afterward they encountered members of the Chicora Nation. The initial meeting proved quite tense, but the Spaniards' gifts and non-threatening demeanor soon allayed the Chicoras' concerns. In the next few days, the appearance of friendship induced approximately 150 Chicoras to accept Quexos and Gordillo's invitation to inspect the Spanish ships. Once on board, the Indians found themselves not entertained as promised but instead faced with Spanish arms. Now prisoners, they were transported to Hispaniola and sold into slavery. As historian Walter Edgar noted, and as many scholars concur, the combined expeditions of Quexos and Gordillo set into motion "what would become an all-too-familiar pattern of European treachery and mistreatment of the Indians in North America."

One captive took an exceptionally keen interest in the strangers who enslaved him and, over the two years that followed, adopted the culture of his captors, mastered the Spanish language, accepted Catholicism as his religion, and assumed the name Francisco Chicora. Chicora's willingness to acculturate and the speed with which he transformed himself attracted the attention of one Hispaniola sugar planter and judge, Lucas Vasquez de Ayllon. Himself desirous of accumulating greater fortune from the Americas, Ayllon in 1523 journeyed to Spain seeking a commission from King Charles V to lead a rather ambitious undertaking to the land of the Chicora Nation. Francisco Chicora sailed with Ayllon and provided the Spanish court with detailed descriptions of the land, resources, and Indian cultures along the southeastern stretch of North America. But Chicora could "play a crowd"—aware of the king's wide-eyed enthusiasm for what he was hearing, Chicora not only embellished his presentation but also concocted elaborate fantasies that held the court spellbound. Excited by the prospect of securing new sources of wealth from the Americas and more than a little intrigued by Chicora's stories, King Charles V authorized Ayllon to establish a Spanish colony of one million acres and instructed him to include priests on his expedition for the religious conversion of the native peoples.

In mid-July 1526, Ayllon's expedition sailed from Santo Domingo with six ships, between 500 and 600 settlers and missionaries, African slaves, livestock, and Francisco Chicora as interpreter. Spanish records suggest Ayllon hoped to settle the area earlier visited by Gordillo and Quexos, but apparent miscalculations and unfamiliarity with the coastline carried the settlers much farther north, presumably to the Cape Fear River at present-day Wilmington, North Carolina. While scouting the terrain, Chicora deserted the Spanish now that he was in the vicinity of his homeland. Unimpressed with the surroundings, abandoned by his interpreter, and confronted with growing restlessness among the settlers, Ayllon turned the expedition southward, passing the present-day Grand Strand, and founded the settlement San Miguel de Guadalupe near Winyah Bay in Georgetown, South Carolina.

The settlement seemed destined for failure from its founding. En route to Winyah Bay, the sea claimed one ship loaded with supplies. It was now too late in the season to plant crops. Moreover, the neighboring Chicora still seethed over Gordillo's kidnapping of villagers two years earlier and posed a very real threat to the lives of Spaniards who ventured too far from the safety of the settlement. Disease also spread among the settlers, killing many, including Ayllon himself. A power struggle ensued for command of the community, and the settlement devolved into chaos and violence. Starving and desperate for provisions as winter bore down on the coast, settlers descended on Chicora villages looking for food and clothing and willing to use force if they were not freely given. The Chicora fought fiercely, easily driving back the

Must-See Sites: Hilton Head Island

South of Charleston is Hilton Head Island, the largest sea island between New Jersey and Florida. "Discovered" in 1663 by English sea captain William Hilton, the island became home to several rice plantations in the eighteenth and early nineteenth centuries, served as part of the Confederate coastal defensive network for Charleston and Savannah during the Civil War, and in World War II was home to an observation post that searched for the German U-boats that were ravaging Allied shipping along the US coast. Development of Hilton Head Island as a resort community began in the 1950s, and today it boasts luxury accommodations, several marinas, championship golf courses, beautiful beaches, and unique shops. Located in Sea Pines Forest Preserve is an Indian shell ring, an ancient refuse heap of shells and animal bones approximately 150 feet in diameter, several feet deep, and dating back to the same era in which the Great Pyramid in Egypt was constructed. For details, see www.hiltonheadisland.org.

Hilton Head © Alexander Glagolev

Spaniards. As the new year opened, only 150 of the original 600-man expedition remained alive. Aware that the colony was lost, the survivors straggled back to Hispaniola.

Aylon's effort to establish a colony failed miserably; nonetheless, Spain persisted in its bid to locate and exploit resources north of Florida. Two more expeditions entered South Carolina over the following 40 years, one for discovery and the other for settlement. Hernando de Soto in 1540 guided 600 men overland from the Florida panhandle through central Georgia, and then meandering through the midlands of South Carolina, crossing the Savannah River, the Congeree River, and the Catawba River before venturing into present-day North Carolina and turning westward to Tennessee. In 1561 Angel de Villefane sailed from Havana under orders from Spain's King Philip II to found the colony of Santa Elena in the Port Royal Sound area of South Carolina. A hurricane swept from the Atlantic and destroyed three of Villefane's four ships as they sailed the Carolina coastline, killing more than 20 of the expedition's 100 men. Given the loss of men and supplies, Villefane scrapped plans to settle Santa Elena and turned toward Santo Domingo. Spanish activity in South Carolina had netted nothing of value for the Crown to date and little profit for expedition leaders. One would suspect, then, that Spain's interest in the area would have waned. Indeed, this might have occurred had France not threatened Spain's exclusive dominance of the American coast and the Caribbean.

France and Spain had watched one another cautiously since Columbus's first voyage to the New World in 1492. The wealth gleaned from Spanish expeditions and conquests in the Americas since the turn of the century had transformed Spain into the military powerhouse of Europe and made Spain's economy the envy of the continent—power and wealth that grew consistently under the reigns of Charles V and Philip II. Both England and France yearned for access to New World riches, but at mid-century only France was capable of testing Spain's stranglehold on American territory.

Spain's concerns about French colonial efforts in the New World were matched by Philip's fear of France becoming a Protestant neighbor. Philip viewed the rising tide of Protestant Christianity across Europe as a serious threat to what he believed was the true word of God espoused by the Catholic Church. He was determined to crush, with military force if necessary, the heretical groups growing within Spain and throughout Western Europe. From the Protestant Reformation in France emerged the Huguenots, and among them were noblemen who enjoyed enough political and popular support to threaten France's Catholic monarchy. Should France fall to the Huguenots, Philip reasoned, a nation of heretics would border his own and perhaps aggressively spread its unchristian agenda. By 1560, Philip perceived France as a dual threat—to New World resources and thus to Spain's military dominance in Europe, and to the supremacy of the Catholic religion defended by Spain. Philip soon realized his fears were well founded.

In January 1562, Gaspar Coligny, a Huguenot and admiral of the French navy, hatched a plan to construct an outpost in America. A colony in the New World, he contended, would likely net substantial wealth for France and concurrently become a home for French Huguenots. The prospect of wealth and a corresponding reduction of the Huguenot population at home convinced France's Catholic monarchy to approve the Coligny plan. Coligny assigned Jean Ribaut as commander of the expedition. Ribaut was a devout Huguenot, an experienced sea captain, and a staunch nationalist—all qualities Coligny believed essential for his plan's success.

Ribaut's two ships, crowded with 150 soldiers, departed France on February 16, 1562 and for ten weeks the tiny vessels sailed the westward currents before making landfall in northern Florida. There, in the area of modern Jacksonville, Ribaut erected a marker that issued French claim to that land and all territory northward. The expedition then sailed along the coast in search of Ayllon's Jordan River (the Cape Fear). En route, however, the French ships entered a sprawling, beautiful harbor into which several rivers emptied. The countryside was lush in vegetation and home to a magnificent array of fowl. He scribbled into his journal that the harbor and network of rivers were filled with "so many sorts of fish that you may take them without a net or a hook, as many as you want."

To Ribaut and his men, "It is one of the goodliest, best and most fruitful countries ever seen, where nothing is lacking." The area seemed so majestic, Ribaut could think of no better name to give it than Port Royal. Having sufficiently scouted the region, the expedition established its settlement, Charlesfort, at present-day Parris Island and within five days the soldiers erected a blockhouse, mounted cannon in well-protected emplacements, felled trees for construction of the fort, and dug a moat to surround the garrison.

Ribaut was convinced that Charlesfort rooted France in the New World and signaled to Spain that her days of unmolested command over American resources were at end. Hoping to expand the fledgling colony, he sailed for home in June to secure more supplies and additional settlers, leaving behind about 30 volunteers to complete construction of the fort, maintain crops, and build strong ties with Indians in the area. He arrived in France on July 20 only to discover his nation shredded by civil war between Huguenots and Catholics, a crisis in part influenced by Spain. More money and manpower for Charlesfort was not a luxury the colony's backers could now afford; the French settlement in America would receive no aid, and the men who stayed behind would be left to survive on their own until, at some undetermined time, rescue ships could sail to Port Royal.

Disillusionment, anger, and fear settled over Port Royal as it became obvious that supplies and reinforcements were not coming. The few crops harvested proved inadequate for the winter that awaited the 30 men, a dire situation made worse when the blockhouse that stored all supplies burned to the ground. Edisto Indians offered some food to their hungry French neighbors but not enough to ensure the colonists' survival. In addition, Captain de la Pierria, who was left in charge of the settlement, proved to be a severely harsh commander. His cruelty ignited rebellion and ultimately resulted in his murder. Despair, a longing for home, and the belief they had been forgotten led to the settlers to abandon the colony. The men pieced together a makeshift boat, stitched together blankets and shirts for sails, and ventured into the Atlantic hoping a ship might eventually rescue them. Only one man opted to stay behind, eighteen-year-old Guillaume Ruffin. Starvation and

Parris Island Marine Corps Recruit Depot

Alexander Parris, English aristocrat and army colonel, purchased the island that today bears his name from Carolina's Lords Proprietors in 1715. In little time he built a profitable rice plantation, and his descendents continued the family business until the Civil War. In April 1861, the Confederate States of America rushed to build a ring of defensive fortifications along the South's Atlantic coast. Anticipating this, the Union Navy swept into the Port Royal area and, under the command of Samuel F. Du Pont, seized Parris Island and from here conducted operations against the Confederacy. Following the war, the US Navy used the minimal facilities there as a southern base for the ironclad fleet and for the training of sailors, and in 1882 converted the base into a fixed defensive installation with long-range shore guns manned by the US Marine Corps. This post was meant to repel any enemy vessels that might threaten the American mainland and to defend ships entering and exiting the Intracoastal Waterway then being built along the length of the East Coast for the safe inland waterborne movement of vital war materiel. Facilities, however, remained rather simple and limited. In 1909 a Marine Officers' School was added at Parris Island, training and graduating 27 new lieutenants in December and another 16 the following year, but this program was transferred to Norfolk in 1911 and replaced with disciplinary barracks to house navy prisoners.

As the Great War in Europe raged and threatened to engulf the United States, the Department of the Navy in November 1915 designated Parris Island as a Marine Corps Recruit Depot (MCRD) to provide basic military training to Marine enlistees. When America entered the war in April 1917, 835 men were in training at Parris Island; by war's end, more than 46,200 marines had been processed through the MCRD and the post had assumed additional training responsibilities. A non-commissioned officers' school graduated 2,144 sergeants, and another 1,500 were processed through the marines' clerical, radio, signal, and cooking schools. The war also brought to Parris Island social services and activities for marines. The YMCA established a full-service operation at the training facility, and the Knights of Columbus provided a recreation center, live shows, a movie theater, sports facilities, and basic comforts to hospitalized marines and those departing Parris Island for other duty posts.

During the war years, Army Colonel and student of history John Millis was stationed in nearby Beaufort. Aware of Parris

Island's history, he scouted and discovered the remains of Charlesfort. Excavations of the post commenced immediately after the war, and in 1926 Congress appropriated $10,000 for the construction of a monument commemorating the 1562 Jean Ribaut expedition. The navy initiated numerous construction projects in the interwar period, and by 1929 a new causeway and bridge connected the island and mainland. The number of training battalions also increased; indeed, in 1938 Congress authorized a substantial rise in marine manpower, and the MCRD training program intensified in anticipation of war.

Japan's strike on Pearl Harbor in December 1941 abruptly raised training demands at Parris Island, from an average of 1,600 recruits monthly to 6,800 in the same time span. The Works Progress Administration of South Carolina committed 100 workers to Parris Island early in 1942 to build new barracks, dining facilities, and training areas. This still proved inadequate. To accommodate the rising volume of new recruits to the available facilities until WPA construction projects were completed, the Marine Corps temporarily reduced basic training to five weeks from its earlier eight-week cycle. During World War II, nearly 205,000 marine recruits trained at Parris Island.

World War II made the United States a global superpower. Since 1945, the size of the Marine Corps and, subsequently, the size of the training battalions posted at Parris Island have expanded and decreased in relative harmony with America's global obligations and endeavors. Parris Island has evolved into one of America's principal and most respected military training sites and today trains 18,000 Marines annually.

For information regarding recruit training, MCDR organization, and visitor information, see www.mcdrpi.usmc.mil or contact the Beaufort Regional Chamber of Commerce Visitor Center at (843) 986-5400.

possibly cannibalism sailed with the men until an English ship spotted survivors in the waters near the European continent and pulled them on deck. Back near Port Royal, Spanish scouting parties discovered Ruffin living with the Edisto and took the lone Frenchman prisoner.

Civil war in France continued to rage, but in 1564 Admiral Coligny once more posited the notion of founding a Huguenot colony in North America and scrapped together adequate funds from previously untapped sources. That year, 300 Frenchmen sailed west, not for Port Royal but instead to northern Florida, where they erected Fort Caroline on the St. John River. Although confronted by problems similar to those that had plagued the French effort two years earlier, the colony endured thanks to aid from England, an unlikely ally but a nation always willing to help any enemy of Spain. Still determined not to let French Protestants establish a threat to Spain in the New World, Philip II dispatched to the region Pedro Menendez de Aviles, who promptly destroyed Fort Caroline. Those Frenchmen who eluded capture and execution fled deep into the woodlands, many of them filtering north toward Port Royal.

Menendez soon heard stories that Frenchmen once more occupied the Port Royal–Santa Elena area, and in April 1566, with a force of 150 soldiers and his prisoner Guillaume Ruffin as interpreter, he moved north to Santa Elena and founded Fort San Felipe on Parris Island. Menendez sent well-armed units inland on exploratory missions throughout autumn and winter. One team of soldiers, led by Captain Juan Pardo, reached present-day Spartanburg and the base of the Appalachian Mountains. These journeys were, indeed, expeditions of discovery, but they also were intended to establish friendly relations with Indians and determine what resources might be exploited for Spain's benefit.

Santa Elena enjoyed a brief period of growth and prosperity. A pleasant climate for farming, plentiful game and fish, easy access to the sea, and the sheer beauty of the environment lured hundreds of Spaniards to the colony. Entire families emigrated to Santa Elena, mostly farmers who hoped for landholding opportunities not available in Spain and who were promised short-term farm subsidies by the Spanish government. The colony also became home to physicians, a variety of artisans, priests, and low-level government officials. A rather lucrative fur trade with local Indians generated profits for settlers, and the sale of timber to Spanish markets brought additional money to colonists' hands. By autumn 1569, Santa Elena's population stood at 325, without question the most promising Spanish effort north of Florida to date.

Despite the colony's apparent progress, turmoil soon compromised its development. Santa Elena was surrounded by land prone to flooding; consequently, farmers failed to produce an abundance of quality crops as expected. Moreover, cattle and other livestock promised by Spanish officials never arrived. Food supplies ran precariously low in 1570. To ensure his soldiers' welfare, the commander of Fort San Filipe appropriated most of the harvested crops, thereby forcing civilian settlers to rely increasingly on whatever they could pull from the harbor and nearby rivers. Malnutrition spread among the settlers, and as the food shortage worsened, the Spaniards raided nearby Indian villages for meat and vegetables. This brought swift retribution from the Indians. A tenuous détente settled over the region for the next six years, a period in which food remained critically insufficient for the settlers, a problem compounded by the lingering presence of typhus in the colony.

In June 1576, several Spanish settlers murdered three local natives for reasons that remain unclear, and, driven by hunger and disease, the Spaniards once again raided several Indian villages. The Edistos retaliated immediately, forging a temporary alliance with other Indian nations along the coast and driving all Spaniards in the region to the refuge of Fort San Filipe. Rather than endure a protracted siege waiting for military support that might not come, colonists fled the settlement for the security of Cuba. With the settlers' departure, the allied Indian nations torched the fort and launched strikes against all Spanish communities as far south as central Florida. Only St. Augustine survived.

Having destroyed so many Spanish settlements, the Indians assumed they had regained mastery over the coastal lands, and their alliance evaporated. Spanish authorities, however, were not ready to relinquish the Santa Elena area to native control. The following year, another Spanish fort was constructed within sight of Fort San Filipe, which now lay in ash. Fort San Marcos was much larger and stronger than its predecessor and was intended to become the Spanish citadel on the North American Atlantic coast. A more vibrant town arose around the fortification, attracting hundreds of new settlers. The community established closer ties to Spanish settlements in Florida and the Caribbean, and regular trade generated considerable prosperity for the reborn colony. Farmers located fertile soil outside flood zones, and abundant grasslands soon sustained a fledgling cattle industry. Equally important, Spanish officials and the military command at Santa Elena not only recognized Indian power in the region but acknowledged the necessity of amicable relations with local natives, at least for the near future. For the first time, it appeared Spain had learned from its previous mistakes and now laid successfully the foundation for a permanent foothold along the Carolina coast. To the settlers' chagrin, this would soon change.

English Efforts in North America

England had long envied the wealth and subsequent power Spain derived from the New World, but it was not until the 1570s, under the reign of Queen Elizabeth I, that the English navy had the capacity to challenge Spain's secured shipping lanes. As the new Santa Elena colony rose from the ashes of Fort San Filipe, English "sea dogs" such as Francis Drake prowled the Atlantic and pounced on Philip II's gold-bearing galleons. Piracy soon gave way to attacks directly on Spanish colonies in the late 1570s as English vessels plundered Spanish communities throughout the Caribbean and along the Florida coast. England's intention to ravage Spanish shipping and settlements became even more evident in 1585, when Sir Walter Raleigh directed the founding of an English colony on Roanoke Island in the northern Outer Banks of present-day North Carolina. Raleigh openly admitted that the colony was partly planned as a base of operations against Spanish interests in the Americas. Spain's far-flung colonies were vulnerable and the king's army and navy so dispersed over the vast empire that the Spanish were unable to counter these devastating

Must-See Sites: Magnolia Plantation and Gardens, Charleston

The first record of the Drayton family dates to the Norman Conquest of England at the Battle of Hastings in 1066, and since then the family has played a prominent role in the history of both England and America. Descendent Thomas Drayton and his wife Ann were among the earliest settlers of the Carolina Colony and there helped establish rice cultivation in South Carolina. In 1676, Thomas and Ann built Magnolia Plantation, one of the first plantation homes constructed in the colony and a major supplier of rice. By the time of his death, Thomas had also created a ten-acre garden of exotic and local plants, a project that was continued by his descendents and today is the oldest public garden in the US. The Drayton family proved central in the state's economic development and in each pivotal moment of South Carolina history: among its members are a signer of the Declaration of Independence, a co-author of the South Carolina state constitution, the first judge of the US District Court (appointed by President George Washington), a governor, and a Confederate Army general. Visitors may tour the magnificent plantation house, the expansive and beautiful garden, former slave housing, the family burial site, and an on-site zoo and nature center. Also available to visitors are boat excursions on the plantation's surrounding waterways and swamps, a Revolutionary War battle reenactment, educational programs, holiday celebrations throughout the year, and numerous other special programs and activities. Magnolia Plantation and Gardens is located at 3550 Ashley River Road in Charleston. For more information, call (800) 367-3517 or see www.magnoliaplantation.com.

blows with concentrated force. Philip II understood this problem and, consequently, ordered that the most remote colonies be abandoned and Spanish forces regrouped to more strategic defenses. The king's decision applied to Fort San Marcos and the entire Santa Elena experiment, despite the returns the community now promised. In mid-August 1587, Spanish settlers burned the fort and homes, boarded ships anchored in the harbor, and vacated the colony.

For more than 60 years, Spain labored to extend its presence into the lower region of modern South Carolina. Both Charles V and Philip II hoped a colony there would contribute to the agricultural base of the Spanish empire and that its settlers would ultimately tap into valuable resources such as gold that would further enrich and empower the nation. Although an uneasy and inconsistent peace marked the colony's relations with the Chicora and Edisto, Spain still wished to convert the native population to Catholicism, encourage them to embrace Spanish culture, and possibly convince them to help the Spaniards seek mineral wealth. But Spain's elaborate vision for development in South Carolina proved grander than its ability to plant a profitable, secure colony. Poor leadership, inadequate preparation and planning, and general ignorance of the region all combined to doom outposts. Moreover, Gordillo's enslavement of Chicoras, the settlers' sporadic attacks on nearby tribes to acquire food, and Spain's dismissal of Indian culture corrupted the possibility of an alliance with local tribes that would have directly benefited Spain's effort to establish a permanent colony in the area. Santa Elena was also a victim of international rivalry—a distant, isolated outpost in a world for which three nations competed. As long as all three nations eyed the same territory, none of their colonies would survive. Over the 80 years that followed, neither Spain, France, nor England attempted settlement of Santa Elena.

As Spain abandoned the Carolina coast, England's colony at Roanoke also faltered and in 1590 collapsed, with more than 100 settlers listed as missing; in this case, however, the financial loss fell on private investors such as Raleigh rather on the national government. Queen Elizabeth I had remained adamant that treasury funds not be spent on colony-building projects in the New World because the nation's resources were more immediately needed to expand defense forces against possible Spanish attack on the British Isles. Indeed, her caution was well founded; in 1588 Philip II launched his Armada against England with an accompanying invasion force of 20,000 soldiers. The Roanoke debacle embittered investors.

Elizabeth I died in 1603, after 50 years on the English throne. Her successor, King James I, openly encouraged the founding of English colonies in North America, but like Elizabeth committed no government funds to support such efforts. He did, however, issue a charter that allowed for the creation of the London Company, a joint-stock corporation to raise private investments explicitly for placing an English colony in the New World. With the funds raised, the London Company purchased three ships, hired John Smith and a small contingent of soldiers to command and protect the expedition, and recruited 100 settlers to establish settlement in America. In May 1607, after nearly three months at sea, Smith's prospective colonists made landfall in Virginia and founded the colony of Jamestown.

Similar to Spanish adventures in South Carolina, England's Jamestown Colony suffered terribly. Disease proved rampant, especially malaria. The settlement sat in marshlands, an area not suitable for agriculture. Malnutrition and periods of outright starvation took many lives, as did the high salinity of the James River, from which the settlement obtained its drinking water. Relations with the Powhatan Indians who surrounded Jamestown were, at best, strained from the outset. Captain John Smith was a strong, competent leader, but serious injury and his subsequent return to England for medical care left Jamestown without anyone capable of command until 1610. In its first year of existence, fully half of the settlers at Jamestown died; another 500 arrived in spring 1608 and over the next two years all but 100 of those had perished. For another five years, Jamestown's grip on life was tenuous, but in mid-decade a new tobacco plant that blended Spanish and Virginia Indian varieties found a receptive market in England. Tobacco quickly became the colony's version of Spanish gold, and Jamestown's survival was assured. By 1620, England boasted a permanent and thriving colony in the New World.

That same year, 1620, nearly 100 men, women, and children in England boarded the ship *Mayflower* and crossed the North Atlantic in an arched route to Virginia. Autumn storms, however, violently whipped the vessel off course and cracked the *Mayflower*'s primary support beam. Lucky to reach shore, the newcomers found themselves stranded in present-day Massachusetts, homeless, with no food but the supplies they carried, and facing fast-approaching winter in a strange land. Unknowingly, those who survived the first year would be the first of nearly 40,000 Englishmen to migrate to Massachusetts over the three decades that followed.

THE FOUNDING OF CHARLES TOWN

As colonies in New England and Virginia grew, British settlement in the Caribbean also took root and expanded in direct challenge to Spain's regional dominance. On Barbados, tobacco and cotton netted limited profits, but by the late 1640s sugar production on the island exploded with unheralded returns. Worldwide demand skyrocketed for sugar and its byproducts molasses and rum, and by the late seventeenth century Barbados had emerged as the richest British colony in the Americas, sustained by African slavery and governed by a planter aristocracy. Among the island's English elite was John Colleton.

Colleton had remained loyal to the Crown during England's Puritan Revolution, and with the restoration of the monarchy to Charles II in 1660, Colleton traveled to London. Rewarded with knighthood for his support of the Royalists, the Barbados planter was honored with a seat on the Council for Foreign Plantations, which netted him close ties to powerful and influential men such as Sir George Carteret, Sir Anthony Ashley Cooper, William Berkeley, and Edward Hyde, all titled men with direct connections to the king.

Colleton's newfound position enabled him to press a plan he had conceived years earlier: a colony somewhere between Jamestown and Spanish Florida. Given the prosperity generated by slave-produced sugar on Barbados and other islands throughout the Caribbean, members of the Council of Foreign Plantations believed an agricultural settlement on the North American mainland might reap similar profits. Tobacco had substantially enriched Jamestown, and profits from its production and sale had a ripple effect on England's larger economy. Surely, council members reasoned, a properly structured and governed colony could make money.

It required little effort to convince King Charles II. He owed Cooper, Hyde, Berkeley, and the others a debt beyond the scope of money and titles for their many years of

Must-See Sites: Charles Towne Landing State Historic Site

Situated on the bank of the Ashley River opposite downtown Charleston, Charles Towne Landing is the site of England's first permanent colony in South Carolina, established in 1670. On the 300th anniversary of its founding, in 1970, the South Carolina General Assembly pronounced the landing site a state historical park. Spanning 664 acres, Charles Towne Landing includes a visitor center with interactive exhibits highlighting the colony's founding, daily life in the formative years of Charleston and South Carolina, and the diversity of settlers, slaves, and Native Americans who inhabited the settlement and surrounding area. Anchored nearby is The Adventure, a full-size reproduction of a typical trading vessel of the seventeenth century. The park also has a 22-acre zoo that features a variety of animals the original settlers encountered, walking trails around the marsh and through an 80-acre English-style garden, the Legare-Waring Plantation House, sugar cane and rice fields, and an ongoing archaeological project. Each April, Charles Towne Landing celebrates Founders' Day, commemorating the establishment of the settlement and featuring militia drills, black powder demonstrations, guest speakers, and special historical programs. The landing is located on SC Hwy 171 between SC Hwy 17 and Interstate 26, about three miles west of the city. See www.charlestowne.org for more information.

support that culminated in his restoration to the British throne. The king also recognized the potential for a financial return that would not only reward those who produced marketable crops in a well-situated colony but would, like Jamestown, benefit the larger English economy. Moreover, a colony considerably south of Jamestown would further challenge Spanish dominance of the Americas and expand England's empire. On March 24, 1663, Charles II issued a charter for the Colony of Carolina, which its custodians named in honor of their king, and assigned title to eight individuals, or proprietors: Anthony Ashley Cooper, George Carteret, Edward Hyde, William Berkeley, John Berkeley, William Craven, George Monck, and the plan's initiator John Colleton. The colony's boundaries were unlike those of any previous colony founded by any other nation. Carolina, by charter, stretched from Virginia south to Florida, and, in direct challenge to Spain, from the Atlantic Ocean to the Pacific Ocean.

The Lords Proprietors, as these men were known, were given extraordinary power. They were entitled to make war, declare peace, establish towns, raise and maintain an army and navy, tax settlers, and serve as heads of the colony's judicial system. The proprietors could control all Indian affairs within the colony, including trade with the native populations, and regulate the import and export of goods. Equally important, the eight noblemen were to own hundreds of thousands of acres of land. Indeed, the king's grant proved more extensive, more empowering, and more enriching than any award given to any individual or collection of Englishmen outside the royal family.

Once the colony was chartered, investors based in Barbados hired William Hilton to scout the Carolina coast. Hilton reported back in 1664, describing in detail the climate, wildlife, plants, soil quality, location of natural harbors and river openings, and the temperament of coastal Indians. His remarks and later published account also highlighted the sheer beauty of the Carolina coast and the potential economic windfall that awaited settlers and the colony's investors. One serious hurdle had to be overcome before the Barbados investors, collectively known as the Barbadian Adventurers, would commit themselves to colony-building in Carolina. The adventurers worried that few Englishmen then living in Barbados would willingly relocate to the new colony unless the proprietors made settlement far more enticing than simply offering the promise of hard work and potential financial gain. The Lords Proprietors acquiesced and conceded to all settlers in Carolina freedom of religion, the right of self-government, and extensive personal land grants. In fact, the proprietors wanted to reap profits more than they wished to establish and rule personal kingdoms; therefore, Colleton and his seven colleagues each contributed an equal sum of money to finance a first settlement in Carolina.

Charlestown was established originally at the mouth of the Cape Fear River (present-day southeast North Carolina) in late 1665 and boasted nearly 1,000 settlers by the following summer. The hostility of local Indians, probably the Tuscarora, raised concerns for the colony's security and in 1667 the colony was abandoned. Two years elapsed before another attempt was made in Carolina. In April 1669 Lord Anthony Ashley Cooper convinced the proprietors to invest substantially more money into the colony-building project. As Walter Edgar notes in his *South Carolina: A History*, each nobleman agreed to contribute the equivalent of nearly $40,000 in 1996 US dollars. A new venture was about to unfold, one that would ultimately succeed.

Cooper and his secretary John Locke penned a document for governing the colony, *The Fundamental Constitutions of Carolina*, in part to assure earlier accepted concessions would be guaranteed by law and in part to attract to the colony a large enough population to ensure its survival and prosperity. The Fundamental Constitutions promised tolerance for diverse religions, including Anglicans, non-Anglicans such as Quakers and Huguenots, and Jews. Catholics, however, were denied religious freedom in Carolina. Despite what seem now like its limitations, Cooper and Locke's statement on religion affirmed the rising spirit of the Enlightenment and appealed to a broader body of potential settlers throughout England, Europe, and the Caribbean.

The issue of private land ownership was also prominent in the Fundamental Constitutions. Land grants of 150 acres were to be awarded to every adult male settler,

John Locke

Although an Oxford academic, a trained physician, and colleague to scientists such as Robert Boyle and Sir Isaac Newton, John Locke is best remembered as one of England's leading philosophers. His 1689 work, *An Essay on Human Understanding*, arguably one of the most influential works in Western philosophy, posited the idea that humans are born with no innate knowledge, only the instinctual needs of all animals; in short, the human mind at birth is a blank slate, or *tabula rasa*. An individual's knowledge is the product of his experiences, experiences based on sensation and reflection, and human understanding and morality are the products of the application of "reason," or critical thought, to those experiences. Locke encouraged people to question the nature of man and of human institutions, including religion, and denounced those who avoided the labor of rational thought. He called for universal education and encouraged humans to pursue truth founded on reason and logic.

Locke's two-volume masterpiece *Two Treatises on Government*, also published in 1689, laid the foundation of a political ideology that soon altered Western civilization. In this work, Locke argued that man is born free in "a state of nature." Contrary to philosophical trends at the time, Locke believed that man was neither good nor evil from birth, but that man seeks certain advantages or protections in life that may cause him to behave in a manner sometimes detrimental to others. Humans, therefore, agree to organize as a society and form a governing structure to protect each person's "natural rights" to life, liberty, and property. This is government's only task, argued Locke. Should that governing system fail its responsibility, it is then the duty of society to end that government and create in its place a system that will protect the people's natural rights. This he termed the "right of revolution." Locke's concept of a "social contract" shaped the thought of later political philosophers and ultimately served as the foundation for the political ideology of the American Revolution.

Locke's immediate connection to the Carolina Colony was through Lord Anthony Ashley Cooper, earl of Shaftesbury, for whom Locke served as personal physician in London. Lord Ashley firmly believed that England's future prosperity hinged on its expansion of trade; the founding and exploitation of overseas colonies were central to England's financial growth and ultimately to the nation's power within Europe. As one of the eight proprietors for the new Carolina Colony, Lord Ashley was in a position to apply his perspective. He believed that to build a successful enterprise in America, it was essential to attract to the colony the noblemen necessary to govern the estate directly and a working-class population committed to the colony's welfare and development.

After reflecting on contemporary English politics and the problems encountered by recent colonies in America, Lord Ashley and Locke reasoned that both noblemen and settlers must have a vested interest in the colony, each in possession of certain rights or privileges that would attract them to Carolina and ensure their commitment to its success. With Lord Ashley's support, Locke in 1669 served as co-author of the Fundamental Constitutions of Carolina. This document created a two-house colonial assembly, an upper chamber of noblemen and a lower division of representatives popularly elected from each district. Property ownership was permitted for all persons, although the right to vote and to hold elected office was restricted to individuals who held 500 acres of land or more. The assembly was to conduct and regulate affairs with native peoples, internal commerce, land distribution, and slavery. With the exception of Catholics, settlers also possessed the right to worship in any manner they chose, provided they believe in God. To be sure, the constitution proved reminiscent of Jamestown Colony's sovereign status earlier in the century and was probably patterned on that; however, Jamestown's situation was based on the settlers' immediate need for survival at a time when King James I of England considered the colony outside his jurisdiction. The Carolina constitution, in contrast, signaled shifting currents of political thought in both England and its American colonies, thought that included the restraint of monarchial authority and the protection of liberties and rights for citizens.

100 acres to each adult female, and another 100 acres to each male under the age of sixteen. Although the land grants were later reduced by half, the opportunity to own land in any amount lured thousands to Carolina from European countries where such opportunity did not exist. Should a truly industrious settler prosper and accumulate additional property, his status in society would likewise be elevated, granting him greater prestige and influence in the colony. All male landowners in Carolina had the legal right to vote, itself a rare opportunity for men in the seventeenth century. Cooper's vision for Carolina was one of steady growth, prosperity, and permanency. Opportunity, responsibility, and security for all settlers, he believed, were essential to the colony's success and survival. The Fundamental Constitutions were completed in July 1669 and within one month the first settlers to Carolina Colony were at sea.

Three ships sailed from England. The journey would normally have required two months' travel, but the expedition encountered numerous delays and difficulties. The ships first stopped in Ireland to take on additional passengers; from there, the vessels plodded through the Atlantic and in October dropped anchor in Barbados, where the Carolina passengers rested, acquired supplies, and bought livestock. The ships again took to sea in late February; one ship ran aground in the Bahamas, and a storm swept another vessel farther north to Virginia. Only one ship landed in Carolina, making landfall in mid-March 1670 near present-day Charleston.

Cooper's colony builders had originally intended to settle in the Port Royal area but, now ashore, concluded the nearby deep-water river was more advantageous. Local Indians, probably the Yamasee, warmly welcomed the newcomers and encouraged them to stay, viewing the strangers as potential allies against their inland enemies. Certainly, the English preferred the friendship readily offered them to the level of diplomacy necessary to foster favorable relations with natives of the Port Royal region, whose earlier conflicts with settlers were well known. Also, the colony site would afford a natural security unavailable at Port Royal. Being several miles up river, the town would not be visible to passing enemy warships on patrol and would be out of range of naval guns should the Spanish learn the village's precise location. A ground invasion of the town by an enemy force would also prove impractical; marshlands extended inland from the Atlantic shore, making the terrain entirely too difficult for an invading force to cross. The only avenue open for attack was the river itself, but the settlement would stand on a bluff protected by a very narrow causeway, on which Spanish troops would have to be concentrated and, consequently, would be easily targeted by the settlers' defenses. Although the colony would not be impregnable, the colonists reasoned that taking it would cost an invading army more lives, materiel, and money than it was worth.

One hundred and thirty Englishmen and women now called Charles Town home. Over the following 30 years, waves of new settlers descended on the community from England, Barbados, and the English West Indies. Charles Town survived and showed early signs of prosperity. Rising wealth in the colony along with the spirit of the Fundamental Constitutions lured thousands of additional settlers to the community. After so many attempts to establish a European outpost in the area of South Carolina, one had finally succeeded.

3

South Carolina in the Colonial Era

Charles Town beckoned Europeans, and the population of both the city and the larger Carolina Colony soon mirrored the Old World's diversity. The Lords Proprietors envisioned a colony that would enrich them personally and concurrently elevate the wealth and power of England. A community of settlers that could supply resources to the mother country and become a western market for English manufactured goods was considered the key to Carolina's economic development. Luring people to the burgeoning Carolina coast was hardly difficult.

The Fundamental Constitutions certainly appealed to Europe's dispossessed and ultimately offered hope to thousands of men and women. The Proprietors also distributed promotional flyers and brochures throughout the continent that highlighted the colony's economic potential, in much the same way American states in the twentieth century conducted booster campaigns to lure industries. Visions of economic opportunity—land ownership especially—crossed national boundaries and class divisions, bringing to Carolina a truly diverse population.

The colony was divided in the 1720s, creating North Carolina and South Carolina. By mid-century, at least eight separate nationalities had rooted themselves in South Carolina. English settlers comprised nearly 37 percent of the total population. Scots accounted for nearly 33 percent of all settlers, followed by the Irish, Welsh, Germans, Dutch, French, and Swedes, in that order. It is interesting that in an English colony more than 60 percent of the total white population was not English. With such diversity came a myriad of religious affiliations—Anglican, Presbyterian, Lutheran, Huguenot, and some Catholics. Moreover, South

Carolina's avowed tolerance for any religious group that simply professed a belief in God in practice extended to Catholics and opened the colony to Jewish settlers as well, many arriving from Spain and Portugal. Most Jewish settlers lived in Charles Town, and South Carolina's Jewish community exceeded that of any other American colony on the eve of the Revolutionary War.

African slaves from the West Indies were brought into Carolina Colony in 1671, just one year after Charles Town's founding, but little time elapsed before large numbers of slaves were imported directly from Africa. This dual path of Africans into Carolina Colony, and later South Carolina specifically, continued throughout the 1700s. Moreover, the African population, like the European, was itself highly diverse. Trading centers dotted the length of the West African coast and drew slaves from a variety of ethnic groups representing numerous languages, customs, habits, values, and spiritual beliefs. Records indicate that about 100 Africans entered Charles Town annually until 1712; over the next half century, however, slave traders imported 600 yearly to meet the labor demands of the rapidly developing rice culture. The slave population also experienced a natural growth rate of about 5 percent yearly throughout the eighteenth century, far greater than the natural increase among white settlers.

Perhaps startling to the present-day observer is the colony's racial composition. In 1680, approximately 1,000 whites and 200 Africans resided in the vicinity of Charles Town, Africans totaling less than 17 percent of the population. By 1775, nearly 70,000 white settlers and 104,000 Africans lived in South Carolina, with Africans comprising roughly 60 percent of the colony's total population, which demonstrates the colony's agricultural focus.

Early Patterns of Economic Development in Colonial South Carolina

The agrarian base of South Carolina's colonial economy provided wealth and fulfilled the Lords Proprietors' intention for the colony: to produce a crop profitable on the world market, following the model of Virginian tobacco. Rice proved most suited to the South Carolina coastal environment and climate and by 1720 gave rise to a "rice

South Carolina's Pirate Connection

Pirates routinely sailed along South Carolina's colonial shore between 1690 and 1725, hijacking commercial vessels, kidnapping persons of wealth, and stealing anything of worth. Blackbeard, perhaps the most infamous pirate, was a constant source of turmoil for South Carolinians. Few people today, however, are aware of Anne Bonny and Stede Bonnet, two pirates who also had South Carolina ties.

Anne Bonny, the illegitimate daughter of attorney William Cormac and his maidservant, was born in County Cork, Ireland sometime between 1695 and 1700. Soon after Anne's birth, Cormac and Anne's mother left Ireland, settling in Charleston, South Carolina, where he restarted his life as a local lawyer and plantation owner. Anne was a rather rambunctious child, given to her own whims, and at age sixteen eloped with James Bonny, a known pirate operating in the Bahamas. Anne soon joined the crew of Captain Jack Rackham, dressing like a man before entering battle, drinking and fighting alongside her companions in taverns throughout the Caribbean, and eventually becoming Captain Rackham's lover. Her wild years came to an end when Rackham's ship was attacked by a British warship; the popular story has Anne remaining on deck to fight British marines while the rest of Rackham's crew cowered below and soon surrendered without a fight. Regardless of the story's veracity, Bonny was taken into custody, tried and convicted of piracy, and sentenced to death. Upon hearing the sentence, she informed the judge of her pregnancy, a condition that spared her life. Bonny was released from prison and was rumored to have returned to the Charleston area where she lived as a respectable married woman until her death in 1782.

Stede Bonnet was not a typical pirate. Born into a life of privilege, he built a highly profitable sugar plantation on Barbados. Boredom, however, drove him to seek adventure. Bonnet purchased a ship, hired a crew, and engaged in piracy along the Carolina coast. Blackbeard and Bonnet joined forces for a short time, but Bonnet soon realized Blackbeard only wanted to use Bonnet's ship and men as a raiding party along the Cape Fear River. After Blackbeard harassed South Carolina shipping throughout the summer of 1718, South Carolina's governor William Rhett organized a naval force, tracked Bonnet to the Cape Fear River, and captured the captain and his crew. After being found guilty of piracy, his crew were hanged in Charleston on November 8, 1718; Bonnet was executed on December 10. For a detailed treatment of Bonny and Bonnet, visit the "Original Charleston Walks: Pirates and Buccaneers." Tickets may be purchased at 45 Broad Street in Charleston. For additional information, call (866) 550-8939 or visit www.piratesofcharleston.com.

culture," an aristocratic planter society that relied on slave labor. Plantations varied considerably in size, ranging from 50 to more than 1,000 acres and worked by 20 to 75 slaves. Exports soared throughout the eighteenth century, reaching a production rate of 6 million pounds of rice per year in the 1720s, surpassing 17 million pounds annually in the 1730s, and exceeding 30 million pounds each season in the 1740s. Indeed, on the eve of the American Revolution, South Carolina rice shipments totaled a staggering 66 million pounds, with an average per acre yield of 1,500 pounds. Truly, the crop earned its reputation as "Carolina gold."

While the economic system of colonial South Carolina may have been largely a "banquet table of rice," there were other sources of wealth for colonists. Indigo, a plant used to produce a blue-colored dye for textile goods, garnered substantial profits. First harvested in the colony in the 1740s, farmers exported only 138,000 pounds to European markets in 1747, but in 1775, just as war with Great Britain commenced, South Carolina supplied more than one million pounds of dye to foreign buyers.

Naval stores also generated positive returns. Throughout the seventeenth century, England enlarged her navy to bolster her defense of home waters, to protect English colonies and challenge Spanish holdings in the Americas, and to secure shipping lanes to European markets. Crucial in this fleet expansion were naval stores—tar, pitch, and turpentine—all used to waterproof and seal wooden hulls. The founding of Charles Town secured land covered in pine forests, from which these products were derived. Production of tar and pitch rose with each year, from 5,000 barrels in 1710 to 50,000 barrels in 1720. Moreover, at the beginning of the 1720s, South Carolina supplied more naval stores than any other English source and reaped profits across European markets that exceeded $6 million. This phenomenal profit ended abruptly in mid-decade, however, as Britain imposed a new series of navigation acts that altogether constrained colonial commerce by forbidding colonies from trading with other nations.

Orange groves also turned a profit in South Carolina's mild winters, and hemp emerged as a major source of income by the 1740s. Hog raising and cattle ranching brought additional wealth. Free-range foraging and grazing in the interior grasslands fattened the animals, and the abundance of rivers and creeks satisfied their thirst. Once slaughtered, meat was preserved in salt for export to New England and to British ports in the Caribbean.

By mid-century, Londoners strolled on sidewalks made of Carolina pine, the British fleet sailed on Carolina timber, English families dined on Lowcountry food crops, and Britain's nobility dressed in clothing dyed blue with South Carolina indigo. Agriculture generated incredible wealth for the colony's landed population, for export-import houses, and for shippers. The port at Charles Town (commonly referred to as Charleston by the mid-eighteenth century) grew into a rich, thriving city and England's most important harbor between Spanish Florida and the Chesapeake.

African Slavery in Colonial South Carolina

South Carolina's wealth rested on the back of slave labor. Regardless of the commodity—rice, indigo, or food crops—slavery was considered vital in producing that wealth. Given the sparse white population and its ultimately dispersed settlement, encouraged by the abundance of free or cheap land, white colonial landowners believed slavery was an essential labor source. As crude and reprehensible as it sounds to Americans today, colonial landowners found slavery cost-effective. The long-term costs of slave ownership fell far short of the hiring of day or seasonal white workers, had white field hands in fact been available in the numbers needed.

African slaves were imported at an alarmingly high rate following the colony's founding. In 1720, there were 535 white settlers residing in Goose Creek, a community just north of Charles Town, but there were also 2,027 African slaves living there. Given the profitability of rice cultivation in the South Carolina Lowcountry and the planters' reliance on slave labor to produce that crop, Goose Creek's racial profile resembled that of most other coastal communities. Indeed, by 1720, fully 65 percent of all South Carolina residents were African slaves.

Ever fearful of slave insurrection, colony leaders contemplated methods by which the number of white settlers in the colony might be increased. Briefly considered was a plan to recruit one white European servant for every

Five generations on Smith's Plantation, Beaufort, South Carolina 1862

ten Africans brought into South Carolina. To be sure, a black majority would have persisted in the colony, but the white population would likewise have grown rapidly and thus provided a larger sense of security to white residents. The measure never gained widespread support because rice planters preferred the less expensive slave labor system to the costs associated with establishing whites as independent farmers at the conclusion of their labor contracts.

Nearly half of all Africans enslaved in British North America before 1775 entered the colonies at Charleston and were held initially on Sullivan's Island before being auctioned in the city's slave market. Said Charleston merchant and landed aristocrat Henry Laurens, Africans "from the River Gambia [Ghana] are preferred to all others with us [in Carolina] save the Gold Coast." Ghanaians were especially well versed in rice cultivation; they brought to South Carolina plantations valuable knowledge acquired from personal experience and learned from previous generations. Their skill and knowledge made them far more expensive on the auction block than other Africans. Carolina planters of the eighteenth century typically paid between 100 and 200 pounds sterling, or roughly $11,500 to $23,000 in today's currency, for Ghanaians. Being such a major investment for planters, Ghanaians generally performed little manual labor and instead supervised small teams, or gangs, of "field slaves" taken from the Niger Delta, the Windward Coast, and Angola.

According to most white South Carolinians early in the eighteenth century, there existed little racial antagonism; without question, this was a one-sided, flawed perception. Through some combination of ignorance, arrogance, and bias, planters and other whites disregarded the harsh reality that defined slavery, preferring to see it as a paternalistic, Christian guardianship. As early as 1702, argued planters, African slaves at Goose Creek received some academic training, from the Reverend Samuel Thomas. Writing one year later, Thomas noted that under his tutelage "twenty slaves have learned to read." His observation in 1705 suggested further gains: "Many [slaves] are well affected to Christianity so far as they know of it and are desirous of Christian knowledge and seem to be willing to prepare themselves for it in learning to read." Benjamin Dennis, an English educator, founded a school near Charles Town in 1712 and there served African, Native American, and white children. Another school was established in 1743, this one in Charleston and expressly for African children, who were instructed by Harry and Andrew, two adult slaves who had been trained as Christian missionaries and teachers to slaves in Charleston.

Efforts to educate African slaves, however, were not commonplace and were roundly discouraged by white South Carolinians. It was widely assumed that Africans "of some learning" would be able to plan and execute successful rebellions or escapes. Although planters countered this argument by suggesting that a carefully constructed educational program actually produced more manageable and compliant slaves, the potential threat of an educated enslaved population seemed too great to permit. Throughout the eighteenth century, communities individually erected laws to ban academic and religious instruction to African slaves.

White colonists also referenced the inclusion of African slaves in the colony's militia. In 1704 the colonial assembly announced its intention to train slaves for military service should the colony ever face invasion by Spanish forces or confront the need to suppress hostile Indians. Although the plan never materialized to the extent first envisioned, many African slaves were recruited into the South Carolina militia for training and combat duty during the Yamasee War of 1715. Again, in 1742, more than 70 slaves were enlisted as combat soldiers against Spanish raiding parties operating near Beaufort. In each instance, slaves served under the command of their owners, in return for minimal wages, or, in some cases, for the reward of emancipation. Regardless of the slaves' motive for service, white colonists who championed African service generally believed militia duty provided slaves with a sense of inclusion and a vested interest in the welfare of the colony, and thus retarded the threat of armed slave insurrection.

As in the case of academic and religious instruction for slaves, South Carolinians largely disapproved of military training for Africans in bondage. The danger of training slaves in military skills was obvious. A population prepared in military tactics, skilled in marksmanship, and victimized by brutal enslavement would be a grave threat to the safety and security of white South Carolinians.

White colonists also highlighted the specialized training many Africans received in what were then termed "the domestic arts"—cabinetmaking, blacksmithing, carpentry, and related crafts. Hundreds of male slaves in eighteenth-century South Carolina did gain these skills and often were hired out to local whites, typically at a rate of one dollar per day. White South Carolinians touted the slave's opportunity to save his wages, ultimately purchase his freedom, and once emancipated establish himself as a

Slaves quarters, Port Royal, South Carolina.

free man employed in a profitable trade. By the end of the century there was, indeed, a growing "free black" population engaged in skilled work and living in Charleston. But, more often than not, the wages of skilled slaves were instead paid directly to the planter, and training in the domestic arts allowed planters to reduce their own overhead expenses by having slaves manufacture items needed on plantations instead of purchasing those goods from a European or colonial supplier.

The colonists' emphasis on the good slavery brought Africans only denied the brutal reality generally experienced by slaves in the colony. The overwhelming majority of Africans were set to work in the rice fields, widely considered the most strenuous labor in British North America. Noted one observer, the slaves stand "mid-leg deep in water which floats an ouzy [*sic*] mud, and exposed all the while to a burning sun which makes the very air they breathe hotter than the human blood; these poor wretches are then in a furness of stinking putrid effluvia: a more horrible employment can hardly be imagined." Their work followed the sun, beginning at daybreak and continuing until dusk, with few periods of rest. Any perceived sluggishness in the field and lack of productivity frequently resulted in reduced rations, loss of their day of rest on Sunday, and sometimes severe physical punishment.

Slave housing in eighteenth-century South Carolina was crude. Huts averaged fifteen feet in length and twelve feet in width, with earthen floors, no fireplaces, roofs made of palmetto fronds, and clay walls that eroded in the excessively wet Lowcountry climate. Homes were unbearably cold in winter and brutally hot in summer. Rather than the "highly organized and carefully arranged" slave houses found on nineteenth-century southern plantations, slaves in eighteenth-century South Carolina commonly built their huts in "loosely clustered settlements," noted one archaeologist. Generally, meals were cooked outdoors and were principally rice-based. Meat was uncommon in the slaves' diet, and, when available, consisted of the least-favored parts of the animal such as the legs, feet, jaw, and skull discarded by the planter. Rarely were slaves entrusted with firearms to scare birds from crops and to hunt small game for themselves.

Given the deplorable housing, grossly inadequate diet, absence of personal and slave community hygiene, and the brutal labor to which slaves were subjected, it is little wonder that a high mortality rate ravaged the slave population. Fully one-third of all African children enslaved in South Carolina died before their first birthday, and two-thirds did not survive to their sixteenth year. Scholars frequently ascribe such a macabre record of slave death to malaria. To be sure, malaria-carrying mosquitoes swarmed throughout South Carolina's hot, wet coastal low lands and infected a large segment of the slave population, but the slaves' complete living and work environment must also be considered. Food preservation proved wholly inadequate for anything but short-term use. Salt curing of meat was certainly a practice common to colonists, but salt rations to slaves were severely limited. The little meat slaves were provided had to be consumed soon after receiving it. Moreover, meat given to slaves by the planter's household was often already spoiled or of questionable quality. Added to this was the heat and damp environment that only hastened the spoiling of meat, vegetables, and fruits and their infestation by disease-bearing pests.

Waterborne diseases also claimed many lives. The coastal region of South Carolina was largely marshland and swamp, making clean water difficult to locate. Many of the rivers that emptied directly into the Atlantic and were widely presumed to be freshwater were compromised by a high salinity level and, consequently, fatal to those slaves who depended on them as their principal water supply. Underground water obtained from "shallow wells" was compromised by a latent salt content along with a high residue of sulfur and other potentially hazardous minerals. Unlike the scholarly work conducted in the Jamestown, Virginia area by historian Tim Breen and others, there exists no record or serious estimate of the deaths caused by contaminated drinking water in colonial South Carolina.

Caught in a system utterly destructive of their lives, African slaves challenged the institution whenever opportunity arose, and they employed a myriad of tactics—some hardly noticeable, others dramatic. Common to most plantations was the slow pace of slave labor, most often a purposeful attempt to limit the planters' profits by

Gullah

The Sea Islands of South Carolina between Georgetown and Beaufort are home to the Gullah people, a people descended from slaves who originated along the "rice coast" of Africa and included various ethnic groups from Senegal, Gambia, Sierra Leone, Guinea, Angola, and Ghana. Scholars believe the name "Gullah" is a derivative of either Angola or Gola, the latter being an ethnic group that lived between present-day Sierra Leone and Liberia. The diversity of West African cultures on South Carolina rice plantations, and the immediate need for these enslaved peoples to communicate and coexist, gave rise to a new language that melded English with their native tongues. Cultural traditions and values blended as a natural consequence of the slaves' newfound living condition. What emerged was something of a hybrid African culture in the South Carolina Lowcountry.

Fiercely loyal to family and community, the Gullah people have fought to retain their African identity despite centuries of enslavement and the acculturative influences of twentieth-century South Carolina; indeed, Gullahs are widely credited with preserving more of their African heritage than any other African-American community in the US. Central to the Gullah diet are red rice and okra soup, both largely the offspring of West African "jollof rice," a style of cooking brought to America by the Wolof and Mande peoples of West Africa. "Root doctors" remain part of community tradition, providing care using herbal medicines similar to traditional African remedies. The Gullah have consciously preserved many skills used in African art, basket making, pottery, and weaving. Their children are often reared on African tales slightly modified to fit the contemporary world, and their unequivocally Christian religion carries some imagery and spiritual inclinations traceable to traditional West African cultures. The Gullah language is English-based, but contains numerous unaltered African words from multiple ethnic and linguistic groups, as well as slightly altered African words, and the spoken language exhibits substantial African influence in sentence structure. In 2005, the Gullah community published a translation of the New Testament in the Gullah language, a project that required twenty years to complete. In recent years, they have also renewed their direct connection with West Africa, sponsoring visits, or "homecomings," to Sierra Leone in 1989, 1997, and 2005.

In July 2004, South Carolina Congressman James E. Clyburn introduced HR 4683 on the floor of the US House of Representatives.

Titled "The Gullah/Geechee Cultural Heritage Act," HR 4683 was based on a report issued by the National Park Service that identified the Gullah/Geechee coast as one of eleven historic sites in the US most endangered by urban sprawl, commercial development, and resort expansion. "The [NPS] study confirmed that extraordinary steps must be taken to preserve this rich and vibrant culture that is rapidly disappearing," said Congressman Clyburn. His bill called for the establishment of a Gullah/Geechee culture heritage corridor, a coastal heritage museum highlighting Gullah culture and history, a $1 million annual appropriation from Congress for ten consecutive years to fund the project, and a commission to manage the program. "The Gullah/Geechee culture is the last vestige of the fusion of African and European languages and traditions brought to these coastal areas," said Clyburn. "I cannot sit idly by and watch an entire culture disappear that represents my heritage and the heritage of those that look like me." Although Clyburn's bill received scant opposition, substantial debate did erupt in Congress over each of the next two national budgets in the context of the Iraq war, homeland security, and national debt; consequently, HR 4683 was not passed until October 2006.

African Americans with direct Gullah roots include football Hall of Fame star Jim Brown, boxing legend Joe Frazier, Supreme Court Justice Clarence Thomas, hip-hop giant Jazzy Jay, and Motown icon James Jamerson.

Several Gullah festivals are held annually in South Carolina. Each February, the Gullah Celebration at Hilton Head Island features exhibitions of art, crafts, food, music, and dance. For information, contact the Gullah Celebration Hotline at (877) 650-0676 or visit www.gullahcelebration.com. A similar event is held in Beaufort each May, the weekend before Memorial Day. See www.gullahfestival.org for more information. To see preserved Gullah culture, visit the McLeod Plantation on James Island, near Charleston. See www.gullahtours.com for information.

producing a smaller harvest than had been expected. Slaves "accidentally" broke the tools with which they worked or feigned sickness, two methods to interrupt the flow of work and the productivity of field hands. Although escape was an option, it was seldom attempted. The network of white landowners and availability of posses on horseback made escape rarely successful, and the punishment given to captured runaways was generally so severe and brutal that it adequately intimidated other slaves who might contemplate escape. Commonly practiced throughout the colony was the branding of a slave who attempted escape multiple times. Moreover, most planters encouraged marriage and family-building among their slaves as one means of discouraging escape. Said one planter, slaves "love their families dearly and none runs away from the other." To be sure, there were occasions when a runaway made a successful escape. These individuals ran not from established society but instead directly toward it, into Charleston itself. The black population of the city was quite large, with slaves living in town and often hired out to local businessmen. Given the continually rising city population, the ever-increasing number of black residents, and the extensive use of African labor brought from plantation to the city, it proved rather easy for an escaped slave to go unnoticed in Charleston. Indeed, said Samuel Dyssli, a white resident of the city, "Carolina looks more like a Negro Country than like a Country settled by white people." While in the city, he could live with friends or estranged family members, work and earn a modest income from a white employer, and eventually hope to secure passage on a ship exiting South Carolina. Planters and overseers anticipated slave resistance, but with a majority slave population in the colony, white South Carolinians feared violent slave revolts. One such event occurred in 1739.

Word sifted throughout the southern British colonies that runaway slaves who successfully found their way to Spanish Florida were rewarded with both freedom and land. Indeed, the rumor was true. Early in the century Spain issued a proclamation that not only encouraged slaves to escape their British masters but also promised that upon arrival in St. Augustine they would live as free, propertied men. The

Spanish announcement, coupled with the ever-present fear of slave revolt, compelled South Carolina's colonial assembly in August 1739 to pass into law the Security Act. White males had always been permitted to carry firearms wherever they went, any day of the week. Such measures were necessary, colonists believed, for local security against thieves, Indians, and slaves. Only during Sunday religious services were men not allowed to bear their weapons. As the Sabbath was generally a day of unsupervised rest for slaves and white men were prohibited from carrying firearms, South Carolinians understandably assumed Sunday mornings to be a propitious opportunity for a mass slave escape or insurrection. Spain's encouragement only made that assessment more serious. The Security Act, then, was intended to permit white men the right to bear firearms during Sunday church services and, consequently, be better prepared to crush an insurrection should one occur. Only a few weeks after the bill's passage into law, the feared scenario unfolded.

On Sunday morning, September 9, 1739, twenty slaves assembled near the Stono River in St. Paul's Parish, about twenty miles outside of Charleston. From there, the slaves stormed a local firearms store, killing the shopkeeper and taking his guns and ammunition. Moving south, ultimately for Florida, they agreed to recruit additional slaves in the rebellion and exact their vengeance on all whites they encountered. At the home of one Mr. Godfrey, they burned the house and killed Mr. Godfrey and his son and daughter. By midday, the group had torched six more homes and murdered 25 whites. Now numbering about 60 runaways, they rested along the Edisto River.

News of the insurrection spread quickly across the Lowcountry. A posse of nearly 100 heavily armed whites, most of them recruited from the church pews, charged south and by late afternoon had encircled the armed slaves and engaged them in battle. Half of the slaves fell dead or wounded in the opening volley of musket balls; the remainder fled into the surrounding swamplands. Over the next month, all but one runaway were apprehended and executed. The Stono Rebellion collapsed, but in its wake lay a swath of death and destruction. Moreover, the South Carolina colonial assembly quickly framed and passed into law the Negro Act, a measure that effectively limited the slaves' free time and banned their pre-rebellion opportunities to assemble in groups, learn to read, and earn money working in local stores after their plantation duties were complete.

The Stono Rebellion manifested the grave threat slavery held for colonists. South Carolina's agricultural wealth depended on African slaves. The labor drained from the lives of those men and women produced the bounty of rice, indigo, beef and pork, timber, and naval stores sold by the white, planter class across Britain's colonies and in Europe, generating a level of prosperity that made Britain's American colonists among the richest peoples globally in the eighteenth century and South Carolinians among the wealthiest of American colonists. That this prosperity depended on a most inhumane, exploitive labor system mattered little to those South Carolinians whose pockets were fattened with profit. As long as this "peculiar institution" existed, the fear of slave insurrection existed. The Stono Rebellion was but the precursor of much bloodier rebellions to come.

The Perils of Prosperity

South Carolina's economy grew rapidly throughout the first half of the eighteenth century. Charleston, the colony's center of activity, enjoyed the greatest profits and as a result attracted new settlers from the British Isles, Caribbean colonies, and communities along the entire North American Atlantic coastline. With 3,500 residents in 1706 and a commercial energy that promised extreme growth, Charleston quickly surpassed Savannah and Williamsburg in wealth and importance and competed directly with Boston. Stacks of animal hides, barrels of rice, and chained Indian captives regularly lined the docks waiting to be loaded on ships bound for ports in England, Jamaica, Barbados, and the Caribbean; entering the city by ship were African slaves of greater financial worth than all of the exports leaving Charleston. Sails dotted the harbor on almost every day of the year, and the level of trade entering and exiting the city gave evidence that Charleston was "as thriving... as any colony on the continent of English America." Indeed, the value of South Carolina's exports attested to the colony's economic strength—nearly $28 million on the eve of the Revolutionary War.

Prosperity and growth had unwanted repercussions. Seaborne commerce lured a "meaner sort of people" to Carolina waters. Although piracy had plagued the Caribbean since Sir Francis Drake harassed Spanish shipping in the late sixteenth century, few pirates ventured farther north until the wealth of Savannah, Charleston, and Wilmington proved too attractive to ignore. Between 1700 and 1720, roughly 6,000 pirates menaced shipping between North Carolina and Barbados; ten percent of these pirates were women. Ed Teach, more commonly known as Blackbeard, commanded a refuge in the North Carolina Outer Banks and wielded considerable influence over that colony's governor; frequently, he and his three vessels threatened Charleston.

Throughout most of June 1718, Blackbeard and his 400 men plundered shipping just outside Charleston Harbor. From the city specifically he demanded 500 pounds of medical supplies. When Charleston officials balked at this demand, Blackbeard and half of his crew entered the city and paraded through the center of town, waving their guns and promising to burn Charleston to the ground if he were compelled to take the medical supplies by force. To assure the safety of town residents and the continued use of the city docks, Governor Robert Johnson acquiesced and issued Blackbeard the materials he demanded. The pirates left the city unharmed and within days they vacated Charleston waters—at least for now. Blackbeard returned regularly to harass shipping outside of Charleston, and other pirates such as Stede Bonnet also found the Carolina waters enticing.

Fear seemed commonplace among South Carolinians generally and among Charlestonians specifically in the first half of the eighteenth century. With rising wealth came a rising population. Indeed, by the 1740s Charleston's population reached nearly 10,000 people. Increasingly, newcomers without marketable skills found it nearly impossible to secure jobs or property in Charleston. Unemployment skyrocketed. Prosperous townsfolk regularly complained of the "number of idle, vagrant... people" wandering the city's streets, engaged not in gainful work but "drinking and debauchery." Crime became a more serious problem for the city as well. The unemployed, constrained by desperate circumstances, occasionally

Sweetgrass Baskets

Sweetgrass basket making is perhaps the oldest surviving African art form in the United States. The skill arrived in Spanish America with West African slaves, and with the founding of rice culture spread into South Carolina's Lowcountry in the late seventeenth century.

Slaves relied on baskets to store and transport harvested rice. They were also used extensively to store shellfish, fruit, cotton, clothing, and household items. The baskets were made of bulrush, a marsh grass commonly referred to as "sweetgrass" for its mild, pleasant aroma and noted as a flexible but durable material.

Sweetgrass baskets were functional and practical, but their intricate, artistic designs made them desirable for display in the finest Charleston homes and for use on the dinner tables of the city's elite. Indeed, the baskets became so popular across the South Carolina Lowcountry that slave women found themselves weaving baskets for their owners to sell at nearby markets.

Following emancipation, the Gullah people supplemented their meager income by weaving sweetgrass baskets and selling them to passers-by and local stores. Moreover, maintaining this skill consciously connected them to their African identity, and the concentration required to produce such artistic pieces offered momentary escape from the grind of daily chores and from the intense racism affecting the Gullah community.

Highway 17, a stretch of road running the length of South Carolina's coast, was finally paved in the 1930s and became the primary artery connecting Charleston to the rest of the state. Basket makers recognized its construction as a golden opportunity to sell their creations to motorists, and from roadside stands lining the highway's shoulder in the Mt. Pleasant area south to Charleston Gullah women sold, and continue to sell, sweetgrass baskets.

For more than 300 years, sweetgrass baskets have remained an integral feature of Gullah culture. When traveling along Highway 17 through Mt. Pleasant, pull off at a sweetgrass basket stand and watch the basket weaver weave the bulrush into a finished basket. Talk with the woman making the basket, and perhaps purchase one of the many she has for sale. For a hands-on experience, visit the Hopsewee Plantation in Georgetown, located about 50 miles north of Mt. Pleasant. Hopsewee offers a three-hour class in sweetgrass basket making for minimal cost, including all materials and instruction. To find scheduled classes or to arrange a private session, call (843) 546-7891 or email mail@hopsewee.com.

If you're visiting the Mt. Pleasant–Charleston area in June, attend the Annual Sweetgrass Cultural Arts Festival, which is part of Charleston's famed Spoleto Celebration. In 2007, more than 5,000 people attended the Sweetgrass Festival. The annual celebration highlights the history of Lowcountry basket making, and skilled basket makers display, weave, and sell their goods. In addition, the Gullah-Geechee culture is celebrated with music, dancing, food, storytelling, games, and numerous other activities. For more information, visit www.sweetgrassfestival.com.

turned to theft, and sailors on short-term leave from their ships were "rowdy" and prone to "immoral behavior." Alarmed by the rising tide of unemployment and vagrancy, Charleston residents insisted the city fund and construct a public workhouse and hospital. Both buildings were erected and in service by 1738. The city also demanded a jail be built and the penal code be made stricter. With money granted by the colonial assembly, the jail was operational by 1740. The assembly also approved public whippings, the burning of a convicted thief's hand with a hot iron, and for more serious offenses the public pillory of the convicted individual with "one ear nailed to the post" and one ear to be removed at the end of the sentence.

Overcrowding in the city further allowed for the rapid spread of communicable disease. A smallpox outbreak in summer 1738, allegedly brought to the city by two slaves, was only complicated by a simultaneous outbreak of whooping cough. By summer's end, fully ten percent of the city's population had died from one or both of these diseases. Yellow fever settled upon the residents the following year.

Fire also nearly destroyed Charleston. Autumn 1740 proved unusually warm and dry. By November, the most casual observer in the city recognized that Charleston had become a tinderbox. On November 18, a small fire accidentally started on the city's southeast side, but embers were soon whipped north and west by a stiff wind. Within only a few hours, Charleston was engulfed in fire; the "shrieks of women and children" were heard all over the city, noted one survivor. The conflagration was made worse at the docks, where barrels of turpentine, deer skins, and rum ignited and crates of gunpowder exploded. The fire raged for three days, destroying more than 300 homes and 70 percent of the merchants' buildings and wares.

Fear of future fires pervaded Charleston's residents and unquestionably contributed to the fierce punishment issued to a slave convicted of attempted arson one year later. In August 1741, Kate, a slave in Charleston, was arrested for trying to set her owner's house on fire. Within 48 hours of her arrest, she was convicted and sentenced to death. Kate escaped the gallows by naming her lover as co-conspirator. He was promptly apprehended and, like her,

Portraits of African American ex-slaves from the U.S. Works Progress Administration, Federal Writers' Project slave narratives collections. Attendants at Old Slave Day, April 8, 1937.

quickly tried and convicted for plotting arson and "domestic treachery." At his trial, he claimed "every white man he should [ever] meet" is "his declared Enemy." Rather than hanging him, the court ordered him burned alive, in the manner of the house and city he planned to destroy. He died "like... the impudent hardened wretch he was," said one white city resident. His method of execution certainly serves as example of the "hardened" community surrounding African slaves and the unspeakable brutality white society directed against slaves. It further demonstrates the depth of white South Carolinians' fear of slave rebellions, a fear lingering from the Stono Rebellion two years earlier. The burning of a man for conspiracy was so vicious, so heinous, that it was meant to serve as a warning to all slaves in the colony.

The years that followed were little better. Rumors of slave insurrection persisted, each rumor the product of speculation and fear. White residents of Charleston worried that the ongoing illegal sale of alcohol to slaves would embolden them to rebel; others were certain that the rising crime wave was the result of slaves securing the money and material needed to launch an insurrection. So frequent and increasingly detailed were these rumors that in May 1745 the South Carolina governor requested a battalion of British soldiers be posted in Charleston "to give heart to our people." Only a small detachment of British marines arrived, and in December another rumor of slaves plotting to "cut the throats of white people in Charleston" while they slept once more sent terror through the white community. Each rumor strengthened white resolve to secure the city and colony. As that rumor sifted throughout the Lowcountry, the requested battalion of British soldiers arrived in Charleston and the alleged ringleaders of the purported insurrection were arrested. The investigation revealed the plot to be nothing more than the imagination of an excited and fearful white population; no rebellion was in preparation.

Word also reached Charleston of a Spanish military incursion into coastal Georgia. In anticipation of a similar strike on Charleston, the colonial militia was called to duty and enlarged with fresh recruits. Money was appropriated without debate for the construction of trenches by slave labor, their owners receiving financial compensation from the Assembly for their work, and the protective wall along the harbor was fortified. The arrival of a British fleet and the fierce resistance of Georgia colonists drove the Spanish force back south to Florida and returned a temporary sense of security to South Carolinians, but another war between England and France was brewing—one that could spill into North America. South Carolina remained on guard throughout much of the 1740s.

The first half of the eighteenth century was one of tremendous economic growth for South Carolina. Fear, nonetheless, shadowed South Carolina's prosperity—fear of a Spanish strike along the coast, of Indian retaliation for the enslavement and sale of nearly 12,000 Native Americans, of slave insurrection from among the tens of thousands of Africans held in bondage, of plunder by pirates in commercial shipping lanes, and of the growing number of unskilled and unemployed residents living desperate, poor lives. Colonists were determined to secure South Carolina and its economy; however, a new threat to the colony's welfare soon surfaced.

4

The Turmoil of Revolution

Great Britain waged four major wars with France between 1690 and 1760, the last of which was the Seven Years' War, or French and Indian War, as it was commonly known in the American colonies. Collectively, these wars drained Britain's treasury and by 1763 it was on the verge of bankruptcy. Saddled with war debt and responsible for a vast global empire, King George III in 1763 announced his intention to erect new commercial trade regulations and rebuild the nation's finances through a series of new taxes. Although the king and Parliament assumed that most colonists in America remained firmly convinced of the king's authority to initiate any policy he wished without direct input from his subjects, a contradictory political ideology had evolved among many over the previous century. Based on the philosophy of Englishman John Locke and amplified by Enlightenment philosophers such as Jean-Jacques Rousseau and Montesquieu, a large segment of Americans now held a liberal body of thought perhaps best termed popular sovereignty.

According to Locke and those who conformed to Lockean philosophy, government is consciously and purposely established by humans to protect their three natural rights. These unalienable rights were the right to life, liberty, and property. Government's only purpose, Locke argued, was to protect each individual's natural rights. Should government abuse its limited power, attempt to increase its authority, or fail in its single mission, citizens retained the right of revolution, meaning they held the right to scrap that governing system and replace it. In short, Locke posited the liberal notion that the people, not the king, held all political authority. King George's intended tight control over colonial commerce and his determination to extract taxes from colonists certainly were within his rights under the banner of royal sovereignty, but his view of authority conflicted sharply with that of popular sovereignty. It was fundamentally this constitutional issue that underpinned the confrontation between Crown and colonists from 1763 to 1783.

Colonial Resistance to King George III

With the end of the Seven Years' War, King George issued his Proclamation of 1763, a royal statement that banned the colonists' migration across the Appalachian Mountains into the Ohio River Valley. Although well intentioned—to prevent a war promised by Native Americans residing in the valley should settlers enter their territory, a war that would require further British expenditures to defend colonists—Americans interpreted the measure as an arbitrary decision by the king that prevented colonists from acquiring property. In essence, the king was not protecting the settlers' liberty to venture into new lands, the right to property, and, consequently, their natural right to life.

Two years later, Parliament crafted its first major tax law, and George III approved the measure. The Stamp Act of 1765 placed a tax on all paper products and on certain government documents. Playing cards, newspapers, birth certificates, and marriage licenses were among the taxable items. Retailers and government agencies were to purchase and affix stamps to paper items prior to their sale and recoup their costs from consumers by raising the price of those goods and documents accordingly. The Crown believed the cost of each stamp to be minimal, but with the tax imposed throughout the British Empire, the revenue generated might repair the damage done to the treasury over the previous decades of war. Moreover, newspapers and playing cards were not essential items; colonists could avoid paying the tax altogether by not purchasing taxable items. Rather than pay the required fee and tax for birth certificates, death certificates, and marriage licenses, individuals could simply record that information in a family Bible and have witnesses confirm those entries. The tax, however, did not go over well in the American colonies.

Long known in the South Carolina Assembly as a hothead, Representative Christopher Gadsden immediately emerged as the assembly's principal and most vocal critic of the Stamp Act. In little time he built a large opposition force in the assembly to Parliament's recent legislation. Gadsden, a Charleston merchant, prided himself on having built his fortune with the sweat and commitment of his own labor. He denounced the Crown's effort to reach into his pocket and relieve him of any amount of personal wealth. If left unchallenged, he argued, the Stamp Act could threaten the financial vitality of Charleston and potentially stymie the city's continued economic growth. Gadsden's prediction of economic doom was clearly exaggerated, but he, like his supporters in the assembly, believed unequivocally that all American colonists enjoyed the "the rights of Englishmen." He announced in the assembly a basic premise of Lockean political philosophy, that it was the "inherent right of every British subject not to be taxed but by his own consent, or that of his representatives." Any tax or any other law created by Parliament or king that did not receive the explicit consent of the colonists violated this most fundamental principle of British rights.

That summer, critics of the Stamp Act in Massachusetts called on each colony to send representatives to New York City for a "Stamp Act Congress," a convention of colonists that would discuss, draft, and present a united call for repealing the tax and stating the limits of the king's authority in the colonies. On September 4, the South Carolina Assembly sent 26-year-old Charleston attorney John Rutledge, Georgetown planter Thomas Lynch, and 41-year-old Christopher Gadsden to New York. Once there, Gadsden took a commanding role in the congress's deliberations and penned both the cover letter to King George and the resolutions that condemned the Stamp Act.

While the congress drafted its letter to King George III, colonists continent-wide took a more aggressive response to the Stamp Act. Starting in New York and Massachusetts, an organization known as the Sons of Liberty was founded to challenge any Crown interference with the rights of British subjects. They considered no tactic too extreme in defense of the colonists. The Sons of Liberty soon spread into every colony, and, in September, its members ignited protests in each colonial capital. In Charleston, tax collectors were physically assaulted and sometimes tarred and feathered;

stamps were burned or stolen. Enraged mobs shattered the storefront windows of merchants who complied with the law, and the governor himself found his home surrounded and threatened with torches.

On October 18, the *Planters Adventure* arrived in Charleston Harbor from England. Aware that the ship carried the colony's supply of stamps, the local Sons of Liberty and their supporters erected a 40-foot-tall gallows near the present-day Battery and hanged an effigy of a stamp distributor next to a sign reading "Liberty and No Stamp Act." The mob spent that evening and the next day ranging throughout the city, ransacking government offices, burning effigies, and disturbing the peace of Charleston. The message could not have been clearer. Colonists in South Carolina and the other colonies would not tolerate this tax. Gadsden and his colleagues from South Carolina attending the congress in New York applauded the protestors.

Acting Governor William Bull, widely liked among South Carolinians, ordered the stamps locked up and protected by armed guards at Fort Johnson, located on the tip of James Island. Aware the stamps had been removed but unsure where they now were, a mob descended on the home of Henry Laurens. Henry Laurens, planter and prominent political figure in the colony, had denounced the Sons of Liberty and insisted their call for "liberty" was nothing more than a cover for their natural inclination to "commit unbounded acts of licentiousness and at length burglary and robbery." He warned Charlestonians that the city would likely incur a stern punitive response from the Crown, possibly the closure of Charleston Harbor by a British fleet or occupation by British troops, should mob action persist. His call for calm and his less-than-flattering description of the local citizenry attracted the attention of the Sons of Liberty as well as their anger. Some suggested that Laurens himself stood to profit from the sale of stamps and that he personally stored stamps for the Crown in his waterfront home. Nearly two dozen disguised men converged on Laurens's home for a midnight visit and "recommended" that he allow them to search the premises for the missing stamps. Over his heated objection, the mouthy and unruly mob stormed into each room, and rifled through every drawer and cabinet seeking any evidence of the stamps. Finding no incriminating

The South Carolina State Flag

Each feature of the state flag relates directly to South Carolina's role in the American Revolution. In 1775, shortly after the war commenced at Lexington and Concord, Massachusetts, Colonel William Moultrie fashioned a flag for the South Carolina troops he commanded on Sullivan's Island. He chose royal blue, the color of his soldiers' uniforms, as the flag's background color. He placed a crescent in the flag's upper left-hand corner, representative of the three-crescent flag carried by the Charleston Patriots in their 1765 opposition to the Stamp Act.

Not until January 1861 was the flag altered; at that time, just one month after South Carolina seceded from the Union, the palmetto tree was added to the 1775 flag. The white tree in the center of the flag commemorated Colonel Moultrie's defense of Sullivan's Island against British attack in 1776, a defense made successful by fortifications constructed of spongy palmetto logs that absorbed or deflected enemy cannon fire. The state flag design with the 1861 addition remains the current flag for South Carolina.

Although the origin of the South Carolina crescent, or "new moon," is considered "lost to history," scholars speculate that it actually has no lunar reference. Some posit that the crescent was part of the Governor William Bull family crest. Others contend that the crescent is a traditional English symbol, representative of the second-born son in a family, who by custom was to inherit nothing from his father. So many emigrants to South Carolina were those not entitled to their father's property; consequently, the crescent honors the building of a colony and a state on the labor and will of the people rather than on privilege. Still others argue that it was simply the emblem worn on pre–Revolutionary War soldiers' caps and around the necks of commissioned officers to signify a particular army unit or an award for courageous military service.

material, the visitors left Laurens but warned him not to support the Crown on the matter of the Stamp Act. They "threatened... to carry me away to some unknown place and punish me" for aiding the Crown, said Laurens. After the mob left, he scribbled in his diary "Riot is in fashion."

Finally learning the stamps' location, a group of 150 Charlestonians armed themselves and forcibly took control of the lightly guarded post. More than 2,000 local residents also gathered in the city, burning an effigy of a tax collector and promising unrestrained force against British agents should the Stamp Act be enforced in the colony. The situation having turned critical, Bull and leaders of the mob agreed that the stamps would be removed from Fort Johnson and returned to England. The potentially explosive reaction to the Stamp Act in Charleston and along the length of the Atlantic seaboard stunned the Crown and their agents in the colonies. Hoping to quell the escalating violence, King George repealed the Stamp Act in early 1766.

The Stamp Act crisis exposed a serious rift within the South Carolinian population. Opposition to the Stamp Act centered in urban communities, particularly in those along the coast, where wealth and direct connections to business interests in England were largely concentrated. People in the Backcountry, the rural inland region populated mainly by small farmers, viewed the crisis as an urban phenomenon and of little importance to their own lives. The conflict was also seen in terms of class—the moneyed interests of the Lowcountry pressing an issue that did not directly affect the working and farming classes. Little sympathy surfaced among Backcountry settlers for the opponents of the Stamp Act.

Soon after he repealed the Stamp Act, King George III issued the Declaratory Act, a statement asserting the king's authority and that of Parliament to create and implement all laws deemed necessary, with or without popular consent. South Carolina's colonial assembly responded, announcing that only it, in accordance with the will of the people, held the right to legislate on internal colonial matters. The ideological division separating Crown and colony could not have been clearer.

Only one year passed before the Crown demonstrated again its determination to raise tax revenue from its colonies in North America, passing the Townshend Acts of 1767 without the consent of American colonists or their representation in Parliament. Unlike the Stamp Act, the Townshend Acts placed a miniscule tax on numerous luxury items typically purchased by the wealthy. Certain paper products once more would be taxed, but levies were added to paint, glass, lead, and tea. Colonists who opposed paying taxes on these goods had easy access to suitable alternatives. Much of the revenue collected by England's agents was to cover the cost of defending the colonies and paying the salaries of government officers and appointed officials. As correctly understood among the colonists, under this provision British officials would no longer be financially dependent on salaries provided by colonial legislatures and therefore no longer be obligated to support the colonists' perspective on matters dealing with the Crown. If British officials were independent of the colonists' control over salaries and other financial matters, it would mean the Crown's appointees would be unfettered by the will of the people being governed—a direct contradiction of Lockean philosophy. Although George III and the sponsor of the act, Charles Townshend, both believed the minor tax placed on numerous goods would hardly be noticed in the colonies and largely be paid by the wealthy elite, they ignored the fundamental argument backed by most colonists who protested the 1765 measure: legislation must reflect the will of the people. The political ideology gaining support among colonists was simply that political authority, or sovereignty, rests with the people; it is the people who establish government and laws can only be enacted by the consent of the people.

The taxes levied by the Townshend Acts were aimed certainly at the colonies' more prosperous residents, but they also affected artisans, cabinet makers, bookbinders, painters, and others of the middle class whose professions depended on paint, glass, lead, and paper. Once again, voices of opposition sounded throughout the thirteen colonies, and the Sons of Liberty called for a ban on the importation of taxable British goods, a complete boycott of the sale or use of taxable items presently in the colonies, and the promise of violent retribution against anyone violating the boycott. Christopher Gadsden organized public

Francis Marion

Born in Berkeley County only a short ride from Georgetown on February 26, 1732, Francis Marion was his Huguenot parents' sixth and final child. His family relocated to a plantation in Georgetown soon after Francis's fifth birthday and there he began his formal education. Always imaginative and curious, young Francis yearned to go to sea and at age fifteen joined the crew of a ship bound for the West Indies. On his return voyage to South Carolina, a whale collided with the schooner, sending the ship under the waves so quickly that the crew escaped without any food or water. Having drifted and suffered for seven days before rescue, Marion vowed that his seagoing career was now over.

Marion joined the South Carolina militia in 1757 and, as a lieutenant under Captain William Moultrie, battled beside British Army regular units to push the Cherokee farther west. War left a profound imprint on the young officer. His diaries and letters vent the horror he witnessed as British troops and militiamen laid waste to Indian villages and killed without remorse. "Some of our men seemed to enjoy this cruel work, laughing very heartily at the curling flames," wrote Marion in one letter to his friend Peter

Horry. "It appeared a shocking sight. Poor creatures!... I could scarcely refrain from tears."

As a member of the South Carolina Provincial Congress in 1775, Francis Marion challenged the colony's continued submission to British authority. In June he was promoted to the rank of captain in the 2nd South Carolina Regiment and the following June served again with William Moultrie in the defense of Charleston against British military and naval forces. Because of his inspiring leadership, the Continental Congress promoted Marion to lieutenant colonel in September 1776.

Until autumn 1780, Marion served with the American Continental Army, battling British troops along the Georgia–South Carolina coast. With the fall of Charleston he organized an irregular force of men—largely local citizens who had abandoned their farms and families to punish the British invaders. Known as "Marion's Men," they served without promise of pay and provided their own horses and arms. For the next several months, Marion led his men against British supply lines, evading destruction and capture by hiding in the swamplands and marshes of South Carolina's Lowcountry. So elusive were Marion's Men that Britain's Colonel Banastre Tarleton referred to Marion as the "Swamp Fox." Marion's union with Continental Army Colonel Richard Henry Lee and their joint interdiction campaign against British supplies throughout 1781 effectively crippled Cornwallis's strength in the South.

After the war and until his death on February 27, 1795, Francis Marion served multiple terms in the South Carolina State Senate, commanded Fort Johnson, and managed his vast plantation, which included 200 slaves. In honor of his long service to the nation and state, the Francis Marion National Forest near Charleston is named after him, as is Francis Marion University in Florence, the Francis Marion Hotel in Charleston, the town and county of Marion, South Carolina, and numerous towns across the United States founded by South Carolinians.

meetings in the Lowcountry in which he and other opponents of British policy chastised the king and Parliament for their persistent affront to popular sentiment, to the rights of Englishmen, and to the emerging ideology of popular sovereignty. The Townshend Acts, he thundered, again threatened the colonists' "liberty and property." Gadsden and his supporters convinced the colonial assembly to unite with the other colonies in the boycott of taxable items and to support calls to ban importation of British goods. In Charleston, Gadsden's "Charleston Patriots" barred the unloading of all British imports at the town's docks, not simply those taxed under Townshend's plan, and resorted to violence against local merchants not honoring the general boycott. Patriot-led mobs ravaged the stores of unsupportive merchants and promised violence toward any shipper determined to unload his cargo on Charleston docks. Individuals who attempted to purchase British imports were verbally and occasionally physically abused. Gadsden and his Patriots, along with others in the city who supported them, burned the king and Townshend in effigy and held bonfire rallies against British taxation. Local newspapers printed scathing attacks on the Crown's alleged abridgement of the rights of Englishmen in America, and broadsides criticizing the king's colonial policy littered city streets. Protestors equated the colonists with "slaves"—slaves to Britain's king and Parliament—and warned of rebellion unless the Crown truly respected American liberty.

The disruption of commerce greatly concerned the Crown, and the threat of rebellion seemed more real than ever before. South Carolina in 1767 imported 50 percent fewer goods than it had the previous year; the Patriots assured British shippers that 1768 would prove even more financially disastrous to England. Flushed by the fury of colonial protest and barraged by the complaints of British exporters and merchants, whose livelihood was threatened by the colonists' boycott, George III repealed most of the Townshend duties, leaving the tax on tea as a symbolic gesture of the king's authority.

Divisions within South Carolina society widened with Patriot action against the Townshend Act. Some Carolinians labeled Gadsden and the Charleston Patriots traitors and urged the Crown to apprehend and punish all who challenged the king's authority. Merchants targeted by boycotters understandably felt the same, but they also felt increasingly alienated from the general community. Their wallets, lightened by the non-importation movement, forced them to choose between violating the boycott and thus suffering the wrath of the Patriots or foregoing profit for survival in the local community. Neither option was satisfactory. In the Backcountry, taxes imposed by the Townshend Act had little effect, if any; rural settlers, therefore, perceived the protests as uniquely urban and, perhaps, a class conflict with the Crown irrelevant to them.

The division between government officials and general citizenry also widened as the decade drew to its close. Some government officers in the colony were appointed to their posts as favors, or "pay-offs," from friends or relatives connected directly to the Crown. Indeed, this practice had become increasingly commonplace. More often than not, these "placemen" held no vested interest in the colony and seldom had experience in the jobs given them. Some, such as Peter Leigh, were widely considered disreputable before coming to South Carolina. Leigh had been a New Jersey lawyer who, through suspicious means, became governor of that colony. Leigh was accused of misconduct in office and literally chased out of New Jersey. Soon afterward, the Crown placed him in South Carolina as the colony's chief justice. Across the colony, placemen such as Leigh generally proved ill-prepared for their assignments and frequently susceptible to corruption and scandal. The Charleston Patriots most vocally pointed to the placemen as clear evidence of the Crown's corrupted political presence in the colony and insisted that a governing system based on popular sovereignty would prevent such unworthy individuals from holding office.

In response to the protests over the Stamp Act, the Townshend Acts, and now placemen, South Carolina's Crown-appointed governor in 1770 dissolved the colony's popularly elected assembly. The governor adhered strictly to the king's directive that colonial governments were to be abolished should they refuse to abide by and to enforce royal decrees and Parliament's laws. The governor's action demonstrated the king's authority in South Carolina and served notice that further signs of disloyalty would be dealt with quickly and severely. While this was certainly the message intended by the governor and echoed by many residents in the colony, it drove many of South Carolina's wealthiest aristocrats directly into the Charleston Patriot camp. William Henry Drayton, for example, viewed the governor's action and the king's directive as an abuse of political authority, the suppression of popular will, and the denial of traditional English rights that Patriots had championed since 1765. Dissolution of the colonial assembly was the watershed event for many in South Carolina.

For the next three years, a tenuous calm settled over South Carolina, as it did across the colonies. Trade through the port at Charleston increased rapidly, with more than 800 cargo ships depositing their wares on the docks in each of the next three years. Historian Walter Fraser, Jr., in his book *Charleston! Charleston*! noted one visitor to the city who remarked, "the number of shipping far surpasses all I had seen in Boston." A wide array of imported goods filled merchants' shelves and rising sales fattened their pockets. More than 10,000 African slaves were moved through the port to auction blocks and garnered unparalleled profits for traders. The city constructed a new jail, more streets, marketplaces, public wells, and a drainage system. A civic consciousness surfaced among city leaders and society's most fortunate residents. The majority of white residents enjoyed a slight increase in their income and general standard of living; high society's elegant dinners and parties made Charleston evenings sparkle. For those outside Charleston, particularly in the Backcountry, life remained very hard. Market prices for farm goods certainly rose, but the labor required to produce crops remained as back-breaking and time-consuming as ever. Indeed, the natural urge to cultivate more land rose in proportion to higher profits. The peaceful, prosperous, and rather slow-paced life of South Carolinians fit well with the seemingly tranquil years of the early 1770s; this peace and tranquility, however, would prove short-lived.

The appearance of calm shattered in late 1773. The Tea Act, issued that year by Parliament and fully endorsed by George III, was intended to enrich the British East India Tea Company with a monopoly on the tea trade to

America. A select few importers were to move the tea from India to the American colonies, giving the importers the full financial benefit of no competition, and prices on the cargo were to be set lower than those typically charged by American shippers. A small tax on the tea would channel American money to the British treasury, an objective that had failed with the Stamp Act and the Townshend Acts.

England stood to gain much. The British East India Tea Company served as Britain's source of entry into India and from there across Southwest Asia. It was widely assumed in London that the resources and potential markets of India, along with the points of entry from India into neighboring territories, would one day generate more profits for Britain than those ever accrued from the Americas. Maintaining Britain's early hold on Indian resources and markets was deemed critical to England's' financial security. Moreover, a tax on tea reasserted the Crown's supreme authority over all British colonies. And, it was reasoned, the tax on tea would be so small, a mere three pence per pound, that Americans would not notice it once the actual price of tea was reduced. The Tea Act seemed to King George III and to Parliament a perfect solution.

Opposition to the Tea Act surfaced immediately in South Carolina and centered itself in Charleston, much as the opposition to placemen, the Townshend Acts, and the Stamp Act had years earlier. As in previous squabbles, the amount of the tax and the item to be taxed were themselves not actually the critical points of resistance. Mint tea and sassafras tea were widely consumed in the colonies instead of East Indian tea; moreover, coffee had long been a popular substitute. Colonists could easily have abandoned East Indian tea and never confronted England's latest tax, but South Carolinians condemned this latest tax measure as one created and enacted without the consent of the people being governed or the approval of their representatives. The Tea Act was another attempt by the Crown to assert its sovereignty, a view of authority in stark conflict with that now expressed by colonists in America. To accept the tax on tea would acknowledge the Crown's right to tax colonists and to implement laws without popular oversight and control. "Their personal independence, property, and the power of their Assembly were again threatened," wrote

Walter Fraser, Jr. To be sure, many in Charleston and across the surrounding countryside did agree that the king and Parliament possessed absolute authority to govern, with or without the consent of the governed.

Arguments surrounding the Tea Act remained largely academic until December 2, 1773. That morning, the *London,* the first of seven ships scheduled to arrive that day laden with tea, appeared in Charleston Harbor, dropped anchor, and awaited instructions for unloading the 260 crates of tea in its hold. Christopher Gadsden, the principal architect of the Charleston Patriots and the local Sons of Liberty, recognized that paying the taxes and unloading the tea would constitute South Carolina's acquiescence to British authority over that of the colonial assembly that represented the will of its constituents. Gadsden quickly printed and distributed a circular throughout the city, informing residents that an emergency meeting would be held the next day at the Exchange Building.

Opponents of the Crown, supporters of the king, and genuinely curious spectators gathered at the Exchange Building on December 3. Within moments even the foggiest brain realized this meeting was aimed at resisting the Tea Act. In quick succession, those in attendance selected a presiding officer, penned an order that prohibited the unloading of the tea, and arranged for committees to solicit support from local merchants.

Informed in advance of the planned Patriot gathering and anticipating a scenario perhaps more confrontational than that which unfolded over the Stamp Act and Townshend Acts, Lt. Governor William Bull ordered all tea arrivals stored under lock and key to protect them from confiscation or destruction by the city's malcontents. Bull's quick action saved the tea from destruction, but it did not prevent the Patriots' physical attack on tax collectors and on town merchants willing to sell the imported tea. Charlestonians soon implemented another boycott of British imports, and once more merchants and customers who violated the ban paid dearly at the hands of Patriots. Newspaper editorials, broadsides, flyers, and petitions denouncing the Tea Act sifted through the colonial population and encouraged all citizens of South Carolina to resist the Crown.

Throughout the American colonies similar responses to British policies unfolded, reaching a climax with the Boston Tea Party. Explicitly responding to the Boston affair, king and Parliament struck back. From the Crown's perspective, England had long worked with the colonies to resolve disputes fairly and to maintain a relationship financially and politically beneficial to each. Had the king not repealed the Stamp Act? Had he not also scrapped the Townshend Acts following colonial opposition? Had Parliament or king repressed the colonists' exercise of free speech, assembly, or dissent, even when it included violence against British officials and the destruction of both private and public property? And, despite years of opposition to its taxes from colonists in America, England continued its military protection of the seaboard colonies. And, in defense of its position on royal sovereignty and the rights of Englishmen, King George III and leaders in Parliament insisted that the colonists' perspective had always been represented in Parliament through the good will of its members. The time had now come, reasoned Parliament and king, to assert the Crown's absolute authority over its citizens living in America and, in the process, to punish Boston for the tea its residents had destroyed.

In early 1774 Parliament fashioned the Coercive Acts, a series of measures American colonists collectively termed the "Intolerable Acts." Boston's harbor was to be closed and all traffic into the city by land would be halted until all financial loss caused by the Boston Tea Party was recouped. Five thousand additional British troops were to be posted in the city and become, in essence, a policing force of 10,000 troops. Boston residents were to fund the construction of barracks for those incoming soldiers, and, until barracks were built, house those troops in private homes. Standing warrants to conduct general searches without probable cause were now permitted. British officials charged with crimes in America were to be tried not in the colonies but in England, and the Massachusetts colonial charter was to be revised to reduce its degree of independence from the Crown. Although the Coercive Acts were immediately and expressly aimed at Boston, Parliament's action was a clear statement to all colonists that the Crown, not the people, was sovereign.

Battle of Cowpens

Some historians regard the Battle of Cowpens (January 17, 1781) as the turning point of the American Revolution in the Southern Colonies—the pivotal battle between British and American forces that led inevitably to the British military defeat at Yorktown the following October and the Crown's agreement to negotiate an end to the war on American terms.

General Nathaniel Greene, commander of the American Continental Army in the South, ordered General Daniel Morgan into the western territory of South Carolina to harass British forces and to extinguish Loyalist activity there. The move compelled Lord General Charles Cornwallis, who was in pursuit of Greene's forces, to divide his army into smaller elements and in so doing weaken the main body of British military might in the Southern Colonies. Cornwallis directed Colonel Banastre Tarleton, known among colonists as "Banastre the Butcher," to destroy Morgan's regiment. Tarleton gave chase and tracked Morgan to Grindal's Shoals on the Pacolet River. Careful to place his own army in an advantageous position, Morgan selected the frontier crossroads Cowpens as the location at which he would turn on Tarleton and confront the British.

The site Morgan chose was a 2,500-square-yard cattle pasture. On either side of the pasture stood sizeable hills on which Morgan posted American sharpshooters and cavalry. He purposely positioned his troops with the Broad River to their rear so that they could not retreat. In earlier battles, his militia units had broken ranks and fled the battlefield; retreat here would be impossible, forcing his militia units to stand and fight. His objective was simple: draw Tarleton into the open land and then allow the cavalry to envelop the British from two sides. Sharpshooters would hold their positions to prevent Tarleton from securing the high ground.

The morning of January 17 was bright and unusually frigid. Tarleton's scouts informed him of the lay of the land, the river blocking American retreat, the number and position of militiamen, and the assessment that victory would come quickly with an all-out attack. Tarleton immediately instructed his men to take no prisoners and issued orders to charge. Morgan's plan, however, worked to perfection and within one hour British forces were decimated. Tarleton himself and his few surviving men fled from Cowpens and linked with Cornwallis. American casualties totaled 12 dead and 60 wounded; the British, however, suffered more than 100 dead, 200 wounded, and 500 soldiers captured. The Battle of Cowpens and the Battle at Kings Mountain three months earlier effectively ended the British military presence in western South Carolina and drove from the region their Loyalist allies.

The Cowpens Battlefield Park is located near Chesnee, South Carolina between Gaffney and Spartanburg. Guests may walk the paved mile-long Battlefield Trail, which includes wayside exhibits open daily, and drive along the four-mile Auto Loop Road that encircles the Cowpens battlefield and includes parking areas with walkways onto critical battle positions. A museum on the property features weapons common to the Revolutionary War, as well as uniforms, maps, and battle dioramas. On July 4, the park celebrates Independence Day with a living history encampment, activities for children that teach colonial-era arts, and a fireworks celebration after sundown. On the weekend closest to October 7, Over-mountain Victory Trail marchers arrive at the park to rest and treat guests as they retrace the path taken by Patriots to battle Major Patrick Ferguson at Kings Mountain in 1780. The park commemorates the Battle of Cowpens each year on the weekend closest to January 17. Among the activities offered at the annual celebration is a living history encampment in which guests witness firsthand the typical eighteenth-century army life. The park also presents a firing demonstration of Revolutionary War–era weapons, a small arms drill by a team of battle re-enactors, lectures by historians and others, a play, and a wreath-laying ceremony to honor those whose lives were lost at this battle.

For more information about the park, write to Cowpens National Battlefield, PO Box 308, Chesnee, South Carolina 29323, call (864) 461-2828, or visit the US National Park Service website at www.nps.gov/cowp.

War Comes to South Carolina

Once colonists learned of the Coercive Acts and recognized the obvious message of the measure, New York's dissidents called for an inter-colony meeting comparable to the earlier Stamp Act Congress. They asked that representatives from each colony attend a Continental Congress in Philadelphia in September 1774 and there discuss the disagreements between Crown and colonists and, they hoped, devise an amicable resolution.

The importance of the Coercive Acts and the Continental Congress was not lost on South Carolinians. Gadsden, the Charleston Patriots, and the local Sons of Liberty saw "these hostile acts of Parliament against Boston" as the first direct assault by the Crown on colonists resisting absolute Crown authority, as a loss of citizen rights, and as a possible financial loss caused by Parliament's economic policies. On July 6, a General Meeting convened in Charleston with 100 members of South Carolina's aristocracy present. It was the first assembly in the colony that included substantial representation from the Backcountry—the inland regions historically at odds with the Lowcountry's wealthy planters and merchants. The delegates, however, were not of one mind. Arguments raged over the prospect of another general boycott of British goods, the purpose of government and the extent of authority commanded by citizens, and the real intent of the Philadelphia convention. After three days of squabbling, the General Meeting instructed its chosen representatives to the Continental Congress to support no action that would substantially harm South Carolina's merchants, artisans, or planters. Elected to represent the colony at the Continental Congress were two veterans of the Stamp Act Congress—Christopher Gadsden and Thomas Lynch. Henry Middleton, who owned a plantation along the Ashley River outside Charleston, and the Rutledge brothers—John and Edward—were also chosen to attend the Philadelphia meeting. Although the General Meeting openly stated its intention to represent the colony's diverse opinions at the congress, all the delegates except John Rutledge were supporters of Gadsden's Patriots. Equally critical, the General Meeting established the General Committee of 99, a collection of merchants and planters chaired by Charles Pinckney to serve as the colony's unofficial political assembly in place of the Commons House, which the governor had dissolved in 1770. It would be, in effect, an ad hoc governing body.

Neither the General Meeting nor the Committee of 99 fully reflected public opinion in South Carolina. Across the Lowcountry, many merchants whose stores were stocked with British imports condemned anyone who called for a general boycott and damned the Sons of Liberty and Charleston Patriots for the destruction of property they promised against those who continued to sell British goods. Others such as Reverend John Bullman of St. Michael's Church chastised the Lowcountry elite for rousing the "idle and illiterate" working population into violent opposition to legal authority, insisting that the lower class should remain in its "place." Similar views were shared by "gentlemen" throughout the region. And, of course, most of the Backcountry's small farmers and emerging elite denounced what appeared to them as a urban crisis generated by the wealthy to protect their own financial security, under the pretense of defending the rights of Englishmen.

The First Continental Congress convened as planned, but it accomplished little. From the meeting came a request that each colony endorse a general boycott of British wares. Beyond this, the opinions expressed by delegates ranged from a call for the colonies' independence from England to their total submission to royal authority. Delegates returned home in October to solicit their constituents' advice before returning to Philadelphia in May 1775 for a second congress.

In January 1775, the General Committee convened in Charleston. Present were six delegates from each South Carolina parish outside of Charleston. Charleston comprised two parishes, and by order of the General Committee each was allowed fifteen delegates, a decision that only reinforced the Backcountry's long accusation of political corruption in the colony and the Lowcountry's heavy-handed control over South Carolina's affairs. Once in session, the Committee renamed itself the First Provincial Congress and following some debate agreed to the boycott recommended by the First Continental Congress. As before, however, delegates to the General Committee were not of one mind, and heated arguments over British policies and the proper colonial response produced no resolution. Before their delegates journeyed back to Philadelphia, blood was shed in mid-April at Lexington Green, Concord Bridge, and along the twenty-mile road leading from Concord to Boston. Although Englishmen in both America and England called for a peaceful, nonviolent resolution to the crisis separating the colonies from the mother country, almost everyone understood that the fighting in Massachusetts had been the opening shots of war.

Learning of the battles at Lexington and Concord one week after they occurred, South Carolina's First Provincial Congress moved to protect Charleston from any British military move directed toward the Lowcountry. It was widely known that Parliament had dispatched more soldiers to the Americas earlier in the month; fear spread in the Southern Colonies that these troops were destined for points between Williamsburg, Virginia and Savannah, Georgia. Late in the evening of April 26, William Henry Drayton led several members of the Provincial Congress to the arsenal near Charleston Harbor, gathered the weapons, ammunition, and powder and hid them throughout the city. Thus any British troops that might arrive would not have access to the stores, but locals would be better equipped to defend the city.

South Carolinians watched the pace of war quicken in New England throughout May and June. The colony's delegates to the Second Continental Congress in these weeks committed themselves and South Carolina fully to the rebellion, even though popular opinion was seriously divided in the colony. When the congress proclaimed itself the de facto governing structure for those in rebellion, South Carolina's delegates offered no opposition. Indeed, they supported the move and voted for George Washington to command a continental army against England.

The revolutionary spirit within South Carolina coalesced in the Lowcountry. Members of the Provincial Congress and its thirteen-man executive council, known as the Council of Safety, publicly pledged their lives and fortunes to preserve the colonists' rights as Englishmen and to chase from South Carolina those who supported the "oppressive" and "tyrannical" acts of king and Parliament.

Must-See Sites: Kings Mountain National Military Park

This military park, located approximately 20 miles southwest of Charlotte, North Carolina on Highway 216 on the state line is the site of the pivotal October 1780 battle between Carolina patriots and a force of British regular troops and local Tories under the command of Major Patrick Ferguson. A museum and video presentation greet visitors, and guests may hike battlefield trails, camp, fish, visit a nineteenth-century living history farm, or ride horses. A wreath-laying ceremony is held on October 7 each year to commemorate the battle and to honor those who fought and died at Kings Mountain. The park is open daily except on holidays, and admission is free. Visit www.nps.gov/kimo for additional information.

Citizens who refused to support the rebellion were pronounced "enemies of their country" and subject to the confiscation of their property and fortunes. The Provincial Congress also voted to raise and fund three army regiments for the defense of South Carolina. The sharp tone, divisive spirit, and stern steps taken by the congress and council horrified more moderate members; Congress President Charles Pinckney resigned his position over his colleagues' intolerant stance. In the weeks that followed, residents supportive of the Crown, also known as Loyalists, found the fervor of rebellion spreading throughout the Lowcountry. Several merchants in Charleston were "tarred, feathered, and carted through the streets," one South Carolina Patriot later recalled. Loyalists were chased from the city and surrounding towns, and those who had not chosen sides in the conflict were advised to do so quickly. Slaves were warned against any behavior that might be construed as inciting insurrection, as doing so would most certainly benefit local Loyalist plans to collapse the Patriot rebellion. Tolerance had no place in this developing civil war.

The Backcountry of South Carolina did not align itself with the rebellion. The turmoil that had rocked Charleston before 1775 had little to do with the region. Many residents of the area still perceived the confrontation as a commercial conflict only relevant to the coast's urban elite. Moreover, they refused to take arms against the legitimate government of the colonies, the British Crown. In September, rumors spread that Royal Governor William Campbell intended to arm Backcountry loyalists and march them against Lowcountry rebels. Members of the Provincial Congress demanded the governor's arrest. Evading capture, Campbell fled South Carolina and sailed to England. Whether or not there was any truth regarding Campbell's plot, the fact that Lowcountry residents considered the rumor true testified to the long-term animosity each region had for the other.

Events continued to spiral beyond the possibility of reconciliation. Soon after Governor Campbell made his exit, a South Carolina rebel regiment moved against Fort Johnson and took military command of the island that secured the southern approach to Charleston Harbor. On November 1, the Provincial Congress ordered the blockading of the Cooper River, which would protect Charleston from British naval bombardment. Earthworks and other defense-related construction projects were begun, local residents were assigned emergency tasks such as fighting fire or policing the city, women were asked to prepare medical kits for their families and to store necessary supplies for their families, and slaves were pressed into defense work.

While Charleston readied itself for British attack, Patriot and Loyalist forces on November 15 clashed at the small community of Ninety-Six, shedding the first drops of blood in South Carolina. Loyalists retreated into Cherokee lands with Patriot forces in pursuit, and in December the Great Snow Campaign in the area of present-day Greenville County pitted 4,000 Patriots against nearly 2,000 Loyalists. The preponderance of Patriot power quelled Loyalist activity in the Backcountry well into the next year.

Not until June 1776 did British troops directly threaten South Carolina, a move that ultimately pressed the colony's moderates to support the call for total independence from

Britain. Charleston Harbor was vital to the British war effort. Through it, British troops and supplies could move inland easily and quickly and in so doing extend the British army's range in both Carolinas and northern Georgia. General Henry Clinton commanded 3,000 British redcoats and a fleet of warships, and he moved to take the harbor and city. John Rutledge, South Carolina's new governor, mustered a rebel militia of 5,000 men under the leadership of Colonel William Moultrie, who quickly constructed a makeshift fort on Sullivan's Island to guard the harbor's entrance. Nearly 500 American Continental Army soldiers under the command of General Charles Lee arrived from North Carolina to offer their support. The defensive structure was made of double rows of soft, almost spongy palmetto logs.

Clinton began his assault on June 28. Redcoats landed on the Isle of Palms just north of Charleston, but they were unable to ford the waterway separating the island from the mainland. Several of Clinton's vessels ran aground and were destroyed by a withering fire from Patriot guns. The remaining British warships bombarded rebel defenses, but cannon shells only bounced off the palmetto logs. Patriot cannon returned fire, sinking one ship and damaging several others. The British retreated without inflicting any significant damage on rebel defenders. To honor their local hero, the earthwork and palmetto structure on Sullivan's Island was named Fort Moultrie. One week later, South Carolina's representatives to the Second Continental Congress affixed their names to the Declaration of Independence.

Although the British threat to Charleston in summer 1776 was reduced substantially by the British debacle at Sullivan's Island, along the western frontier the Cherokee launched a series of stunning raids on Backcountry settlements. It is likely that the Indians would have eventually warred with settlers in the region, but their strikes in July 1776 were encouraged by one British agent, John Stuart, who was ordered by the Crown to unite Cherokees with the British war effort against rebel forces. Stuart's ignorance—his assumption that all South Carolinians were rebels— carried serious repercussions for the British effort in the Backcountry. Indians struck both

Must-See Sites: Historic Camden Revolutionary War Site

British forces under General Lord Cornwallis soundly defeated American troops under General Horatio Gates at the Battle of Camden in summer 1780. While in Camden, Cornwallis appropriated a local home for his headquarters. The Kershaw-Cornwallis House, as it is known today, is open for tourists visiting the battlefield. At the historic site are log houses common to the Revolutionary era, a powder magazine, and walking trails around the battle site. In November each year, the community holds its Revolutionary War Field Days at the site, featuring crafts, living history demonstrations, and regimental drills. The battle site is open Tuesday through Saturday. Call (803) 432-9841 or email hiscamden@camden.net for more information.

rebel and Loyalist communities in the Backcountry. Their attacks only drove those settlers into rebellion against England. With little difficulty, Colonel Andrew Williamson in August assembled an 1,800-man force and pressed a counterattack with a ferocity and brutality that surpassed Cherokee depredations. Indians fled into the western mountains, ceding to South Carolina exclusive ownership of present-day Greenville, Pickens, Anderson, and Oconee counties.

For the next three years, South Carolina remained rather quiet. War still raged throughout New England and the Middle Colonies, but England did not threaten the South. The tenuous peace collapsed, however, in August 1779 as Britain abandoned its failed military strategy and implemented a new plan for victory in America. With a large navy and army, supplemented by the abundant Loyalist base that remained in the region, British forces decided to conquer Georgia and then roll northward through the Carolinas, eventually linking up with British armies in New York. In short, as each southern colony fell to British military power and political authority, rebel forces would retreat north and at some point become pinned between two massive British armies. An American surrender would result.

Savannah fell quickly to British military and naval might. A fleet of 32 ships and 4,000 French and American troops were rushed to the South Carolina coast but their commanders failed to agree on a counterattack strategy, squandering any chance to push British forces from Savannah. General Clinton used the American–French delay to fortify the coastal city with reinforcements and to collapse the rebel presence inland. At the same time, small skirmishes dotted the South Carolina–Georgia border, but in May a British force of 3,000 soldiers sat on the outskirts of Charleston. Only the arrival of General Benjamin Lincoln's American army of equal strength prevented a British strike against the city at this time. With the city momentarily secured, local Patriots vented their rage against Loyalists who still resided in the city. Planters and wealthy merchants who preferred reconciliation with England were assaulted on the streets, suffered home invasion and the theft of their household goods, and occasionally were forced to watch their property destroyed. General Lincoln was more concerned about the city's defenses. His army held few supplies, and he knew that British reinforcements would soon outnumber his own army. Lincoln persistently begged the American congress for greater manpower and more supplies; not until December did congress give him a portion of what he needed.

In February 1780 General Clinton finally moved against Charleston. He encircled the city with 10,000 soldiers and blocked the harbor with a British fleet. Over the next three months, British cannon laid siege to the city. No quarter was given to Charleston's civilians. Historian Walter Fraser reports that one Hessian officer attached to Clinton's army heard "A terrible clamor among the inhabitants" and the "wailing of female voices" coming from the city following a prolonged bombardment in mid-April. Food, medicine, and clean water were soon in short supply among the city's residents. Not a dog, cat, or rat was safe with human survival in doubt. On May 7 Fort Moultrie fell to the British, and one week later Charleston itself capitulated. Clinton took 5,000 American soldiers as prisoners of war, confiscated the American army's supplies, and took control of the last port open to American and French fleets on the Atlantic coast. It proved to be Britain's brightest victory in the war.

British cavalry now ranged deep inland, patrolling the countryside and countering any rebel force that challenged them. Colonel Banastre Tarleton commanded one such unit. In present-day Lancaster County, Tarleton cornered a regiment of Virginia Patriots and slaughtered the entire unit despite the white flag it hoisted and its shouts of surrender. Rather than compelling Patriots in the area to lay down their arms and submit to British authority, as he assumed such brutality would force, Tarleton's actions only enraged Backcountry men and drove the entire section of South Carolina into the rebel cause.

At the same time, Clinton turned over the operational duties of his command to Lord General Charles Cornwallis. Reaching Camden near present-day Columbia in July, Cornwallis utterly crushed a Continental Army commanded by General Horatio Gates. Surviving Americans fled, leaving behind 650 dead Patriots. Gates himself retreated 150 miles to Hillsboro, North Carolina. Days later, Colonel Tarleton followed Cornwallis's victory at Camden with the rout of another American force, one commanded by South Carolinian Thomas Sumter, affectionately known as "the Gamecock" for his fighting spirit. By summer's end, British forces occupied Charleston and much of the Backcountry. Through the harbor came materiel and manpower for pressing the war inland against rebel forces across South Carolina.

Lengthening supply lines worried Cornwallis, and rightly so. Following the Battle of Camden, General George Washington dumped General Gates, replacing him with General Nathaniel Greene. Greene was untested in battle, but his superb organizational skills, his ability to inspire devotion among his soldiers, and his determination to fight the British were all traits Gates lacked. Greene based his new command in Charlotte, North Carolina, about 70 miles north of Camden. He then dispatched Colonel Richard Henry Lee to the areas north and west of Charleston, ordering him to join forces with local militia units in the swamplands commanded by Francis Marion and Thomas Sumter. Their task, Greene said, was the interdiction of British supplies moving from Charleston to Cornwallis's inland units. The campaign of Lee, Marion, and Sumter became legendary, Marion and Sumter quickly becoming heroic figures among South Carolinians and Marion earning the nickname "Swamp Fox" from his admirers.

Greene then began a slow, tactical retreat from Charlotte to the northeast, purposely enticing a British pursuit. To secure the western flank as his army chased Greene, Cornwallis dispatched Major Patrick Ferguson into the Carolina foothills to rally Loyalist support and to crush the few rebel units in the area. Ferguson, a firebrand, failed to control his use of derogatory terms toward rebels. He openly doubted the honesty and loyalty of Backcountry settlers, promised to hang all Patriot leaders he apprehended, and guaranteed that he would lay waste to all communities not absolutely obedient to the Crown. His sharp words enraged colonists in both Carolinas and in the Tennessee mountains and in response they massed a 1,000-man force to chase him from the region.

British scouts and Loyalists informed Ferguson in early October of the approach of "Overmountain Men" who were filtering out of the Appalachian Mountains and crossing the hill country toward his army. They advised the major to seek a suitable defensive position immediately. British troops and their armed Loyalist allies hurried to the top of Kings Mountain, located on the border of the two Carolinas. On October 7, 1780, without resting from their long march, the Overmountain Men charged Ferguson's troops. In only one hour, the battle was decided. More than 800 British and Loyalist soldiers lay dead, including Ferguson, and another 300 were taken prisoner. The Overmountain Men hanged some of the captured soldiers as retribution for the actions of other British commanders, particularly Banastre Tarleton.

Only three months later, Tarleton himself was targeted by rebels. General Greene ordered an interdiction campaign in the South Carolina Lowcountry and commenced his methodical retreat from Charlotte, and at the same time sent a regiment commanded by General Daniel Morgan into western South Carolina to draw away from himself part of Cornwallis's army. On Morgan's heels was Tarleton, armed with 1,000 redcoats and Loyalists determined to kill every rebel and brand the region with the king's authority. On January 17, 1781, Morgan and Tarleton collided. In a masterfully crafted battle plan, Morgan's army trounced the British, killing or capturing more than 900 British soldiers and sending the remaining 150, including Tarleton, scrambling back to Cornwallis in a disorganized and panicked retreat. These two battles, Kings Mountain and Cowpens, effectively sealed the western Carolinas under Patriot control. Continued harassment in the Lowcountry by Marion, Sumter, and Lee prevented Cornwallis from getting the reinforcements and supplies he desperately needed inland.

Cornwallis continued his pursuit of Greene. Along the route, frequent ambushes bloodied and demoralized the redcoats. At Guilford Courthouse (Greensboro), General Greene turned to fight the weary British and, although Cornwallis claimed victory in the battle, inflicted a 25 percent casualty rate on the redcoats. Battered, weakened, fatigued, and demoralized, Cornwallis's force broke off its pursuit of Greene, slipped southeast to Wilmington on the coast, and then moved north to Yorktown, Virginia, where French and American military and naval forces surrounded him, forcing his surrender in October 1781. The campaign in South Carolina proved pivotal in the Patriots' claiming victory in the South.

Despite Cornwallis's surrender, the war officially continued while diplomats in Paris strove to negotiate an armistice and peace treaty. In these months, Greene moved his army into South Carolina, slowly pressing British units back to Charleston. Battles again flared at Camden, Ninety-Six, and Eutaw Springs. Not until December 16, 1782 did the British finally evacuate the coastal city. With the regular army went nearly 4,000 South Carolina Loyalists and their 5,000 slaves. South Carolina was now free of British rule. What had commenced as a debate over the source of power to govern inside the colonies ended in 1783 with a treaty that granted independence to a new nation, the United States of America.

5

Postwar Directions

With a little ink scribbled onto parchment followed by a few polite nods of agreement, diplomats at the Paris Peace Conference in 1783 announced the end of hostilities between Great Britain and her former American colonies. "The World Turned Upside Down," a little ditty played two years earlier at the surrender of General Charles Cornwallis at Yorktown, Virginia seemed so appropriate now. A minority of American colonists had initiated rebellion against the most powerful nation in the Western world, tenaciously stalled British military conquest of the colonies, founded a revolutionary government based on a liberal political ideology, doggedly pursued and ultimately gained an alliance with France, and eventually secured a victory whose reward was far greater than originally anticipated—independence. The monarchs of Europe, including the French king, now pondered the implications of America's revolution on their own peasant masses and their distant colonial possessions. America's Enlightenment-inspired political ideology valued the worth of all men and theoretically shifted the seat of government authority from the anointed few to the people themselves. A revolution had, indeed, occurred; the crowned heads across Europe now cautiously eyed their own realms and studied with interest America's postwar course.

Addressing Postwar Problems

As remarkable and exhilarating an achievement as victory in the war had been for South Carolina's Patriots, the conflict left in its wake a reality few had considered seriously just eight years earlier. The coastal cities of Charleston, Georgetown, and Beaufort all bore the physical scars of battle, their business districts lay in shambles, and urban residents had fled for the relative safety of the countryside.

British forces had razed small towns and villages aligned, or thought to be aligned, with the Patriot cause. Banastre Tarleton's rampage through the Backcountry along with Patrick Ferguson's vicious swipes against the frontier population left homes and farms leveled, thousands of acres of crops destroyed, mills torched, and much of the region cast into poverty. The war had also taken the lives of many South Carolinians—farmers, merchants, manufacturers, traders, and planters alike. By 1783, the war of rebellion had fractured South Carolina's social, economic, and political structures.

To complicate matters, general lawlessness plagued the Backcountry. Assaults and robberies were frequent, most conducted by newcomers to the territory who believed the remote farms and isolated travelers offered easy pickings. Wartime animosities also lingered, as they do after all civil wars. Former Tories, or Loyalists, who aided Colonel Tarleton or Major Patrick Ferguson were remembered for the brutality British forces wreaked on American soldiers, militiamen, and civilians. Some of these former Loyalists were chased from the Backcountry and their property was auctioned to Patriot supporters; more than a few endured the pain of physical retribution. No longer a colony but now a state with nearly the power and responsibility of an autonomous nation itself, South Carolina's government entered the postwar period more than a little apprehensive but determined to assert its newfound authority, stabilize society, and establish peacetime prosperity.

The new state government wasted little time addressing an immediate issue—securing South Carolina's economy. Within months of the Peace of Paris, it incorporated the city of Charleston and in so doing allowed its residents to form a local government. A city council was soon formed, and its representatives quickly moved to protect local business from exploitation by foreign creditors and former Loyalists. In 1784 the General Assembly created a uniform tax rate on land, based on assessed value, and the following year the state permitted South Carolinians to repay their debts with land rather than strictly cash. This act alone enabled many merchants, planters, and farmers to repay their debts. The assembly also authorized the issuance of secured loans ranging from

$2,000 to $17,000 for rebuilding or expanding private business in the state. This particularly aided South Carolina's exports. With the war's end came the virtual collapse of the indigo trade that before 1775 had been buttressed by British subsidies. Moreover, the export of all goods from South Carolina directly to England or to the British West Indies ended with the war's conclusion; England now acquired many of the same goods from non-American producers.

State loans to individuals and to the newly organized Charleston Chamber of Commerce financially supported efforts to open new overseas markets. These steps helped calm the citizenry. Financially strapped coastal and Backcountry farmers who had banded together immediately following the war and violently prevented the foreclosure of properties, threatening open rebellion, now saw the state provide debt relief and the promise of a stabilized economy. Planters and merchants whose investments had teetered on the brink of collapse now saw before them a path toward financial security and possibly renewed prosperity.

The General Assembly also worked to restore order in the general society. In 1785, for example, the state demanded all wartime Loyalists leave South Carolina. This order was issued in part to remove from the state a segment of the population thought to be untrustworthy, undependable, and perhaps corruptive to South Carolina's progress. It was also intended to reduce postwar violence within the state, thus leading to social stability, and to divest the state's previous enemy of its local property, in order to sell it to those who had supported the state and the American cause. The assembly also commanded the founding of local paramilitary units in the Backcountry to protect citizens from thieves and to assure the enforcement of law in that part of the state. It further acted to reduce longstanding tensions between the state's two regions. For decades Backcountry residents had bitterly complained that they were the victims of a coastal elite that fashioned law and channeled funds to suit its own ends. This divide had underpinned the sectional conflict present in South Carolina throughout the Revolutionary War. The General Assembly in 1786 relocated the state capital from

Andrew Jackson

South Carolinians claim the seventh president of the United States, Andrew Jackson, as their native son. Born on March 15, 1767 near Waxhaw just south of Charlotte, he was reared in Lancaster, South Carolina. His childhood was difficult, though not uncommon for the times. Only days before his birth, Andrew's father was killed in a logging accident. His mother, Betty, moved the family closer to her parents in Lancaster. Andrew assumed the normal responsibilities of farm boys on the Carolina frontier, but at night his family tutored him in the basic academic subjects.

When the Revolutionary War came to South Carolina, Andrew's older brother Hugh enlisted in the American Continental Army and in late June, following the Battle of Stono Ferry twenty miles south of Charleston, died from heat exhaustion. Andrew, only thirteen, and his remaining brother Robert enlisted in the Continental Army the following spring. Together they served as couriers and, together, in April 1781, were captured by British troops. One English officer commanded Andrew to clean his mud-caked boots—according to legend, in language most vile. Andrew refused, using similarly colorful expressions. Enraged by the insolence, the officer wielded his saber toward the youngster, slicing Andrew's hand to the bone. The officer then retreated issuing a flurry of derogatory terms about

Jackson, the Backcountry, and Americans generally. For reasons that remain unclear, Andrew and Robert were released from captivity several weeks later.

Robert died only days after his release, apparently from smallpox he'd contracted while a prisoner. The boys' mother left Lancaster and journeyed to Charleston. She took a job at a hospital nursing American prisoners of war, but many within her extended family and some scholars today believe she ventured to the Lowcountry to be near the grave of her oldest son. Little time passed before she, too, died—probably from cholera. Andrew, now fourteen, remained in Lancaster for the next three years.

At seventeen, Andrew traveled to Salisbury, North Carolina to study law, passing the bar exam in 1787 and becoming a prosecuting attorney in the state's westernmost city, Nashville. He earned the reputation as an aggressive but fair prosecutor and built a network of influential friends. In 1796, Tennessee was created from North Carolina's western territories, and Jackson was elected as the state's first representative to the US House of Representatives, followed by a term in the Senate and on the Tennessee Supreme Court.

Jackson also built a thriving plantation known as The Hermitage and was made a major general in the US Army. He led troops in war against the Creek and Seminole Indians in which his ferocity was praised by his superiors but condemned by Native Americans and others even today. He was given command of all American forces along the Gulf Coast during the War of 1812, and in January 1815 Jackson's 6,500-man army soundly trounced a British force of 8,500 men, halting British activity in the region. Old Hickory, as he was now called by admirers for his stern discipline and confidence, was a national hero.

Jackson vied for the presidency in 1824 but lost to John Quincy Adams. Four years later, he challenged the incumbent and, building a strong grassroots campaign, won handily. He served two terms, from 1828 to 1837. His presidency has been termed "the age of Jackson" and "the era of Jacksonian democracy," and, indeed, he inaugurated sweeping democratic reforms. In response to a new tariff law in 1832, the Palmetto State issued its Ordinance of Nullification, giving the state the right to declare void any federal law in conflict with South Carolina wishes. Jackson blasted his home state for its posturing and assured South Carolina that the United States Constitution was, in fact, the supreme law of the land. In Indian affairs, he supported the Indian Removal Act that forcibly removed the Cherokee and other tribes to Oklahoma, freeing 100 million acres of land in the South for white settlement but causing the Trail of Tears, among the most deplorable actions perpetrated against Native Americans. Jackson retired to The Hermitage in 1837 and lived his remaining days in relative quiet. He died on June 8, 1845.

Charleston to a town yet to be constructed but more centrally located—Columbia. Some suggested the move was intended to appease more western residents and in so doing diminish significantly the intrastate wrangling so common to the state's history. Others posited that relocating the capital was a genuine, well-intentioned plan to make government more accessible to all South Carolinians and perhaps more responsible to the citizenry, certainly values consistent with Lockean political philosophy. Perhaps the move was also an effort to separate South Carolina psychologically from its colonial past, a symbolic start to the new, post-British era.

Regardless of the assembly's motives, an immediate backlash whipped across the Lowcountry. Charleston was the founding point of South Carolina; the city specifically and the surrounding region more generally had historically been the seat of political authority and the center of wealth. Lowcountry residents feared that the relocation of the state capital 100 miles inland would mean a corresponding loss of political influence in state politics and finance. In spite of these initial concerns, Charlestonians soon realized that real power in South Carolina remained where wealth resided, and for now that continued to be in the Lowcountry's aristocracy. Fear and anger soon dissipated along the coast; anticipation among Backcountry residents grew as construction of a small, wooden statehouse began in 1786. Altogether, the steps taken by the postwar General Assembly brightened the prospects for social and economic stability.

Toward a More Perfect Union of States

The United States' first national governing system, the Articles of Confederation, disappointed most propertied South Carolinians. Charles Pinckney, himself a member of the national congress, believed there were serious problems with the governing system that demanded immediate attention. Each state held the right to coin its own money; each state regulated its own Indian affairs; each established its own foreign commercial ties; and each state raised and maintained its own military force for defense. Moreover, there existed no national court system. With the latter, interstate legal issues often went unresolved. The Articles also required unanimous consent among congressmen

Captain Charles Pinckney, engraving by Charles Balthazar Julien Fevret de Saint-Mémin, 1806.

before a bill could be passed into law. Congress had no power to issue direct taxes on the states, which crippled it financially; instead, it could only request states contribute funds to the national government. Although the Articles largely conformed to the ideals of the Revolution, in practice the thirteen states were more like separate independent nations responsible solely for their own affairs.

Pinckney suggested in 1786 that the Articles of Confederation be revised to increase the authority of the national government to strengthen the union of states and contribute to the development of a prosperous state and national economy. His was not a lone voice; from a meeting of state representatives in Annapolis, Maryland came the same call. In response, Congress authorized a convention to be held in Philadelphia in May 1787 and expressly charged it with the duty of making necessary changes to the existing governing structure—nothing more. It required little effort for Pinckney to convince the South Carolina General Assembly to participate in the convention. The assembly sent four of its own to represent the state—Charles Pinckney, his cousin Charles Cotesworth Pinckney, John Rutledge, and Pierce Butler—all men of wealth from the Lowcountry who favored a more aristocratic republic.

Contrary to the charge issued by Congress, little time was wasted at the Philadelphia convention before delegates invoked John Locke's "right of revolution" and agreed to draft an entirely new governing system for the nation. Throughout the stifling heat and humidity of summer, working in rooms closed to the public and to fresh air, representatives offered their ideas, debated feverishly, and hammered out a series of compromises framed in a new document, the United States Constitution, which fundamentally reconfigured the location and scope of political authority and the rights of the individual states.

Several critical discussions in the convention focused on southern issues. First, some delegates wanted the new government to prohibit slavery in America. It was, they contended, a labor system incongruous with Enlightenment philosophy and the ideals for which the Revolutionary War were fought. Much of the South's agricultural economy, however, depended on this cost-efficient labor source. South Carolina's delegation spared no words in defending the "peculiar institution." Portending a future crisis, Charles Pinckney and his colleagues all warned that a constitutional ban on slavery would erase South Carolina's membership in the Union. Heated arguments nearly brought the delegates to blows, but eventually they reached a compromise. Slavery would remain the prerogative of the state, but the federal government would halt the importation of African slaves twenty years after the new constitution became the law of the land. Pinckney and his colleagues were not troubled by that provision. The South Carolina General Assembly, on its own initiative, had recently outlawed further importation of Africans. Rice production had already reached its limits within the state, no other crop required such an extensive supply of laborers, and consequently there was diminishing need for slaves.

Another critical issue concerned congressional representation. Smaller states feared representation based solely on population; states with more residents would certainly command greater influence in governmental affairs than states with a small population. Intimately tied to this matter was the issue of slave representation. Southerners insisted the slave population be counted in determining House representation; slaves resided in the states and their labor produced the states' wealth. States without slavery believed this gave an unfair political advantage to the South. Slaves, they countered, were not citizens of the United States and therefore would not be included as part of a state's constituency unless southern states accepted the federal tax liability for them. The Three-Fifths Compromise broke the impasse—three-fifths of all slaves would be counted for both representation and taxation. South Carolina's delegates to the convention agreed.

Pinckney and his colleagues from South Carolina also favored an executive branch stronger than that created under the Articles, but they championed a six-year term for the president rather than the four-year term written into the Constitution. The Pinckney group also suggested the president be chosen by a vote of the members of Congress instead of being elected by the duality of popular and Electoral College votes. South Carolina accepted the bicameral legislature but argued that congressional representation be based on the value of state property rather than on population, a position that, if adopted, would have made South Carolina possibly the most powerful state in Congress in 1788. The Pinckney group also pressed the idea that congressional representatives not receive pay for their service. Theoretically, uncompensated service would keep representatives and senators relatively independent of influence and encourage office-holding in the spirit of civic virtue rather than self-interest.

South Carolina Ratifies the Constitution

In September 1787, the convention completed its self-imposed task. After nearly four months of sweltering in Philadelphia the delegates affixed their names to their

President Washington's Journey through South Carolina

Leaving the new nation's capital in spring 1791, President George Washington journeyed into the southern states, as he said, "to become better acquainted with their principal characters and internal circumstances." Entering South Carolina on April 27 and traveling along the coast through Little River, Myrtle Beach, and Georgetown on a route that today is Highway 17, Washington was struck by the area's general lack of development. The region is "pine barrens," he noted in his journal, "with very few inhabitants… [and] a perfect sameness" everywhere he looked. With the exception of Georgetown's center, Charleston, and parts of Beaufort, "there is not within view… a single house which has… an elegant appearance. They are altogether of Wood and chiefly of logs… being small and badly provided either for man or horse." The president noted that "the people, however, appear to have abundant means to live well" given the availability of land and the soil's fertility.

Washington, most often by necessity rather than choice, dined or spent evenings in the homes of private citizens along the length of his journey. On April 27, for example, the president rested in the home of Jeremiah Vereen, which stood near the present-day intersection of Highway 17 and Lake Arrowhead Road in North

Myrtle Beach. Following a hearty breakfast, "Mr. Vereen piloted us across the Swash (which at high water is impassable, and at times, by the shifting of the Sands is dangerous) onto the long Beach of the Ocean.... Immediately upon crossing this you enter upon Long Bay [today's Myrtle Beach]." Washington and his small entourage continued southward for another 22 miles, moving along what one of the president's contemporaries described a "lonely and desolate" stretch of road, "without shade and with no dwelling in sight." In late afternoon, Washington reached the home of a personal acquaintance, George Pawley. Pawley was a delegate to the First and Second Continental Congresses in Philadelphia and to the South Carolina First General Assembly in 1776. After a pleasant meal and equally pleasant conversation, the president's troupe ventured a few more miles before settling in for the night at the home of Dr. Henry Collins Flagg, "it being about ten miles from Pauleys and thirty-three from Vereens." Flagg's home stood in what is now Brookgreen Gardens near the "Alligator Pool."

On April 30 President Washington "crossed the Waccamaw [River] to Georgetown" and was well received "under a Salute of Cannon, and by a Company of Infantry handsomely uniformed." There, he enjoyed a midday meal with the citizens of the community, was entertained by the town's leading ladies at a tea party, and presented at a formal ball that evening. After leaving Georgetown, Washington rested and dined at the plantation mansions of Governor Charles Pinckney and South Carolina's political giant Edward Rutledge, reaching Charleston on May 2.

Washington spent one week in Charleston. To be sure, he was kept in the city's most elegant homes and entertained by Charleston's elite. He spent some time with the general citizenry, attending a communitywide barbeque on May 3 and religious services over several consecutive days along Meeting and Broad streets. The president also toured local sights, including Fort Moultrie on Sullivan's Island and Fort Johnson on James Island.

Finally, on May 9, President Washington left Charleston for Savannah, Georgia, a journey that took another three full days before he exited the state at Purrysburg on the Savannah River. His trip through the Palmetto State was a rather quick one, lingering only in the harbor city. He was surprised by the sparse settlement of Horry and Georgetown counties and the limited wealth common among coastal residents, especially when he considered the abundance and availability of rich farmland and timber tracts. Charleston Harbor, he concluded, ultimately was the source of South Carolina's prosperity, development, and, consequently, its national political influence.

South Carolina swampland © Natalia Bratslavsky

work, wiped their collective brow, and looked anxiously at the next step in the process—state ratification of the United States Constitution. South Carolina's General Assembly called a state convention in early 1788 to review and either accept or reject the proposed governing structure. Gathering in Charleston, those men selected by the legislature to attend the convention disproportionately represented the propertied class of the Lowcountry, but even among them the Constitution was read with suspicious eyes.

Chief among their concerns was the enhanced power the Constitution granted Congress; the ability to expand its own authority should the need arise seriously concerned the delegates. Although the South Carolina state government was itself highly centralized and managed by a tight-knit collection of merchants, planters, and lawyers, the centralization of power on a national level far removed from the state as proposed in the Constitution appeared threatening to the South Carolina power base.

Representatives of the Backcountry expressed particular concern for the Constitution's provision for the Electoral College. Might this not subvert the will of the people? they asked. They understood too well that membership in that body would largely be to the Lowcountry's favor, and that those in the Electoral College would be in position to select as president their preferred candidate regardless of how voters, especially common people in the Backcountry, might prefer. It seemed, they said, that the Constitution was created by the wealthy for the benefit of the wealthy, an argument fully developed by historian Charles Beard in his early twentieth-century classic *Economic Interpretation of the United States Constitution.*

To be sure, the 55 men who framed the Constitution in Philadelphia were arguably the richest in America. Among the southern delegates generally and South Carolina's representatives specifically were planters, slave owners, and merchants with vested interests in international trade. They not only anticipated the correction of commercial problems imposed by the Articles but also benefits to their own commercial class: interstate commerce would be stabilized, and international trade would receive federal government protection. Competition for trade among or between states would be minimal, with the national government holding

authority to resolve any dispute that might arise. A single monetary system eliminated questionable exchange rates, and a federal court system assured the resolution of interstate legal issues. Inclusion of the Electoral College protected the will of the higher social and economic class, and slavery itself remained unmolested and reserved as a state's right. A permanent standing military was now available to suppress any rebellion that might arise. What concerned Lowcountry and Backcountry alike was the understanding that South Carolina would be legally subservient to and responsible to the national government. In effect, adoption of the Constitution meant a corresponding loss of state independence.

The state convention nevertheless ratified the Constitution on its first vote, 149 to 73, making South Carolina the sixth state to do so. The vote reflected the sectional split present in the state. One observer estimated that 80 percent of Backcountry residents openly denounced the new governing system because it seemingly protected the wealth and power of the Lowcountry and concurrently left western residents vulnerable to Indian warfare. Historians readily agree that had the Constitution been put to popular vote, it would have most surely been rejected in South Carolina. The split within the state proved comparable to that in most other states. Those who formed the Lowcountry elite in South Carolina and those of the urban merchant class in more northern states generally banded with the emerging Federalist Party, while Backcountry residents aligned themselves with the Democrat-Republican Party. South Carolina's Charles Cotesworth Pinckney and John Rutledge, both delegates at Philadelphia, quickly surfaced as powerful Federalists—Rutledge as a United States Supreme Court justice and Pinckney as ambassador to France and later as the party's nominee for vice president in 1800 and for president in 1804 and 1808.

Distrustful of the power enjoyed by the state's elite under the Constitution and fearful of the direction the new national government might take, Backcountry residents called for a broad rewrite of the state constitution. The General Assembly agreed to consider revisions and authorized another state convention, but it held firm to the apportionment of representatives arranged for the state's earlier ratification convention. Once more, this meant that

one-fifth of the white population, who held three-fourths of the state's wealth, controlled the convention. Once in session, delegates clashed, and sectional conflict spawned a series of debates.

Among the first initiatives put forth by Backcountry delegates was reapportionment. Fair representation of the Backcountry was fundamental to a democratic system, they insisted. They were grossly outnumbered, and the Lowcountry majority, determined to retain political power, defeated the measure. On the heels of this came an effort by coastal representatives to return the state capital to Charleston, and by a mere four votes the motion was defeated. Despite Backcountry efforts to democratize the state's political process, the Lowcountry elite retained its position of power. The right to vote remained tied to property ownership; to vote, a man must own a minimum of 50 acres of land or a town lot. This alone excluded most Backcountry farmers. Moreover, membership in the State House required at least 500 acres and 10 slaves, and twice that for a seat in the State Senate, stipulations that prevented all but a few inland residents from holding any place in state or national government. The legislature, not the general population, elected the governor, presidential electors, United States senators, and state judges. Moreover, both houses of the General Assembly exercised authority over numerous offices of local government. Little wonder the Backcountry feared centralized state government.

Sectionalism within South Carolina, present in the twenty years before the Revolutionary War, was alive and well long after America's independence from colonial rule. Many inlanders argued that England's colonial relationship with South Carolina was replaced with Lowcountry colonialism of the Backcountry.

New Economic Direction for South Carolina

Following the Revolutionary War, South Carolina was restored to a level of social and economic stability, assumed a leading role in the adoption of the United States Constitution, and crafted a new state constitution that more fully entrenched the Lowcountry elite as the economic and political center of state affairs. Seemingly adrift and at the

mercy of the wealthiest planters and merchants were residents of the Backcountry; a new current, however, soon swept over the state.

In 1785 the South Carolina Agricultural Society was organized with the aim of finding a staple crop to replace indigo. Rice production, too, suffered in the immediate postwar years. Competitors in nearby Georgia muscled themselves into the market, but the greater challenge came from planters in Southeast Asia and India who sold their crops at cheaper prices. Moreover, Britain no longer was a guaranteed purchaser of Lowcountry rice.

The society was aware of the incessant global demand for cotton and that for years one variety of cotton—long-staple cotton—had been grown along the entire South Carolina coast and sold to markets worldwide. In 1791 alone, the Lowcountry harvested, baled, and sold 1.5 million pounds of cotton. Although it was a strong but fine, soft fiber, "Sea Island Cotton," as it was termed, was susceptible to sudden shifts in the weather and particularly suited to the sandier soil of the Lowcountry. Less soft and a much weaker fiber was short-staple cotton. Although short-staple cotton was less at the mercy of the weather and grown easily in the clay-like soil of the Backcountry, or "upcountry" as the territory around Columbia was now known, the process of removing seeds from the fiber was entirely too slow and difficult. One slave could spend as much as one entire day deseeding, or cleaning, a single pound of cotton. Upcountry cotton, then, did not appear to be the potential moneymaking crop sought by the society until Connecticut inventor Eli Whitney developed the cotton gin in 1793.

The "cotton engine," or "gin" as it later was termed, contained giant rollers on which were fixed thousands of metal bristles. The rollers were cranked by hand to spin in opposite directions and shred the cotton, removing seeds with ease. The gin required only one person to operate it and was capable of cleaning 50 pounds of cotton in a single day. A rapid, easy system of deseeding the fiber made short-staple cotton more marketable worldwide.

With Whitney's cotton gin, the South Carolina Agricultural Society trumpeted short-staple cotton as the new principal cash crop for the state. It was a crop well

suited to the upcountry, the sandy coastal plains, and the western foothills. Conversion to cotton was rapid indeed. Statewide, South Carolina shipped 20 million pounds of the "white gold" to foreign ports in 1800 and 50 million pounds only ten years later. In Richland District (Richland County), Wade Hampton grossed nearly $1 million (1990 dollar value) with his first harvest in 1799 and almost twice that in 1810. Cotton production, however, relied on slave labor. Harvesting the crop demanded an extensive labor force, and an equally large number of workers were needed to clear and cultivate new lands. The newfound demand for slavery mirrored the staggering profits earned by Backcountry planters. In 1800, just as the section's farmers were converting to short-staple cotton, 25 percent of the area's farmers owned slaves; in 1820, nearly 40 percent did. As wealth expanded westward across the state, so, too, did South Carolina's black population. Noted historian Walter Fraser, "This agricultural revolution... silenced Back-country opposition to slavery and blunted Lowcountry hostility toward the Backcountry."

South Carolina's fortune rested on cotton as the state pushed into the antebellum period. Central to the new cotton economy was slavery; slavery and wealth were so intertwined that the combination would eventually shape the state's relationship with the rest of the nation.

Postwar prosperity allowed Charleston Harbor to teem once again with both foreign and domestic shipping, elevating both the city's and state's wealth to unparalleled heights. As South Carolina's wealth increased and continued to command national attention, the federal government founded a branch of the First National Bank in Charleston. For aristocrats and those simply looking from a distance at the city and region, rising wealth made life seem grander. Cabinetmakers, furniture makers, silversmiths, and other skilled craftsmen descended on the Lowcountry, offering their talents to the established blue-blood society and the nouveau riche alike. Indeed, the number of elegant mansions multiplied as the region's

Browntown Cotton Gin, Johnsonville vicinity, Florence County. Photo by Jack Boucher.

wealth rose. Chandeliers and windows imported from England, furniture handcrafted in France, and fine clothing from across Europe moved through Charleston Harbor into the homes of area aristocrats. Cobblestone streets became the norm not only in Charleston but in Beaufort and Georgetown. Gentlemen gambled at local horse-racing tracks, and beautiful playhouses visited by traveling acting troupes from Europe lined the main roads of coastal communities.

The general population of Charleston and the surrounding region grew as the potential for profit became evident. European immigration increased slightly, and migration from less prosperous areas of the United States moved steadily upwards. By 1800, South Carolina's Lowcountry was one of the most heavily populated stretches along the Atlantic coast. Charleston was now the nation's fifth largest city. Its 9,000 white citizens and 10,000 blacks ranked it slightly behind New York, Philadelphia, Baltimore, and Boston.

As the population of the city and region grew, so too did concern for the community's social development. Charleston was vital to the state and to the nation as an economic center, and the College of Charleston was founded in 1790 to serve the demand for higher education among area residents and to support the commercial and political needs of the community and state. And throughout the decade and into the early years of the nineteenth century, citizens increasingly attended to the needs of parentless children and impoverished residents. An orphanage and a poorhouse for the white community opened in 1801, financed largely by the city and supplemented with private donations. The start of these services initiated efforts in Charleston to aid the "less fortunate" that would continue through the antebellum era. Aid to free blacks was also available as the new century dawned, but funding for African-American services was generally the product of contributions made by local churches.

Historic mansion in Charleston © Brian Patterson

6

Antebellum South Carolina

Christian evangelical fundamentalism washed over states north of the Mason-Dixon line between 1820 and 1860 and spawned a myriad of social-cleansing movements collectively known as the "Age of Reform." Crusaders lashed out at Americans' excessive alcohol consumption and campaigned to outlaw the Devil's brew. They derided the mistreatment and improper care of the insane, denounced dehumanizing living conditions in prisons and the excessively punitive policies in those institutions, voiced disapproval of the inadequate educational opportunities available to the nation's children and the misguided curricula commonly found in public schools, condemned urban poverty and squalor, criticized the gender inequality that pervaded society, and called for the immediate abolition of slavery in the South. Although the religious-based movement only captured the immediate involvement and open support of a few, it nonetheless effected substantial reforms across the region. Most Northerners not directly tied to the fundamentalist initiative or sympathetic to the more radical crusades such as abolitionism still shared the belief that a redirection was necessary for the welfare and prosperity of the region and the nation; unlike fundamentalists, the majority of Northerners championed a reform agenda founded on economic development. They promoted rapid expansion of railroads, harbors, and canals; international trade initiatives such as protective tariffs; urban development; and an economy based on manufacturing. Evident, too, was the North's growing national identity, supplanting the traditional state focus with a national perspective.

The Christian fundamentalist agenda slipped into southern society also, but not to the extent or with the fervor found farther north. South Carolina was significantly different from any of the states found above the Mason-Dixon line. While urban growth and manufacturing increasingly defined northern society, South Carolina remained solidly rural and agricultural. Only five communities in the state had a population greater than 1,500 in 1860: Charleston with 40,500; Columbia with 8,000; Georgetown, 1,700; Camden, 1,600; and Greenville, 1,500. Fully 93 percent of South Carolina's 660,500 citizens lived on the state's 33,000 farms and plantations in 1850. Vast cotton plantations and small farms reached from the Atlantic seaboard westward into the mountains. Slavery, a labor system that historians have consistently argued was relatively cost-efficient until the 1850s, underpinned cotton production and stood in sharp contrast to the "free labor" system of northern states. The population continued to be rural in residency and in perspective. White South Carolinians gave allegiance to their state above all; neither time nor circumstance significantly altered their social values, and the Old Guard politics long embedded in the Democratic Party still ruled. Although the Christian fundamentalist reform agenda gained some supporters in the Palmetto State and achieved some critical reforms, the basic structure of South Carolina's society endured as it had been since its founding.

Columbia and Charleston

Columbia, the state capital, was born in the 1780s from the sectional conflict that for decades pitted the Lowcountry against the Backcountry. Although the town's population grew rather slowly, reaching only 3,600 by 1840, it acquired increasingly greater influence in the state's economic, political, and social network throughout the pre–Civil War years. Cotton's productivity pumped new wealth into the region, bringing more residents, new businesses, and increased public services. Planters, farmers, merchants, bankers, and attorneys called Columbia home by the 1840s, transforming the area from the often unruly and independent-minded Backcountry into the more settled, developed, and respected upcountry. The extension of railroad lines to the town in the 1840s contributed to the city's growing importance in the cotton trade, and further railroad construction in the 1850s made Columbia a transportation crossroads for South Carolina. The state

South Carolina Population, by Race, 1800-1850

Demonstrating Importance of Slave Labor in Cotton Production (rounded to nearest thousand)

	1800	1810	1820	1830	1840	1850
White	196	214	237	258	259	275
Black	149	201	265	323	353	394

capital now boasted three major rail lines, connecting it to Charleston to the southeast, to Greenville to the northwest, and to Charlotte, North Carolina to the north. Following the harvest season, city warehouses bulged with cotton yet to be cleaned, and gins rattled around the clock trying to keep pace with demand. In the weeks that followed, the lonesome wail of steam whistles echoed through the countryside and plumes of black smoke lingered in the air. Railroad cars filled with cleaned cotton chugged through Columbia to the Charleston ports or through Charlotte to northern textile mills. By mid-century, Columbia had emerged as a vital marketplace built by cotton, and by 1860 more than 8,000 people called the city home.

A new statehouse was under construction, to replace the 40-year-old facility now deteriorating with age and too small to house the assembly, and to reflect the growing prestige and power of Columbia. Seven hotels offered rest to merchants temporarily trading in the city and to visiting political figures, and an equal number of churches tended to the spiritual needs of Columbia's residents and guests. A farmers' market located near the statehouse kept city residents and restaurants supplied with fresh vegetables and fruits, the R. L. Bryan Bookstore served the area's literate population, and a carriage manufacturer produced buggies sold in faraway cities. The Palmetto Armory employed 40 skilled workers and manufactured military hardware such as swords, bayonets, handguns, and muskets. Numerous other, smaller enterprises hired hundreds of local residents and sufficiently served the community's diverse needs. To be sure, the city flourished from the expansion of cotton and railroads into the upstate and did so in a manner consistent with the state's past.

The spirit of social reform that pervaded northern communities and increasingly found a kindred sentiment among Southerners also contributed to the transformation of antebellum Columbia. City residents actively encouraged the establishment of public schools and envisioned Columbia as a center for higher education in the state. An educated society directly benefited the state and local economy. Reform-minded residents, in concert with the Christian fundamentalist movement presently in northern communities, believed that educated youngsters would be less susceptible to Satan's temptation and also be more capable witnesses for the faith. And a college in the state capital was considered essential, its libraries and faculty providing critical services to political figures, judges, lawyers, and members of the General Assembly. By the 1820s residents' expectations were largely met. The South Carolina College (the present-day University of South Carolina), founded in 1801, expanded rapidly and by the century's second decade was the preeminent college in the state. The student population was small, but the college library nonetheless gloried in having a collection of 18,500 volumes, more than the earlier-established and much-respected Columbia University in New York and Princeton in New Jersey.

Socially conscious South Carolinians also insisted that the state care for its population of "mentally fragile" citizens. Using a Christian fundamentalist argument, mixed with the Southern code of honor and sense of responsibility, and buttressed by the advantage such a facility would provide for Columbia, the General Assembly authorized the founding of the State Asylum for the Insane, to be constructed on Bull Street, just north of SCC. South Carolina was not unique among southern states in providing an asylum; North Carolina, for example, founded a similar facility in its piedmont community of Dix Hill. But South Carolina was the first southern state, and one of only three states nationwide at the time, to fund a facility for the insane with state appropriations. And unlike most other institutions, which simply housed the insane, the South Carolina state asylum aggressively attempted the treatment of patients.

Columbia in the antebellum era was transitioning into a modern southern city. The city's numerous unpaved streets still turned into a muddy quagmire during heavy rain, assemblymen from eastern districts regularly complained of the city's few cultural events and outlets for "gentlemen's" entertainment, visitors routinely criticized the coarseness they found in residents' manners, and almost everyone complained of the merciless summer heat and humidity. Nonetheless, the city was changing. By 1850, most city streets were paved and lined with gaslights. Troupes of traveling actors regularly journeyed to the state capital, parks and gardens offered a charm that mirrored that associated with coastal towns. Business and politics commanded the city's interests, giving Columbia greater centrality in the affairs of the state and making the city South Carolina's commercial center. Still, nothing could be done about the summer heat and humidity that enveloped the city.

Small towns littered the inland and upcountry by 1860, most being service centers to area farmers. Darlington, founded in 1826, was representative of these communities. Central to the town were its cotton warehouses and markets, through which area planters and small farmers sold and shipped their cotton to northern textile mills and to European buyers. A small general store brought local farmers the tools of their trade and a variety of goods they could not manufacture themselves, such as washtubs, lamps, buttons and sewing thread, sugar, coffee, and finer fabrics. A church or two, a very small schoolhouse, a blacksmith, a ginning mill, a post office, a hotel, a restaurant, and several taverns all tended to the farmers' souls and earthly requirements.

Antebellum Charleston, however, remained South Carolina's preeminent city. Its natural beauty and aristocratic elegance distinguished it among US cities. Ancient oaks draped in Spanish moss lined the city's cobblestone streets and partially concealed equally magnificent homes dating to the late seventeenth century.

Gold Mining in South Carolina

In 1799, just across the state line in North Carolina, a twelve-year-old boy named Conrad Reed literally stumbled over a seventeen-pound gold "nugget" as he waded in the stream behind his family's house. Unaware of its value, the Reeds used the rock as a doorstop for nearly three years before selling it to a Wilmington "rock collector," as he termed himself. The buyer quickly cashed in on his purchase, and the cry "gold" soon echoed throughout the Carolinas and the length of the continent; within months, Europeans, too, learned of the discovery. By 1802, North America experienced its first gold rush, with tens of thousands of people flooding the Carolina Backcountry.

In that same year, prospectors found the precious metal in the area of Greenville, South Carolina. Hollywood films typically focus on the lone, crusty prospector crouched over a shallow, cold-water creek, panning for gold. Some certainly used this method, but most miners in the Palmetto State found "placer mining" much more productive. They realized that gold nuggets most often were located near deposits of quartz. Once they spotted the milky pebbles, they took shovel in hand and scooped shallow pits, similar to half-moons, and sifted through the dirt looking for gold nuggets and flakes. Once they made a find, they dug deeper, excavating pits ten to twenty feet in depth and twice that in width.

The most productive placer mining occurred at the Tanyard Pit at the Brewer Gold Mine in Chesterfield County, with 22,000 ounces unearthed. At the Martin Mine

Washing gold, circa 1916

in York County, individual nuggets were found weighing from nine to seventeen ounces. Gold embedded in quartz generally contained as much as ten ounces, although one piece of quartz was discovered with about 200 ounces in it. Highly productive placer digs were expanded further, the owner of the claim hiring skilled miners to sink shafts and construct tunnels for a full-scale mining operation. Gold discoveries were made in eighteen counties across the state. Fifty mines operated in York County alone by the mid-1820s. The Haile Mine, near Kershaw in Lancaster County, began operations in 1827 and eventually became the largest gold producer in the southeastern US. Between the mine's founding and 1942, more than 280,000 ounces of gold were extracted from it. The city of McCormick was built over the mine owned by Cyrus McCormick, inventor of the reaper. His mine produced 44,000 ounces between 1852 and 1880 at a value of $1 million. The Ophir Mine in Union County generated an excess of $100,000 in gold nuggets from 1844 to 1900.

As cotton production expanded westward in South Carolina in the early nineteenth century, gold mining lured thousands of others into the upcountry; railroads that carried the state's vital cash crop to market also hauled gold to the US mint established in Charlotte, North Carolina in 1830. By the eve of civil war, South Carolina had produced more than 320,000 ounces of the precious metal, and mining operations continued through World War II. Since 1945, several mines have continued to be worked for the gold; however, the high costs associated with the business have forced owners to concentrate on other metals necessary to the nation's industries yet cheaper to extract.

Visitors strolled along the river walk overlooking a majestic Charleston Harbor and enjoyed other pleasures such as the city's museum, horse races, theaters, and numerous topiary gardens. Bathhouses were scattered throughout the city, and elegant hotels, a few of which were owned by free blacks, served the white, moneyed class. Churches also lined Charleston's streets, serving large congregations and beckoning visitors. Their spires were visible to the naked eye miles inland. A certain air of refinement pervaded much of Charleston, visible in the gracious hospitality and deference residents accorded important visitors.

Guests and residents alike were struck by the appearance of wealth and progress. The financial district ran the length of Broad Street, compelling some historians to dub the stretch "South Carolina's antebellum Wall Street." Import and export houses operated along the Ashley and Cooper Rivers, which emptied into the harbor; small manufacturing concerns shipped their wares to coastal cities from Boston to Jacksonville; and merchants and artisans flooded the Lowcountry with an array of goods.

But Charleston was also in a period of transition. The city witnessed a population decline from 43,000 in 1850 to 40,500 one decade later. Although the loss was modest, depopulation reflected two emerging patterns. First, cotton growing was moving westward throughout the antebellum period. The upcountry initially benefited from the migration of planters and farmers, but by 1850 it was obvious that cotton farmers were seeking fresher lands beyond the state's borders. Approximately 200,000 of South Carolina's white citizens moved to other states in the antebellum era in pursuit of fresh lands, most relocating to western Georgia, Alabama, Mississippi, and Louisiana. But the out-migration from Charleston also hinted that the city's splendor veiled fundamental problems. As upstate cotton production drew more wealth and business from the coastal city, with it went some of the political clout earlier enjoyed by the Lowcountry elite. Also, diseases such as malaria, tuberculosis, and cholera haunted residents. Rats infested the community, living comfortably in the city's refuse. City leaders gave scant attention to the sources of disease, and as a result many citizens escaped Charleston for more healthful environments. Charleston did take steps to address the city's medical needs, opening Roper Hospital in 1856, but epidemics continued to threaten the general population. Yellow fever, for example, struck more than 250 residents and claimed nearly 100 lives shortly after Roper opened its doors.

In addition, Charleston virtually isolated itself from the rest of the world and was largely self-absorbed. As historian Walter Edgar wrote in *South Carolina: A History* (1998), "Whereas eighteenth century Charleston had prided itself on being a city of the empire and the world, the nineteenth century city aspired only to be the cultural capital of the American South." Their narrowing perspective ran counter to the widening vision of other South Carolinians and the expansive reach of the United States. The myopic nature of Charleston compelled many middle-class residents to seek their fortune and to rear their families in a more modern and progressive setting.

But Charleston retained an unrivaled economic position in the state. The harbor and the import-export businesses flourishing there provided thousands of jobs and generated much of the state's wealth. In 1828, the Lowcountry's largest-ever export of rice and to that date the city's second-largest cotton shipment moved through the city: 215,000 bales. These rates, however, were misleading. Cotton prices fluctuated considerably from year to year as rising global production increasingly threatened America's agricultural base. Rice production was in a worse state for the Lowcountry. Most planters, merchants, and exporters understood that the days of prosperity resting on cotton and rice were numbered. Aware of this, city business leaders in the 1830s encouraged a transition to manufacturing, a call mirrored in the post–Civil War "New South Creed."

Little time was wasted in developing a manufacturing component to the city and Lowcountry's agrarian economy. By the early 1850s, Charleston and the surrounding area boasted six iron foundries, more than one dozen grist mills, dozens of saw mills, six turpentine producers, and a railroad machine shop. Also located on the city's outskirts were wagon and buggy manufacturers, boat builders, metal-working shops, rice mills, and makers of railroad cars, furniture, silverware, bricks, and numerous other luxury and essential goods. Indeed, by the mid-1850s

Charleston had emerged as South Carolina's manufacturing center.

Manufacturing also spread across the state in the antebellum period. Mill towns, such as Graniteville in Aiken County, were more the product of advanced planning than evolution. Cotton usually followed a fixed path from southern fields to northern textile manufacturers; southern planters profited from the sale of raw cotton and northern mill owners from the marketing of finished goods. Realizing the potential for financial gain if South Carolina produced both fiber and finished goods, and sensing the need for economic diversification in the state, a small collection of investors ventured into unfamiliar territory. William Gregg, for example, saw a three-way benefit from the founding of cotton mills within South Carolina—wage jobs for poor whites driven from the land or unable to purchase their own, economic diversity for a state still dependent on cotton and rice, and, of course, profits for himself as a mill owner. Toward these three goals, Gregg founded Graniteville Mill in 1849 and challenged other business owners in the state to follow his lead.

Graniteville Mill emerged as a pattern soon replicated across the upcountry. Around the mill stood a self-sufficient community—a mill town—built by Gregg's personal investment and company profits. Small cottages, constructed at mill expense, housed 300 workers and their families; two churches served town dwellers, a school educated non-employed children, and a mill-owned store provided minimally priced essential goods. Wages averaged 70 cents per day for a six-day work week, comparable to wages paid in northern mills. Gregg served as company president and town patriarch. With absolute control over the mill, store, housing, and school, Gregg reaped a financial windfall that placed him among the state's richest men. By the eve of the Civil War, Graniteville Mill stood as the largest textile operation in South Carolina, and it would flourish well into the twentieth century.

Other mill villages arose between Aiken and Greenville Counties. Many surfaced in response to falling market prices for raw cotton and the displacement of small farmers driven from nutrient-depleted soil. Each year, cotton stripped vital minerals from the earth and rendered poorer quality harvests in succeeding seasons. Commercial fertilizers were expensive and not widely available. Farmers instead depended on a variety of cover crops and grasses such as clover to replenish lost nutrients, but this only slowed the inevitable failure of the soil. As long as market prices for cotton remained high, farmers toiled the land regardless of its diminishing returns. Once a farmer conceded defeat, he had several options: focus exclusively on food crops, abandon the land for property father west, or seek employment in a nearby mill. Food crops generated little income. By the late antebellum period the little land still available was prohibitively expensive. For most small farmers, then, the answer was rather simple—take employment in the cotton mill.

By the eve of the Civil War, cotton was still the economic foundation of South Carolina's coastal cities and market centers such as Charleston, Beaufort, and Georgetown, but manufacturing was annually assuming greater importance. In the upcountry, Columbia had emerged as a modern city and, being surrounded by cotton and at the crossroads of interstate and intrastate commerce, had displaced Charleston as the center of state economic influence. Now scattered across South Carolina were towns such as Darlington, serving the market needs of planters and farmers alike, and mill towns such as Graniteville, the latter showing the direction the Palmetto State would pursue following civil war.

Education in the Antebellum Period

South Carolina's illiteracy rate exceeded that of any other state in the Union during the antebellum era. Farming families often depended on the labor of their children to produce crops; consequently, regular school attendance was considered an unnecessary luxury. Moreover, many families viewed formal, public education as irrelevant to youngsters destined to farm the land. Of what importance to farming were Aristotle and Socrates, Greek and Latin, and advanced math and sciences? A common problem, too, was the cost of attending school. Certainly high tuition prevented most South Carolina children from ever enrolling in a preparatory academy, but the price of texts and other required fees, minimal as they were, proved an obstacle for those parents still reluctant to educate their offspring.

Dueling in South Carolina

South Carolinians widely believed any challenge to one's integrity was a most serious offense. Gentlemen—men of wealth and high social standing—often defended their questioned honor by deuling, although it was illegal under South Carolina law.

Former governor John Lyde Wilson in 1838 published a short defense of dueling and enumerated the rules by which gentlemen could defend their reputation. In *The American Code: Code of Honor, or Rules for the Government of Principals and Seconds in Dueling,* Wilson wrote, "If an oppressed nation has a right to appeal to arms in defence [*sic*] of its liberty... there can be no argument... which will not apply with equal force to individuals." The "first law of nature," he wrote, is "self-preservation"; in the Palmetto State, as across the South, honor secured a man's place in society. A man whose honor was openly questioned must either "submit in silence" or demand and receive a public apology from the offender, with the threat of a duel if necessary.

Wilson's rules for dueling were simple. Arrangements were to be made by each gentleman's representative, or "second." Refusal to duel branded the offender as a coward in the community. On the appointed day, the "second" for each dueler carried his own loaded pistol "to enforce a fair combat... and if a principal fires before the word or time agreed on, he [the "second"] is at liberty to fire at him." Wilson suggested at least one surgeon be present at the duel and one gentleman serve as judge. "Seconds" prepared the weapons under the judge's watchful eye and placed them in the duelers' hands, muzzles pointed to the ground, and the duelers moved to their assigned positions on the field. Once they were ready, the judge issued the word to fire. If either party was wounded, the duel ended; if neither was harmed, the challenger could call for another round of shots or acknowledge the honor of the offender.

Duels often resulted in no physical harm to either party. The smooth-bore pistols of the era were notoriously inaccurate even at short distances. Often, combatants considered honor preserved simply by showing up for the duel, making the duel itself unnecessary. Nonetheless, some duelers suffered hideous wounds, and many others were killed on the field.

The last known duel in South Carolina occurred in 1880. Camden attorney Colonel William M. Shannon in September 1879 charged the wife of Colonel E. B. C. Cash of Chesterfield with fraud in a land transaction. Outraged, Cash reminded Shannon of their twenty-year friendship that included service in the Confederate Army. Shannon responded that Mrs. Cash's honor was never questioned, only the confusing details of a contested land sale. Colonel Cash was satisfied.

A Darlington County court ruled against Mrs. Cash on February 7, 1880, and she immediately filed an appeal. Although she won her appeal, she felt the charges made against her tainted her honor in the community. Within days of her courtroom victory, Mrs. Cash became ill and on April 4 died. Grieved by the loss of his wife and hurt by the allegations that challenged her integrity, Cash now believed Shannon had, in fact, consciously impugned the honor of the late Mrs. Cash, and challenged him to a duel. Shannon refused. Dueling was outlawed in South Carolina, and he still considered Cash a friend. Cash persisted, and Shannon eventually felt compelled to accept the offer to duel in order to preserve his own honor in the community. On July 5 the two men faced each other. Cash's bullet fatally wounded Shannon. He was charged with murder, but, in October, the judge hearing the case declared a mistrial. At a second trial on June 21, 1881, the jury acquitted Cash, placing honor above the law.

The South Carolina General Assembly in 1811 passed into law the Free School Act, which allotted some state funds for the construction and maintenance of rural schoolhouses, but appropriations were generally quite small. Tiny one-room schoolhouses dotted rural South Carolina, but qualified teachers were rare, classroom supplies proved virtually nonexistent, and the buildings were often unhealthy for youngsters in winter months. The Free School Act, although admirable in its intent, delivered little of substance.

Towns and cities obviously offered greater opportunity for children to receive an education. Child labor was not in as much demand as in the farmlands, and parents of both the middle and lower socioeconomic classes urged their children's attendance in school. Charleston's leaders funded eleven public schools with a total of 600 students in 1856; only ten years later, the city's schools served 2,800. Columbia, too, introduced a minimal system of public education in the antebellum period, but it never reached the level provided by Charleston before the Civil War. These urban schools provided basic instruction in reading, writing, mathematics, and history. Their goal was fairly simple: prepare children sufficiently for low-level skilled positions in the city's business community. They also promised a modicum of social control over youngsters, training children in an approved code of conduct that would later meld favorably with the interests of the community. Historian Walter Fraser quotes one Charlestonian who said in the 1850s, "The ignorant and uneducated are always the first to engage in outrage and violence." The public schools founded in South Carolina in the final decade before civil war never attained much respect and never served even half of the state's white children; in fact, South Carolina's public schools were commonly thought inadequate at best, and more often than not, simply disgraceful.

The children of some "free blacks" in Charleston also gained an education, some attending the few schools funded by city leaders, and others enrolling in schools established independently of local government. These efforts were remarkable since the schooling of African Americans—slave or free—violated South Carolina state law. State authorities tried to close black schools in the 1830s and succeeded in shutting down most of them, but by the 1850s the schools had reopened with the financial support of the coastal white elite. Urban slaves were routinely "hired out" to local manufacturers, retailers, and service providers—the greatest portion of the slaves' wages being given to the slave owner. A slave capable of reading and writing and trained in the basic skills required by Charleston businessmen fared better in the local job market. Indeed, it became a common sight in antebellum Charleston to see black children strolling to and from school. Slave owners also educated their wards on the plantation, but the general explanation given by planters was a desire to teach slaves how to read the Bible and in so doing learn Christianity and the submissive traits it encouraged.

The wealthy elite of South Carolina sent their youngsters to private academies. These schools each typically enrolled 50 to 80 students, and many required the children's full-time residency during the academic year. Some, such as Richard School near Columbia, drew students from throughout the South and a few from northern states. Willington Academy in Abbeville, founded in the late eighteenth century, prided itself on such graduates as Preston Brooks, a future US congressman, and John C. Calhoun, who became a US senator and later the vice president of the United States. Academies prepared adolescents for college, giving them sound training in advanced math and sciences, ancient and contemporary literature, philosophy, debating techniques, politics, history, and classical languages such as Latin and Greek. "Female seminaries," academies for girls, were the equivalent of "refinement schools." Madame Talvande's French School for Young Ladies, located in Charleston, instructed young girls in music, dancing, literature, French, and etiquette, all with an eye toward preparing little darlings for their role as proper wives for future South Carolina leaders.

Like her immediate neighbor to the north, South Carolina moved in the late eighteenth century to provide a system of higher education for her citizens. The state chartered the College of Charleston in 1785 and five years later opened the college's doors to students. Beaufort College was founded in 1795. Neither school built a sound

John Caldwell Calhoun

Born near Abbeville on March 18, 1782, John C. Calhoun was the child of a very prosperous cotton-producing, slaveholding family. As was common to young men of his social standing in the state, he enrolled in a private academy, Waddell's Log College in Georgia. He completed his formal academic training at Yale University, returned to South Carolina, and was admitted to the state bar in 1807. Young attorneys from the state's elite considered it obligatory to enter politics; Calhoun wasted little time. He was elected to the state legislature in 1808 and to the US House of Representatives two years later.

In Congress, Calhoun joined the ranks of strident nationalists who demanded war with Great Britain in 1812 in response to its persistent impressments of American sailors into the British navy and its continued interference with American commercial trade with Europe. Like his hawkish colleagues, he also believed Great Britain was purposely stirring Indians on the frontier to violently resist America's westward expansion. As a nationalist he promoted the use of federal authority to expand American business, erect protective tariffs against foreign imports, issue supplemental funding for the construction of roads, canals, and harbors, and establish a national bank. Calhoun's extreme patriotism and promotion of federal power within the states won him the attention of James Monroe and earned him the position of secretary of war in the Monroe administration in 1817. In 1824, he lost his bid to become president, but was elected vice president under John Quincy Adams and was reelected in 1828 to serve under Andrew Jackson.

While serving as vice president, Calhoun's political views began to change, probably as a result of the nation's growing debate over slavery and states' rights. In 1828 Calhoun authored the South Carolina Exposition and Protest, a document that endorsed a state's prerogative to nullify, or disavow, any federal law within its borders the state legislature considered unconstitutional. Over the following four years, Calhoun and Jackson clashed sharply in heated debates on the vice president's position, and in 1832 Calhoun resigned his position as a form of public protest and returned to his home state.

Voters sent Calhoun to the United States Senate in 1842, and he held a seat there until his death in 1850. He proved himself to be an outspoken proponent for the institution of slavery, its expansion into western territories, and states' rights. He personally directed passage of the Gag Rule that prevented debate of slavery on the floor of Congress and fought a losing battle in opposition to the Compromise of 1850 that admitted California as a "free state." He briefly stepped from the Senate to serve as secretary of state under President John Tyler (1844–1845) and in that capacity he was instrumental in the annexation of Texas as a slaveholding state.

Calhoun died on March 31, 1850 following a lengthy and debilitating illness and not long after he had been wheeled onto the Senate floor and had a colleague read a prepared statement in which he denounced excessive federal authority and defended both slavery and states' rights. He was hailed in South Carolina as the state's leading spokesperson and across the South as a regional hero. His body was laid to rest in Charleston.

Must-See Sites: Fort Hill, Clemson

Fort Hill is the antebellum plantation home of John C. Calhoun, US senator and later vice president under Presidents John Quincy Adams and Andrew Jackson. Calhoun's son-in-law, Thomas Clemson, bequeathed the plantation for the site of Clemson College. Fort Hill is situated in the middle of the Clemson University campus. Admission is free, and the home is open for touring every day except holidays. Call (864) 656-2475 or email cuvisit@clemson.edu.

academic reputation during the antebellum period, their level of instruction for the most part no more developed than that provided in the academies. In a bid to reestablish itself as a true institution of higher learning, the College of Charleston closed its doors in 1836, restructured its entire curriculum, hired notable professors, reopened two years later, and soon built a strong reputation.

South Carolina College (now USC) in Columbia, however, may have grown slowly early in the antebellum era, but the quality of its instruction was never seriously questioned. Established in 1801 to train future state leaders, SCC received financing from the state assembly and generally attracted its students from the upcountry planter aristocracy, although some of its students hailed from coastal plantations. The college employed only eight professors and enrolled about 200 students in 1850, but it was respected and boasted a faculty that included nationally admired scholars. It had a strong and deserved reputation for liberal arts instruction, and worked diligently before the Civil War to build equally strong programs in engineering and the sciences.

As SCC grew, the General Assembly in 1824 funded and opened the School of Medicine in Charleston, the first medical school in South Carolina. Among the reasons the assembly selected Charleston, one was perhaps most urgent—the coastal city was notorious for disease. Malaria, tuberculosis, and cholera regularly ravaged the city's population, and many other deadly diseases struck periodically. A school of medicine in such a location could serve a community in desperate need. Moreover, the city could be treated as a large medical laboratory for young doctors and their mentors. The school grew quickly, and in 1831 the assembly elevated its status to "college," changing the institution to the Medical College of South Carolina, today's Medical University of South Carolina.

In 1842, two more colleges were opened to students, each receiving some funding from state appropriations and the bulk of financing from private contributors—Columbia's Arsenal School and Charleston's South Carolina Military Academy, or the Citadel. Each provided excellent academic training, particularly in subjects such as engineering and military history, but both the Arsenal and the SCMA were charged with additional duties. They were to warehouse the state's armaments and prepare men as officers in the state militia. Only four years after opening, the Citadel was forced to cease operations temporarily because so many of its students left school to fight for the United States in the Mexican War. Peace in 1847 returned students to campus, the college having earned statewide praise for the patriotism and service exhibited by its cadets.

The direction of higher education in the state concerned many leading citizens. Since its founding, South Carolina College had refused to identify itself with any particular Christian denomination. Its secular position was barely tolerable to the more devout in the state, but the rising influence of one faculty member, Thomas Cooper, and the simultaneous rise of Christian fundamentalism brought the college and Cooper under fiery criticism. Cooper had been a friend of Thomas Jefferson's and shared Jefferson's Enlightenment philosophy that valued reason and science over emotion and belief. Both Cooper and Jefferson were avowed deists, not Christians. Cooper, like Jefferson, never concealed his perspective or softened his views, which only angered those in the state who insisted the college's curricula be Christian. Unable to remove Cooper because of his popularity among the faculty or to purge SCC of its secularism, religious groups established colleges that based instruction on denominational preferences. Among these newly founded institutions were Erskine in 1839 (Due West, Presbyterian), Furman in 1851 (Greenville, Baptist), Wofford in 1854 (Spartanburg, Methodist), and Newberry in 1856 (Newberry, Lutheran).

Religion, Morality, Reform, and Social Control

Organized religion never commanded much influence in South Carolina prior to the nineteenth century; indeed, church membership was never a serious concern for South Carolinians. Only eight percent of white settlers claimed any specific denominational affiliation as late as 1799. Churches certainly were present in Charleston and outlying towns in the colonial era, but the majority of colonists—and later citizens of the new state—for several reasons belonged to no one faith over another. First, the bulk of the

Must-See Sites: Boone Hall Plantation, Mount Pleasant

Major John Boone built his plantation in 1681 at the time of Charleston's founding. The plantation produced rice but converted to cotton in the early 1800s. The original home was destroyed, and a new house was constructed in 1935 based on archival information about the original house. Slave houses are also present on the grounds, and beautiful gardens surround the property. The John Jakes TV miniseries *North and South* and Alex Haley's *Queen* were both filmed here. Boone Hall is located at 1235 Long Point Road in Mount Pleasant. The plantation is open daily, with admission fees. Call 843-884-4371 for more information or visit www.boonehallplantation.com.

population was dispersed over a vast region of semi-developed frontier or wilderness land. Establishing a church at a point central to most residents in such an environment would still require many members to journey long distances to attend services, a trip complicated by possibly unpredictable weather, angry Native Americans, rebellious slaves, and highwaymen. Complicating this was the diversity of the population. As noted previously, South Carolina became home to a noticeable variety of Europeans, among them Huguenots, Catholics, Jews, Lutherans, Baptists, Methodists, Presbyterians, and others. What denomination would be represented in such a remote, isolated setting? Also, farm work and basic family survival in the colonial period took precedence over all other affairs, including religion. A family could worship God within its own home, in its own manner, without forgoing a day of labor or rest. Finally, many South Carolinians adopted the same Enlightenment values as Thomas Cooper, Thomas Jefferson, and others—reason and science, not religion, best explained nature and humankind.

By the early nineteenth century, conditions changed in South Carolina. The frontier line now stood in mid-state;

wilderness lay not far beyond Columbia. With the state relatively settled, travel much more secure between farms and towns, an agrarian economy based on slave labor continuing to grow, and the population steadily rising, it became easier to attend religious services outside the urban centers and increasingly expected that residents affiliate themselves with a church. And the American people nationally, much like Europeans, were turning their backs on Enlightenment philosophy and accepting a more romantic, spiritual-based perspective of life in which God, faith, and emotion were again central. By 1810, 23 percent of all South Carolinians openly aligned themselves with a specific Christian denomination and regularly attended church services. The age of Protestant revivalism that swept northern states, as noted earlier, sifted into the South by the end of the 1820s, igniting a passion for religion among state residents. Migration patterns also affected religion in the Palmetto State. Presbyterianism washed over South Carolina by the 1830s as Scot-Irish settlers infused the upcountry; Lutherans from North Carolina's piedmont filtered southward into the Columbia area. Baptists, who took immense pride in their informal structures, their intensely personal connection to the Almighty, and their belief that God's ministers were called, not trained academically in an institution of man's, commanded wide appeal among small farmers, who helped plant churches wherever and whenever they could ordain a local man as minister. Less visible but still present were Catholics and Episcopalians (former Anglicans) who dominated coastal communities, their ties to their traditional, European roots remaining firm. And continuing its eighteenth-century presence in Charleston and spreading toward Columbia in the early nineteenth century was a sizeable Jewish population. In fact, South Carolina's Jewish population exceeded that of any other southern state before the Civil War. Methodists, however, were the largest single group of faithful by 1860. Circuit-riding ministers served a district of congregations and were supported at the local level by trained laymen. Their message of "free will" and "grace" to those who admitted their sinfulness attracted ambitious businessmen, planters, and farmers alike.

The rapid spread of organized religion in the state was partly the product of a spirited evangelical revivalism similar to that found in the North during the same period, but there were visible differences between the movements. In South Carolina, as in the northern states, religious revivalism attacked sinful behavior. Alcohol, gambling, fighting, spousal abuse, and adultery were all targets of Christian ministers. Revivalists in northern states generally agreed that sin was to be purged completely and swiftly from society prior to the imminent second coming of Jesus. South Carolinians, however, were less convinced of Christ's immediate arrival and championed the regulation of sinful behavior. Alcohol itself was not sinful if consumed in moderation; abuse of alcohol was. Gambling was a sporting affair for people of means and was permitted provided one met his financial responsibilities to family, community, and church. Under that guideline, gambling was entertainment, not sin. Fighting in defense of honor, family, or state was acceptable and not a sinful behavior.

It was strictly expected that no behavior remotely considered sinful occur on the Sabbath, and to enforce the Sabbath South Carolina drafted and religiously enforced "blue laws" that forbade business activity, sporting events, liquor sales, and all behavior that might be construed as sinful or disrespectful to worshippers. The General Assembly's intervention on behalf of Christian morality was not necessary. Businessmen had always closed their shops on Sundays because of custom, personal preference, religious belief, or absent market activity. The ban on Sunday alcohol sales and gambling also mattered little. Both were enjoyed among all social classes and considered non-threatening to one's moral fiber if enjoyed in moderation. Moreover, those who wished to drink on Sunday usually imbibed in the privacy of their homes or with small groups of like-minded friends.

Far more serious in the eyes of the devout was adultery. As each South Carolinian understood, adultery violated God's commandment. It was, however, a commandment frequently ignored within aristocratic society, and, provided the male adulterer conducted his illicit affair discreetly, high society said little about the matter. Adultery within lower classes was less tolerated. The presumption

Must-See Sites: Colonial Cup Racing Association and National Steeplechase Museum, Camden

Camden hosts two nationally renowned steeplechase races, the Marion DuPont Scott Colonial Cup Race each autumn and the Carolina Cup Steeplechase each spring. Prior to the races, visitors may enter the stands and watch thoroughbreds going through morning workouts. The nearby Steeplechase Museum includes interactive exhibits highlighting the history of steeplechase racing and the sport's history in Kershaw County. Only a short distance away is the Fine Arts Center of Kershaw County, which offers live concerts, chamber music performances, and theatrical shows. The center also serves as an art gallery, and art classes for both adults and children are available. In tandem with the Colonial Cup Weekend, the Fine Arts Center directs an annual fundraising event open to the public, titled "Bluejeans, Bluegrass, Barbeque, and Oysters." Call (800) 968-4037 to learn about racing events and special museum exhibits.

was that a sense of propriety and the Southern code of honor would be sufficient to handle indiscreet behavior among aristocrats; lower social classes, however, were thought to be less in control of their emotions and more inclined to brawling and murder in such cases. In an effort to reduce the incidence of adultery, church leaders throughout the state, along with their congregations, pressured the General Assembly to uphold God's law with earthly, civil law. In 1844, 1856, and again in 1860 assemblymen considered legislation criminalizing adultery, but each attempt failed. Many of the men who cast their votes in the statehouse had themselves engaged in extramarital affairs; others believed such a statute exceeded the state's authority, that it was not the government's duty to determine a code of morality and impose it on all citizens. Adultery was a personal issue between man and

God, between husband and wife. If made into a public matter, it was to be handled properly by the offended party. A man was expected to cast off his adulterous wife to preserve his honor in the community. She was expected to leave the city without her children—her husband having full custody—and she would be disgraced forever in its memory. Divorce was not legal within South Carolina until 1948, but a humiliated husband might have his marriage annulled. The same option was not permitted to an offended wife; indeed, she had little recourse in the case of a wayward husband. It was tacitly understood in southern society that men and women had different natural urges and needs, and that a wife was a "purer sort" and should not be bothered by her husband's frequent sexual needs. She could punish an adulterous husband by taking a separate bedroom, abstaining from sex, or other methods, provided her response remain private, not a public spectacle.

Houses of prostitution were common in South Carolina and served patrons of all social classes. City leaders openly condemned the brothels but tacitly condoned the business. It was generally accepted in coastal communities that prostitution allowed sailors to secure sexual services without threatening or endangering "proper women." The money prostitutes earned eventually filtered back into the local economy. They purchased goods and services within the community, and frequently contributed large sums of money to local charities and community-building campaigns. City leaders also insisted, off the record, that the purveyors of illicit sex confine their trade to sections of the city removed from the heart of commerce and less traveled by women and children. These districts in both Charleston and Columbia, later referred to as "red light districts," remained unaffected by local law and social contempt well into the World War II years. Churches, however, occasionally sent parishioners into the boardinghouses and brothels, even those of the "lowest and degraded character," and there spread the word of redemption to prostitutes and clients alike.

Antebellum society also focused attention on the "less fortunate," with Columbia and Charleston each constructing poorhouses and funding them with tax money. This, like so many of the reform efforts in South Carolina, mirrored similar efforts pressed by Christian evangelicals in the North. The poorhouse was intended to take in "the victims of misfortune" and provide them temporary shelter and food. The facilities that first opened in the early 1850s required aid recipients to undergo a "corrections" program, which attempted to identify the cause of misfortune and then direct the aid recipient along an appropriate course of recovery. It was assumed that "worthy paupers" were hard workers, reliable, and responsible individuals who had fallen on hard times. Many men and women seeking aid could not secure a place in the poorhouse because demand proved so high late in the decade. On the eve of the Civil War, government documents in Charleston showed nearly 1,000 "paupers" resided outside the poorhouse and daily received at government expense bread and a little meat. This commitment proved costly to the city, with annual appropriations throughout the 1850s hovering around $12,000 ($220,000 in 1998 US dollars). Charleston was not unique; Beaufort, Georgetown, and Columbia all aided their "unfortunates" with funds supplied by local government allocations.

In addition to the service provided by government, private citizens involved themselves in support of those in need. To many, the system of honor so cherished and defended among South Carolinians carried with it an obligation to those who, through no fault of their own, suffered and endured misfortune. Numerous benevolent societies consequently formed in South Carolina's cities, more than 50 in Charleston alone in the mid-1820s. Among the more prominent and successful associations was Charleston's Ladies' Benevolent Society, which provided aid and comfort to the city's working-class white women. Many of these women entered the labor force to supplement their families' mediocre income or to become sole providers for their children following the death or abandonment of their husbands. Wages were typically half that paid to men and, interestingly, less than those earned by free blacks. The Ladies' Society sent its members directly into Charleston's seamiest neighborhoods, determined the most desperate cases, and later returned bearing food, clothing, and occasionally cash to the working women considered in most need. In 1861, the

Ladies' Benevolent Society raised an endowment of $4,000, or $70,000 in 1998 US dollars, from the city's elite.

Antebellum Recreation

South Carolina's laboring class may have spent most of the day working, but recreational outlets were necessary and available. As one would suspect, farm towns and mill villages periodically sponsored events enjoyed by local residents and farmers from the surrounding countryside. Political rallies, such as the Gallivants' Ferry Annual Democratic Party Rally held each June since the early 1820s, generally drew large crowds. Rallies afforded citizens the opportunity to congregate at a local spot, see and hear candidates address their campaign platforms and solicit local votes, mingle with friends not frequently visited because of distance, hear a sermon from a circuit-riding minister, or learn the latest market trends from local businessmen. While political rallies today are scripted, those in antebellum South Carolina were wildly unpredictable. A candidate promised whatever the assembled crowd desired and delivered his speech in a manner more befitting a "hellfire and brimstone" minister at a revival than a politician pursuing elective office. Whiskey was a regular guest at these events, and brawls between drunken spectators supportive of opposing candidates were not uncommon. A candidate on occasion would descend his platform to separate pairs of fighting men and himself get slapped, gouged, and otherwise abused. Local musicians played their fiddles and sang, gathering listeners to sing and clap along. Music and dancing usually continued into the evening hours, and families spread their homemade banquets for a picnic.

County seats such as Conway and the state capital in Columbia hosted annual fairs, usually after the season's harvest. Friends and family gathered and enjoyed an array of entertainment provided by traveling musical troupes, jugglers, magicians, circuses, and a myriad of sideshows. Contests determined who had hand-stitched the prettiest quilt, shucked the most corn, or produced the tastiest pickles and pies. Local merchants hawked items at discounted prices, and area residents set up tables from which they invited passersby to purchase homemade bread, cakes, dresses, or bedding. Cockfighting attracted an exclusively male audience and gambling carried the evening for many men. Sometimes the fairs coincided with "court week," during which time pending legal cases would be tried, a criminal convicted of a capital offense might be hanged, and property in tax default might be auctioned.

Fairs in Columbia and Charleston were particularly enjoyed for the entertainment options not found in county seats such as Conway. Horse-racing tracks lured the gentleman class, and fortunes were sometimes made or lost. The theater drew large evening crowds. The New Charleston Theater, founded in 1837, accommodated 1,200 people in a three-tier, horseshoe-shaped seating arrangement. Shakespearean tragedies were the highlights of its offerings and drew the expected aristocratic audience. The theater also attracted internationally renowned singers such as Jinny Lind, "the Swedish Nightingale," who performed during the Christmas season of 1850. Her concerts attracted far more people than the theater could seat, many patrons having to sit on the stage itself. Following her final performance, she donated $3,400 to local Charleston charities. Smaller theaters, similar to the vaudeville houses popular much later in the century, offered a more democratic environment, playing to customers from the middle and lower classes and encouraging "audience participation." Jugglers, dancers, singers, musicians, comedians, actors performing a soliloquy from *Hamlet*, and animal acts all reaped immediate feedback from the audience—boos, hisses, vulgar jeers, rotten tomatoes, or enthusiastic applause and coins tossed on stage.

Communities of all sizes across South Carolina celebrated Independence Day with parades, marching bands, flag displays, patriotic speeches delivered by local officials, dances, games, and barbecues. Local militia units often sponsored the celebrations and frequently performed close-order drill for spectators and registered new members. For Christmas, wreaths adorned front doors in Charleston, Columbia, and other communities, area residents gathered at local churches, families and friends partied, carolers strolled city sidewalks, and a gracious, warm, and generous spirit settled over South Carolina's cities, towns, and villages. Slaves were given extra beef,

Must-See Sites: McKissick Museum of the University of South Carolina, Columbia

McKissick Museum, located on the "Horseshoe" of the USC campus, is the largest university-sponsored museum in the southeastern United States. Its collections date to 1801, and both rotating and permanent exhibits generally feature South Carolina and the South's material culture, the arts, and natural sciences. The museum is located at Pendleton and Bull Streets. Admission is free, and the museum is open daily. For additional information, call 803-777-7251 or visit www.cas.sc.edu/MCKS.

sometimes small gifts, and possibly a few days free from work.

In the first half of the nineteenth century, South Carolina's economy remained inextricably tied to cotton and slave labor. The cotton culture spread westward across the state and ultimately provided South Carolina with a level of wealth unmatched by most other states. South Carolina remained an agrarian-based state, as it had been since its founding—its government, civil society, and economy all connected to the land. But the state's economy and character also showed signs of change. Manufacturing was becoming a more important segment of the economy, and the expansion of railroads and the business growth it encouraged promised an economy more connected to national rather than simply regional interests. Indeed, economic diversification was becoming more real within the state.

The social and cultural landscape of South Carolina was also changing. By 1860, the Palmetto State's population included a religious diversity heretofore most closely associated with Middle Atlantic States. Presbyterians, Lutherans, Methodists, Baptists, Episcopalians, Catholics, Jews, all called the Palmetto State home, many of them having relocated into South Carolina from northern states. They often brought with them manners, experiences, and values that broadened the worldview of South Carolinians. There was also an out-migration of citizens, relocating to Tennessee, western Georgia, Alabama, Mississippi, and Louisiana. Although neither in-migration nor out-migration cut deeply into the power of the state's old guard, both weakened its influence and permitted the rooting of contrary views.

South Carolinians had successfully instituted a number of reforms, including aid to the poor, education for both black and white children, founding institutions of higher learning, initiatives to combat prostitution, as well as cleaning and lighting city streets. This is not to say that South Carolina was yet a truly humane, egalitarian, or progressive society. The ongoing existence of slavery itself condemned South Carolina and maintained its connection to the archaic past. But the state's citizens and businessmen nonetheless occasionally lurched forward, linking the state to a broader, national consciousness and reformist impulse. South Carolina was neither rigidly fixed in the past nor reaching enthusiastically to the future. Throughout the state's history, it has consistently had one foot in the past and one in the future; it remains that way today.

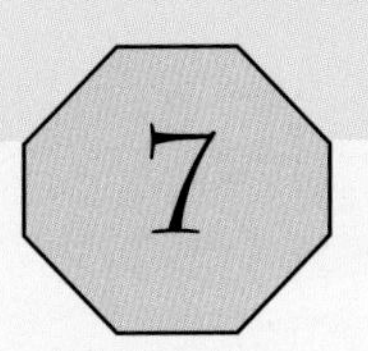

South Carolina and the Coming of Civil War

Between 1820 and 1860, the relationship between the states of the South and the North grew ever closer to rupturing. The break that ultimately resulted in war in 1861 was due as much to poor leadership as malice. Several issues surfaced in those four decades that confounded politicians and divided the two regions.

Slavery in South Carolina

Oaks veiled in Spanish moss line either side of the drive that leads to a magnificent mansion in Greek revival style, complete with giant columns; a wealthy cotton planter and his wife, both immaculately dressed, sit on the wrap-around porch, rocking in their chairs and sipping mint juleps served by their devoted house servant; contented slaves bagging cotton in distant fields sing a soothing melody; an air of tranquility and patriarchy prevails over the scene—these are the romanticized perceptions of antebellum southern plantations, perhaps best popularized by Margaret Mitchell's representation of neighboring Georgia in *Gone with the Wind*. Popular images of the past contain some truth, but truth is typically far more complex and less glamorous than Hollywood suggests.

As discussed in chapter six, manufacturing was emerging in Charleston and across the Lowcountry as an important segment of the economy. Farther west, in and around Columbia, railroads and warehousing made the state capital one of the leading distribution centers in the South. The state's economy was clearly showing signs of diversification, but agriculture—cotton and rice production—remained the dual pillars on which the state's wealth rested. The agricultural economy itself depended on slave labor.

HONOR SYST

Hopsewee Plantation, Slave Quarters, Georgetown County, SC, Historic American Buildings Survey

The antebellum plantation was first and foremost home to a business—the business of producing either cotton or rice for sale. Although most plantations in South Carolina raised cotton, the greatest wealth was derived from rice cultivation. Of the 560 rice plantations spread along the southeast Atlantic coast in 1860, 446, or 80 percent, were located in the South Carolina Lowcountry. But whether the plantation produced cotton or rice, the planters' income relied on slaves.

Slavery was most concentrated in the rice-producing region of South Carolina. In 1860 slaves were fully 85 percent of the population in Georgetown County, for example. But even cotton-producing areas often had a black majority: from the rice fields of the coastal marshes deep into the upland cotton regions of Laurens and Union Counties blacks totaled more than 50 percent of the population. Thirty to fifty percent of the population in northern-tier counties was slaves; only in Horry County in the extreme northeast corner of the state and Oconee County in South Carolina's westernmost territory did slaves make up less than thirty percent of the population, neither county being focused on either cash crop. In 1860, blacks, the overwhelming majority of whom lived in forced bondage, represented 60 percent of the total population statewide.

Across the South, on average 25 percent of whites owned slaves. In South Carolina, however, in 1860 almost 46 percent of white families owned one or more slaves. Slightly less than two-thirds of slaveholding families in South Carolina owned fewer than ten slaves, a pattern fairly consistent with slave owning in other southern states and clearly contrary to popular images. As one would suspect, the wealthiest South Carolina planters were the largest slaveholders. On the eve of the Civil War, nearly 1,200 families owned 50–99 slaves, 360 families owned 100–200, 55 owned 200–300, 22 owned 300–400, and 7 families owned 500–999. Only one individual, Plowden Weston of Georgetown, held more than 1,000 slaves.

Many planters employed the "task system" for both rice and cotton production. Each day, a slave was assigned a certain amount of work to accomplish, generally confined to a quarter-acre stretch of land. When his duty was completed, he was granted the remainder of the day to rest, work in his own small garden, or concentrate on other household chores for himself and his family. If he chose to double his tasks and complete those in a single day, he then had the following day entirely for his own pursuits. The built-in rewards of the task system encouraged attention to work and generally proved the most effective system for the planter.

In the "gang system," the use of slave labor most commonly imagined by Americans today, slaves worked most of the day in the fields with few breaks and under the observant eye of the overseer. There was no reward for working hard, and thus no incentive to be productive. Overseers often resorted to threats, intimidation, and sometimes brutal punishment to make slaves meet the day's goal.

Farmers who owned fewer than ten slaves often worked in the fields themselves, frequently laboring alongside their slaves. The day was divided into regular periods for work, meals, and rest, with slaves and owners on the same schedule. Although their labor was still forced and they still lacked basic freedoms, slaves sometimes assumed a common investment with their masters in the production of cotton. Moreover, slaves belonging to small farmers *typically* received less severe treatment than those who worked on the gang system employed by larger planters. This in no way diminishes the brutality of the "peculiar institution" nor the fundamental inhumanity on which slavery rested; it is, however, a reality of slavery rarely recognized, just as it is not widely discussed that some emancipated slaves became slaveholding planters themselves, others worked as overseers, and others manufactured and sold cotton gins that only perpetuated the cotton culture. To be sure, these instances were uncommon, but collectively they indicate the complexity of this labor system. As we condemn this system today, we should also understand it in as much detail as possible so that slaves' experiences are not lost again to history.

Contrary to Mitchell's representation of contentment, slave life was indeed brutal. Food was often limited, long hours of strenuous work over the course of years bent the strongest of men, adequate clothing was rarely available, and the overseers methods were often unpredictable and cruel. A mild infraction of plantation rules brought immediate punishment; additional work deprived the slave

Lucy Chambers, ex-slave, taken December 4,1937

of what little free time he otherwise enjoyed under the task system, or weekly meat allotments might be reduced or curtailed completely. More serious violations resulted in whippings, sometimes so severe the slave required medical attention and missed days of work. As counterproductive as whipping may have been on immediate work demands, it was used to signal a grim message to the plantation's slaves that strict obedience was demanded and would be enforced. The greatest threat hanging over the slave community was the sale of one or more individuals to other planters in the area, shattering families; equally feared was the possibility of being purchased by an upstart planter on the Gulf Coast where the lifespan of slaves was horrifically short.

Devastating for slaves, too, were the frequent sexual advances and assaults many white planters made on women. Single women, married women, and girls just shy of their teen years all were quite aware that they might be visited by their owner. Some women and girls acquiesced to spare themselves reprisals from a rebuked planter, and some were coerced with the threat that a close family member might be sold at auction unless she complied with the planter's wishes. The violations dehumanized the women, and caused intense anguish for husbands and fathers, who could not protect their wives and daughters from the planters.

For white planters and middle-class farmers, slaves constituted a cost-efficient labor force for cotton and rice production and by law were identified as physical property. Africans enjoyed no rights and no legal protection. They were subject to sale and commonly considered less than human. It seems disturbing to Americans today that in the antebellum era so few whites acknowledged slave suffering; in fact, most whites were oblivious to the pain and fear blacks lived with daily. It was a shock when radical abolitionism challenged the peculiar institution.

Slavery as a Cause for the Civil War

Abolitionism grew from the dogmatic base of the Second Great Awakening, or Christian fundamentalist evangelicalism, that swept over the North and parts of the South in the 1820s, a movement that rested on the premise of Jesus's impending return—the second coming. American society was so filled with sinful behavior and immoral structures that Americans surely faced damnation, argued the movement's proponents. The goal of Christian fundamentalists, then, was to purge the United States of all sinful ways and institutions, among them slavery.

Abolitionists called for the immediate eradication of slavery in the United States and the full equality of blacks in America. Between 1820 and 1860, abolitionists trumpeted their message of freedom and brotherhood in every venue possible. Reverend Theodore Weld, for example, conducted a series of tent revivals in the Midwest calling on the devout to unite against the evil of slavery. William Lloyd Garrison founded his anti-slavery newspaper *The Liberator* in 1831 and printed stinging indictments of the South's peculiar institution based on the testimony of former slaves; he also condemned all those who profited indirectly from the institution and lumped into the group of sinners all those who did not involve themselves directly in the abolitionist crusade. This included not just Southerners but Northerners as well, particularly northern textile mill owners, mill workers, garment distributors, and everyone even remotely connected to the textile industry. Other abolitionists held public rallies and gave sharp, emotional tirades against slaveholders and their accomplices, and some attempted to blockade railroad lines on which cotton traveled to northern factories, or interfered with the unloading of baled cotton at northern docks. Across the North, abolitionists raged against slavery and the sinful profit derived from this most immoral source, all the while calling for the grace of God to cleanse America's errant ways. Abolitionists may have been a numerical minority, but their aggressiveness made the movement seem omnipresent.

South Carolinians defended the peculiar institution with equal fervor and intensity. They frequently retorted that slavery was, in fact, a "positive good" for blacks. The system resembled that of a father and his children, they argued: the father is responsible for his children's moral training; slaves were instructed in the Christian faith. A father is expected to instill in his offspring a productive work ethic; slaves learned the value of work. Children were to be disciplined when they violated their father's rules;

slaves, similarly, were punished and reminded to be obedient to their caregiver. Moreover, planters added, the Bible did not demand the abolition of slavery. South Carolina's slave owners, and those who anticipated owning slaves, deflected the abolitionists' condemnation, arguing that God blessed slavery. Indeed, many of the largest slaveholding planters were leaders in South Carolina's churches, especially among Episcopalians. Numerous men of the cloth statewide voiced support for slavery, frequently citing chapter and verse from the "good book" that suggested slavery's propriety.

Beyond the moral issue, South Carolinians responded with a legal and economic defense that actually carried some weight in the North. The United States Constitution did not prohibit slavery; therefore, it remained a legitimate source of labor and a prerogative of the state, protected by the tenth amendment. In addition, federal courts nationwide consistently ruled slaves to be property under the law, and government had no authority to deprive anyone of his fundamental right to property. Nor was government entitled to deprive anyone of his right to life. Without slave labor, many South Carolinians claimed, the agrarian economy of the state would collapse and with it the means to sustain their lives. And, they continued, failure of the South's economy would trigger tremendous financial loss in the North if slave labor could not produce the cotton northern textile mill owners and factory workers required.

The abolitionists' crusade strained the tolerance of many South Carolinians, and their sponsored activities across the North only exacerbated the rising sense of attack. The legislatures in nine northern states in the mid-1820s labeled slavery an ungodly institution that threatened the moral foundation of the United States and called for its immediate, unconditional abolition. At the same time, Senator Rufus King of New York called on Congress to purchase slaves and then emancipate them. In 1852 Harriet Beecher Stowe's *Uncle Tom's Cabin* incited the antipathy of Northerners who, before its printing, had been moderately opposed to the peculiar institution for its immorality and rather silent about their profitable connections to the region's textile manufacturing. Warfare in Kansas in 1856 between armed abolitionists and supporters of slavery further fueled the

The Grimke Sisters

Sarah (1792–1873) and Angelina (1805–1879) Grimke were two of fourteen children of one of Charleston's leading citizens, Judge John Faucheraud Grimke. Judge Grimke had fought in the Revolutionary War, built a prosperous cotton plantation, and held office in the South Carolina General Assembly. The girls' mother also hailed from Charleston wealth, and the family alternated residency between their Beaufort plantation and their Charleston townhouse. Sarah and Angelina were surrounded by slaves throughout their childhood. Slaves worked the fields and tended to household duties, and they were cared for by black nursemaids and played with slave children—a common practice for white youngsters on southern plantations. Judge Grimke educated his daughters in the fundamentals of law, although this subject was considered a man's realm.

Sarah and Angelina were never comfortable with the institution of slavery. On numerous occasions they saw overseers punishing slaves brutally, sometimes for the mildest infractions, and they witnessed the dehumanizing treatment of blacks outside the plantation environment, in Charleston.

In 1818 Sarah traveled with her ill father to Philadelphia and then to Bordentown, New Jersey in 1819, where he later died. Following his death, she returned to Philadelphia, and there saw a society without slavery. She found a spiritual home in the Quaker religion, which encouraged female leadership, promoted nonviolence, and vehemently denounced slavery. She settled in Philadelphia and officially converted to the Quaker religion.

With Sarah gone, Angelina cared for her widowed mother, but was not content. Slavery surrounded her at home and across the state, and she detested it, its violence, and the inhumane treatment of free blacks. She was also disturbed by the rigid constraints placed on southern women, affecting everything from their role in society to the clothing they wore. When Sarah visited in 1827, Angelina found in her sister the qualities she herself longed for—simplicity, nonviolence, feminism, and respect for the equality of all persons. Angelina also converted to the Quaker faith, but rather than relocate to Philadelphia, the religion's home, she remained in the South and attempted to spread Quakerism locally. Ostracized by Charleston society for her views, Angelina joined Sarah in Philadelphia in 1829.

As the abolitionist movement gained influence in the 1830s, Sarah and Angelina worked full-time with the American Anti-Slavery Society (AASS), forgoing marriage and family. Angelina's letters were printed in William Lloyd Garrison's abolitionist newspaper *The Liberator*, and Sarah participated in a boycott of goods produced directly or indirectly by slave labor. Their activism drew them to Providence, Rhode Island in 1836, where they published a series of attacks on slavery, condemning it as contrary to the teachings of Jesus and Christian principles. Their writings also called for greater participation by women in the AASS and the reform efforts then sweeping the nation. In addition to their writings, they traveled to dozens of cities to deliver public speeches, which was not widely considered proper for women at the time. Angelina also addressed the Massachusetts state assembly, the first woman in American history to speak before a state legislature.

Angelina married Theodore Weld, a widely respected abolitionist, in 1838. She chose not to include the phrase "to obey" in her vows, and Weld openly renounced claims to her inheritance. The Welds, along with Sarah, established a farm in New Jersey where they raised Angelina's children, but the sisters continued to write articles and to draft speeches for others to present at anti-slavery rallies. The Grimkes' combined work certainly advanced the abolitionist argument to a much larger audience. And because they were Southerners and of the planter class, they had a wider readership in the South than such views would otherwise have found.

The Grimke sisters spent the postwar years founding a coeducational school in Boston and championing minority rights. They continued to call for equal rights for women, and in March 1870 Sarah, age 79, and Angelina, age 66, marched with 40 other women to cast ballots in a local election. The bitter cold, the snowstorm, and the harassment by men lining the streets did not prevent the elderly women from voting. Sarah died in 1873, and Angelina followed six years later. The Grimke sisters committed their lives to the battle against slavery, the cause of racial equality, and the struggle for women's rights.

presumption of an impending violent clash, and John Brown's bid to take the federal arsenal at Harper's Ferry, Virginia in 1859, arm area slaves, and initiate a slave rebellion gave evidence of the depth of abolitionist commitment. In the wake of the Harper's Ferry incident, most South Carolina communities organized watchdog committees to keep tabs on any and all strangers, and frequently these vigilante groups questioned, assaulted, and forced outsiders to vacate the state. Little wonder, then, that South Carolinians saw in the abolitionist movement a real threat to their state's established social and economic order. In addition to these overt acts were numerous developments within the state that some South Carolinians presumed to be covert operations supported by abolitionists, or at the least directions applauded by abolitionists.

Denmark Vesey, a Charleston slave who was permitted by his owner to earn money hiring himself out to area planters in his spare time, saved enough cash to purchase his freedom in 1800. Vesey chose to remain in the city, living as a free man and working as an independent carpenter. On Sundays, he attended the city's African Methodist Episcopal Church and regularly led a morning devotional class during which he often read passages from the Bible that emphasized the worth of all men. One of his favorite stories was that of Moses leading his people from bondage to the promised land. In 1822, Vesey and his closest followers plotted a slave insurrection in Charleston slated for June 16. Unknown to him, a co-conspirator turned informant, fearing that a rebellion, successful or not, would have fierce consequences for those who remained enslaved in South Carolina. Vesey and 78 other slaves and free blacks were arrested on June 14 and tried and convicted two weeks later. Thirty-five were sentenced to death, and the rest were to be sold to planters outside of South Carolina. Vesey went to the gallows on July 2, and by month's end the remaining plotters who had received the death sentence were also hanged. There was no evidence of abolitionist complicity, and none has surfaced since. Nonetheless, rumors pervaded Charleston society that Vesey had been in communication with outside "agitators."

Suspicion grew in 1829 when a similar planned slave revolt was compromised in Georgetown. Over the four

Must-See Sites: Denmark Vesey's House, Charleston

Denmark Vesey, a slave in the Virgin Islands, was purchased by a Charleston planter and brought to South Carolina in the early nineteenth century. Vesey was permitted to hire himself out to local merchants when his labor was not required on the plantation, and with his accumulated earnings he eventually purchased his freedom, taking residence in a house on Bull Street and working as a carpenter. In 1822, Vesey was accused of plotting an armed rebellion by local slaves and free blacks, was arrested, convicted of the charges against him, and hanged with more than 30 alleged accomplices. His former home is located at 56 Bull Street. Call (843) 953-7609 for more details.

years that followed, rumors circulated throughout the state of slave plots, and stories appeared in most newspapers of violent attacks by slaves on whites in Marion, Lancaster, and Sumter. Copies of Garrison's *The Liberator* filtered into the state as these developments unfolded and lent some credence to the charge of an abolitionist association with slave rebellions and assaults in South Carolina. Long before the pivotal 1850s, South Carolinians were convinced that their state was imperiled.

Westward Expansion & the Coming of War

Soil quality declined annually in South Carolina's cotton-growing region, and as a result more than 200,000 farmers and planters exited the state in the antebellum period for fresh lands on which they could continue producing the valued fiber. With them went their slaves. A large percentage of South Carolina's emigrants relocated to the Gulf Coast states, a few traveled into Missouri. As the white population settled into the trans-Mississippi West—Missouri, Texas, Oregon, California—the issue of slavery weighed heavily on America. From each new state to the Union went two senators to Congress. Southerners and Northerners alike feared an imbalance of power in the

Senate, an imbalance that would permit one or the other section to gain political control and press the United States in its own direction. Would national or state interests dominate? Would the nation be pushed toward an industrial economy or would agriculture remain the national base? Would slavery be displaced by the free-labor system championed by northern interests? Whose view of the United States and the nation's future would prevail? Given the seriousness of these concerns, both North and South concluded that it was imperative that a balance of power be maintained in the Senate. In the nation's first test of slavery's expansion, the North and the South reached a compromise, allowing Missouri to enter the Union as a slaveholding state and Maine to be created as a free-labor state. The balance of power in the Senate was preserved.

Although content with the compromise, Charles Pinckney, South Carolina's venerable delegate to the Constitutional Convention of 1787 and current member of the US House of Representatives in 1820, expressed concern about what he believed to be the federal government's interference with the institution of slavery. Congress held absolutely no authority to determine the fate of slavery in the states or territories, he argued in a speech on the House floor. Slaves were considered property under the law; Congress could not deny anyone his right to carry his property to a new residence.

Despite Pinckney's argument, slavery once again became an issue in Congress with Texas's application for statehood in 1848. Northern representatives insisted slavery had reached its natural limits in Louisiana. Texas, they contended, was entirely too arid for the expansion of agriculture, particularly cotton production. Southerners rebutted the argument, pointing to the success of cotton in eastern Texas in the 1830s—success in part driven by slave labor. South Carolina's congressional delegation and its citizens statewide defended slavery's expansion. Nature, not Congress, they said, determined the limits of agricultural development in the West, and the Constitution protected the right of Southerners to own slaves; wherever cotton could be grown profitably, Southerners held the right to produce it using slave labor. They echoed Pinckney's position of 1820, stating that the federal government did not possess the authority to halt the spread of slavery anywhere in the United States or its territories and that any discussion of the subject itself violated the intent of the Constitution's framers. Moreover, the blood of South Carolinians had been spilled in Texas and Mexico. The Palmetto Regiment alone suffered 440 deaths in combat, about 40 percent of its total complement of 1,000 soldiers. South Carolinians argued that given the state's sacrifice in securing Texas and the rest of the Southwest from Mexico, Congress had no moral right to deny slaveholders from taking their property into the newly acquired regions. Noted Benjamin Perry, at the time one of the state's most vocal supporters of the national government, any effort by Washington to deprive South Carolinians of their slave property and the movement of slavery into the West required "an immediate dissolution" of the bonds joining the North and the South. He and others also accused abolitionists of fomenting the current crisis. The South Carolinian's critique and similar arguments from across the South carried the issue, and Texas won admission to the union as a slave state. Despite this success, another challenge to slave interests loomed large.

In 1848, gold was discovered near Sacramento, California. The ensuing "gold rush" the following year brought tens of thousands of men and women to the West Coast, and in 1850 California met the criteria for statehood. Again, debate swirled in the halls of Congress and once more resulted in a negotiated settlement, the Compromise of 1850. To balance power in the Senate, California entered the union as a free state. To placate southern interests, the compromise included passage of the Fugitive Slave Act, which permitted slave owners the legal right to pursue runaways virtually anywhere in the United States, and required local law enforcement personnel in free states to detain for repatriation all escaped slaves in their jurisdiction. Clearly, the compromise only added further discord between the North and the South. Abolitionists were livid over the Fugitive Slave Act, a move, they argued, that extended the reach of slaveholders, perpetuated the immoral institution, and implicated more Northerners in the sinful system. Rather than purge the nation of this particular sin, the compromise sustained it and permitted its growth.

Must-See Sites: Slave Market Museum, Charleston

This market was one of several sites in Charleston where African slaves were auctioned and today is the center of the African American Heritage Museum. The last auction of slaves at this market occurred in 1863. The museum includes exhibits on Lowcountry slavery, the "middle passage" of the slave trade, emancipation, reconstruction, and the Civil Rights Movement in South Carolina. The museum is located at 6 Chalmers Street and is open daily. Admission fees are required. Call (843) 958-6467 for additional information.

Although the compromise gave the South one item it had long desired, the very notion of a compromise itself infuriated South Carolinians. James Hammond voiced his argument that California's admission as a free state was the North's most recent attempt to secure control of the Senate and in so doing secure control over the South. Once empowered in the Senate, a federal government dominated by northerners and backed by the abolitionist crusade would ultimately destroy the South's economy and social structure; in short, death awaited the South. Leading figures in South Carolina's cities, towns, and villages along with newspaper editors and ministers all warned their listeners of the threat to the state and succinctly posited a simple alternative—relinquish slavery or quit the Union.

In December 1850 the South Carolina General Assembly convened for its annual meeting, and secession was on the lips of many representatives. The assembly called on all southern slave states to hold a Southern Convention in Montgomery, Alabama in January 1852 to discuss a unified response to northern "aggression" against the South's agrarian interests, including slavery. South Carolina voters would decide in an October 1851 election whom to send to Montgomery. But, extremists in the assembly worried that the Southern Convention might not produce any unified or viable response and called for a separate state convention to meet in April 1852, three months after the Montgomery meeting. No southern state agreed to a January convention, however, which disconcerted South Carolina protagonists, and at the state convention in April the secessionists were soundly trounced by more moderate voices. The crisis of secession dissipated, but South Carolina had moved further toward disunion than any other southern state to date.

Radicals in South Carolina remained active, however. Extremists raised money to support pro-slavery activities in Kansas, and hundreds of men temporarily emigrated to the territory in 1856 to fight in the civil war that exploded there between pro-slavery and anti-slavery forces. At the same time, tempers flared in Congress, and an exchange of stinging speeches between Southerners and abolitionist-supporting representatives further alienated the two sections of the nation. Senator Charles Sumner of Massachusetts on May 19, 1856 not only rebuked slavery's supporters in Kansas but also launched a scathing personal attack on South Carolina and its Senator A. P. Butler. Sumner's tirade went well beyond the scope of slavery, southern rights, and territorial expansion; the senator challenged the one thing most valued among South Carolina's gentlemen, a man's honor—in this case, Butler's. Butler took no immediate action, but his cousin, Congressman Preston Brooks from Edgefield, did respond. On May 22 Brooks left the House floor, burst through the Senate's doors, spotted Sumner, and caned senseless the Massachusetts senator. Sumner's remarks on the 19th had been considered at the time too harsh, too personal, and unwarranted by many of his northern colleagues; Brooks's attack, however, recast Sumner as a victim and martyr of southern aggression. Brooks's star also rose among Southerners who championed the congressman as the defender of southern honor. South Carolinians prided themselves on having a man in Congress who did the "right thing," defending the honor of both Butler and the state. A House vote fell short of the necessary number to expel Brooks, but the congressman nonetheless resigned his seat. In a special election held in July to fill the vacant position, Brooks won an uncontested reelection.

SECESSION

The concurrent moralistic crusade of the abolitionists heated the political and economic confrontation to a much greater emotional intensity and compromised rational debate, complicated further by paranoid, reactionary Southerners. As support for the eradication of slavery drew a wider audience among Northerners in the 1850s, especially after the publication of Stowe's *Uncle Tom's Cabin* and civil war in Kansas, extremists in both the North and the South only hardened their positions. By 1860, then, Americans stood on the precipice of a potential national calamity.

The Democratic National Convention in May 1860 was held in Charleston, much to the chagrin of northern delegates. No city in the South was more defiant of federal authority; no city in the South embodied more fully the radical, pro-slavery stance that had contributed to the series of crises over the preceding 40 years. Shortly after the DNC convened, a proposed plank for the November presidential campaign was presented to the floor. Despite the longstanding argument that slavery was not an issue for congressional debate or action, the plank would have required Congress to create legislation explicitly protecting the extension of slavery into the western territories. Northern delegates, predominantly proponents of free labor and manufacturing, vetoed the proposal. Alabama's delegation stormed away from the convention, led by William Yancey, who had earlier emigrated from the Palmetto State. South Carolina and six other southern states followed Alabama's lead. The convention was in shambles, and the Democratic Party was now split. Northern Democrats organized a separate convention in Baltimore and selected Stephen A. Douglas as their contender for the White House; Southern Democrats assembled in Richmond in late summer and placed John C. Breckenridge as their candidate.

Radicals, willing to secede from the union if necessary, controlled South Carolina's Democratic Party. Moderates reluctantly inched toward the extremist position, largely driven by popular opinion, but hoping to act as a brake on the secessionist impulse. By portraying the upstart Republican Party as the home of abolitionists and promising secession if that party's candidate, Abraham Lincoln, won the election, they believed levelheaded

Northerners would move from the Republican Party to support the National Democrat Party to preserve the Union. The plan rested squarely on the presumption—in fact, the correct presumption—that most Northerners were not in the abolitionist camp, although they certainly preferred free labor to slave labor.

During the campaign of 1860, Lincoln insisted repeatedly that he had no intention of abolishing slavery where it already existed and that he, as president, would not possess the authority to end the peculiar institution even if he did desire to do so. However, he openly and unequivocally stated that he opposed slavery's extension into western territories and believed Washington had the power to prevent this. This was the best abolitionists could expect from any political party in 1860, and in response they gave Lincoln their unified support.

Aware of abolitionist support for the Republican Party, South Carolina's press vehemently denounced Lincoln as a man not to be trusted and one who fully intended the abolition of slavery and the promotion of racial equality, points consistent with abolitionist rhetoric. But the collective voice arising from South Carolina proved more than a political tactic to encourage Northerners to support the National Democrats. Fear was real for South Carolinians. They truly believed a Lincoln victory would bring with it the utter destruction of the southern economy through the eradication of slave labor, and that the collapse of the South's agrarian base would directly lead to the demise of southern institutions and culture. On the November election hinged everything of value to white South Carolinians.

The election-day scenario desired by South Carolinians failed to develop. On November 6, 1860, Lincoln won the presidency; the very next day, South Carolina's congressional delegation resigned from Congress and left Washington, and the General Assembly called for a state convention in Columbia for December 17. Days before the convention assembled, reports of a smallpox outbreak in the capital compelled the assembly to switch the site to Charleston. Although there remained voices urging moderation, all 169 delegates voted for secession on December 20.

South Carolina was alone at the moment, having taken the final, desperate act of a state that believed its way of life—its very existence—was in jeopardy. Delegates in Charleston, bolstered by public opinion, saw secession as the only means by which they could preserve their economic base, social structure, and culture, and escape the inevitable political dominance of northern manufacturing interests and excessive federal authority. They believed that the ideology of the American Revolution, that government must protect one's natural rights of life, liberty, and property, was clearly threatened by a Republican victory. South Carolinians, therefore, invoked John Locke's theory of the "right of revolution," that should government fail to protect the natural rights of the people, the people, then, have the right to dissolve their bonds with the governing system and replace it with a new one. Secession was their recourse. Two questions now pervaded the state: "What will the other slave states do, and how will Washington respond?"

Beautiful and well-preserved buildings line the streets of Charleston
© Michael Smith

8

The Civil War

Upon hearing the news of the convention's vote on secession, South Carolinians roared their enthusiastic approval and celebrated independence from the Union. As they rejoiced, convention delegates penned "A Declaration of the Immediate Causes" and "An Address to the People of South Carolina." The declaration stated that secession was the state's response to the North's repeated attacks on slavery and the damning effect abolition would ultimately have on the state financially and socially; to preserve the state, South Carolina had no alternative but to separate from the Union. The address focused entirely on the federal government's alleged abridgement of the Constitution. Together, the documents framed the two central points of contention between South Carolina and the North over the previous 40 years. Delegates also called for another convention of all slaveholding states for the purpose of erecting an independent confederation.

Not everyone in South Carolina was delirious with joy. As noted by historian Walter Edgar in his masterful history of the state, James Pettigrew said, "South Carolina is too small to be a Republic, and too large to be an insane asylum." His colleague Benjamin Perry reluctantly accepted secession and added that since South Carolinians were "now all going to the devil… I will go with them." Indeed, many in the Palmetto State contemplated what course to follow—support an independent South Carolina or remain faithful to the United States.

While many South Carolinians considered their response to secession and possible war with the United States, the secessionist convention pursued one additional matter—what to do with the federal military installations that ringed Charleston. It appointed three respected men to negotiate the fate of the forts with federal authorities, and they arrived in Washington the day after Christmas. That same evening, Major Robert Anderson, who commanded federal troops in Charleston, quietly slipped his garrison from Fort Moultrie on Sullivan's Island to Fort Sumter centered in Charleston Harbor. After learning of Anderson's move the following morning, Governor Francis Pickens ordered the state militia to seize Fort Moultrie, the arsenal, and all other federal properties in the city. A wire was immediately telegraphed to Washington informing the White House of the governor's action, and the negotiations between the state's delegates and President Buchanan's representatives scheduled for December 27 collapsed.

South Carolina's secession set the tone for other southern states, and by February 1, 1861, Mississippi, Florida, Georgia, Louisiana, Alabama, and Texas had quit the Union. As the Charleston convention requested, the seceded states assembled in Montgomery, Alabama on February 4, formed a government for the Confederate States of America, and elected Jefferson Davis of Mississippi as president. The Confederate Constitution resembled that of the United States, with a few alterations. Davis and future presidents would serve a single, six-year term in office; states retained greater authority than the national government; and slavery was a state prerogative. Interestingly, the Confederate Constitution openly acknowledged its willingness to admit non-slaveholding states on the same basis as slaveholding states, the consent of two-thirds of both houses of the Confederate Congress.

In Washington, federal officials and Congress (minus the southern delegations) worked feverishly to reach some compromise that would resolve the crisis satisfactorily for all states. President Buchanan, a lame duck in the White House, offered little effort and displayed less concern; nonetheless, several measures were introduced and debated in Congress, but all were found lacking in substance. President-elect Lincoln reiterated his pre-election position: he assured the South that slavery was protected where it already existed and that he had no intention to abolish the system; he did, however, remind Southerners that he would not tolerate its expansion into western territories. He added one additional point, that no state had the legal right to secede and therefore the United States government did not recognize the Confederate States of America.

Events in Charleston exacerbated the crisis. The resupply ship *Star of the West* entered the harbor on January 9, 1861, bound for Fort Sumter. Cadets from the Citadel (formerly the South Carolina Military Academy) manned a battery of cannon and fired several warning shots over the ship's bow. Understanding the point, the ship's captain reversed course and exited Charleston Harbor. President Buchanan was promptly informed. Rather than move a fleet of warships to the South Carolina coast and escort future resupply vessels, the president chose not to antagonize the Confederacy and refused to authorize any further effort to secure the federal posts. Fort Sumter was, for all practical purposes, left to the mercy of South Carolina.

The First Shots of War

On March 4, Abraham Lincoln was inaugurated as the nation's sixteenth president, and in his address he once more succinctly stated his view of secession and his promise for the protection of slavery in the South. Lincoln's speech received little interest in South Carolina; the Palmetto State had proclaimed itself a member of a separate, independent nation, and Lincoln's words carried no weight on the Confederacy. But in meetings with the War Department, the new president insisted that Fort Sumter would be held at all costs. To abandon the fort, he believed, would signal the United States' recognition of Confederate authority. He expected Fort Sumter to be resupplied, but no additional troops would reinforce the garrison in Charleston; Lincoln did not wish to provoke the South into committing an overt act of war but rather encourage a compromise with the errant states.

South Carolina understood clearly that it could not tolerate a foreign force within its territorial boundary, and on April 11, 1861 a delegation of Confederate officials sailed to the fort and demanded Major Anderson's surrender. Anderson refused to abandon his position but added that his provisions would be depleted within one week and he would then have to evacuate for the sake of his men. The delegation, however, was aware that Lincoln's navy was already en route to Charleston Harbor with fresh supplies and Anderson's command would therefore be salvaged.

Must-See Sites: Fort Sumter, Charleston

In the 1830s, the United States began in earnest to build coastal fortifications for the defense of vital harbors. Charleston's port was the largest and most active along the southern coastline, so important that the War Department ordered the construction of a second fort to supplement Fort Moultrie, which already guarded American shipping from its position on Sullivan's Island. Fort Sumter arose on a manmade island within one mile of Moultrie and was nearly completed when on April 12, 1861 the Confederate battery in Charleston opened fire on Union troops posted there. The shelling of Fort Sumter officially started the American Civil War, and from summer 1863 through spring 1865 when the war concluded it was under constant siege by Union gunboats.

Over the years that followed, Fort Sumter remained an active military facility. During World War I and World War II, a United States garrison manned the compound, in both conflicts serving as a defensive position against German U-boat activity and in the latter war as an air observation unit that searched for enemy aircraft. At war's end in 1945 Fort Sumter was decommissioned, and three years later Congress proclaimed the fort a national monument.

Today Fort Sumter is a prominent attraction for visitors to Charleston. Approximately 340,000 tourists visit the landmark annually, and the National Park Service budget for both Fort Sumter and Fort Moultrie exceeds $1.5 million each year. Information regarding tour boat schedules and costs, hours of operation, and park services is available at various visitor centers in Charleston and at the National Park Service website, www.nps.gov/fosu.

For additional color photographs, biographies of notable Civil War officers and enlisted men, battle reports, and archival material, visit the following sites: www.us-civilwar.com/sumter.htm and www.americancivilwar.com.

Montgomery ordered General P. G. T. Beauregard, who commanded 6,000 Confederate troops in Charleston, to cripple this obvious delaying tactic and force the issue. At 4:30AM on April 12, 1861, the Confederate battery in Charleston opened fire on Fort Sumter. Local citizens were roused from their slumber, and rushed to their windows to witness the commencement of war. Throughout the day, gentlemen and ladies in their finest clothing and workers covered in dirt and grime stood on rooftops and fire-escape landings to observe the burst of cannon shells over Fort Sumter. Servants filled champagne glasses for their aristocrat masters while the middling folk took swigs of whiskey. Politicians heralded the beginning of a new era in southern history; their rhetoric gushed with flourishes of "states' rights" and "honor." The worst war in American history had begun. Charlestonians saw not the impending death and destruction but the commencement of a promising new age.

Thirty-four hours of constant bombardment drove federal troops to the lowest depths of the fort, cannon shots shattering the top tiers of the structure into absolute rubble. On April 14, Anderson raised the white flag and surrendered Fort Sumter. Upon learning of the events in Charleston, Lincoln immediately called for 75,000 volunteers to crush the southern rebellion and preserve the Union, a move that compelled the remaining slaveholding states to consider their options. In the weeks that followed, Tennessee, Arkansas, Virginia, and North Carolina joined the Confederacy; four slaveholding states—Maryland, Missouri, Kentucky, and Delaware—did not secede but remained in the Union for the war's duration.

By mid-May, Union warships lined the southern coastline to block key Confederate ports. Charleston's harbor, long considered one of the largest and most active facilities in the United States, faced layers of enemy ships stretching deep into the Atlantic. Northerners reasoned that if they closed Charleston, South Carolina's economy would likely collapse and the flow of supplies to and from the state would halt—control Charleston and cripple the state's war effort. The city was also a symbolic target for Union forces. It was home to the secessionist impulse, "the vipers' nest" of rebellion. Facing the Union's obvious plan to take the city, the Confederate government ordered its defense to the last man.

A blockade of Charleston was essential to the North, but the United States War Department believed that to conquer the city, they would first have to take the surrounding towns. Beaufort and Georgetown residents soon viewed northern sails on the horizon. Slaves were quickly put to work building earthwork defenses around these communities and on the string of barrier islands outside Charleston to keep federal troops from landing. Fortifications in the Beaufort area were soon tested.

On November 7, Union vessels sailed into Port Royal Sound 50 miles south of Charleston, intent on establishing a federal supply base on the southern coast. The Federal force included some 13,000 troops on 36 transports and 15 warships. Confederate guns opened fire on the invading fleet at 9:00AM, but by noon the contest was decided in favor of the Union. Fort Walker on Hilton Head Island and Fort Beauregard on Bay Point were abandoned, and the Stars and Stripes flew once more in South Carolina. Beaufort's white citizens sought refuge in Charleston; their slaves in open defiance refused to evacuate. Union troops who entered Beaufort two days later found blacks resting comfortably in their masters' houses. With little further effort, Federal troops soon occupied the "sea islands" along the southern stretch of the state. The war that so many South Carolinians presumed would be won by Christmas was now perceived more realistically; it would be a long, brutal war and one that would certainly bring its devastation to the Palmetto State. Only extreme measures could save South Carolina and, perhaps, the Confederacy.

The Early Course of War

Throughout 1862 South Carolina maintained both its legitimate government, framed by its state constitution, and a separate wartime council established by the Secession Convention. In practice, the council commanded far greater authority. To instill order within the state, the council instituted martial law in coastal communities and closed taverns located near military encampments. To prepare the state more fully for a lengthy war, bolster defenses on the home front, and still provide manpower to

Mary Boykin Chesnut Observes the Civil War

Perhaps no diarist of the Civil War era is more renowned than Mary Boykin Chesnut. A member of one of South Carolina's most elite families, Chesnut detailed daily her impression of Confederate military commanders and politicians, Northerners and President Abraham Lincoln, and the common soldier defending the South. The following is an excerpt from that diary:

> April 12, 1861:
> Anderson [Major Anderson, commander of Fort Sumter] will not capitulate.... I do not pretend to go to sleep. How can I? If Anderson does not accept terms at four, the orders are he shall be fired upon. I count four St. Michael's bells chime out and I begin to hope. At half past four the heavy booming of canon [*sic*]. I sprang out of bed, and on my knees prostrate I prayed as I never prayed before.... [Chesnut, along with family members, friends and servants, rush to the rooftop of her house to observe the battle]. The shells were bursting.... The regular roar of the canon, there it was. And who could tell what each volley accomplished of death and destruction? The women were wild there on the housetop. Prayers came from the women and imprecations from the men. And then a shell would light up the scene.... We watched up there, and everybody wondered why Fort Sumter did not fire a shot.
>
> Last night, or this morning truly, up on the housetop I was so weak and weary I sat down on something that looked like a black stool. "Get up you foolish woman. Your dress is on fire," cried a man. And he put me out. I was on a chimney and the sparks had caught my clothes.
>
> April 13:
> Nobody has been hurt after all. How gay we were last night. Reaction after the dread of all the slaughter we thought those dreadful canon were making.... Fort Sumter has been on fire... These women have all a satisfying faith. "God is on our side," they say.

the Confederate Army, the council in March 1862 began the conscription of men into military service, a step taken just one month before the Confederate government initiated compulsory military service. This included white men for military service and black men for manual labor. Conscription required South Carolina to both provide 3,000 slaves for the construction of forts and earthwork defenses along the southern coast and to meet whatever quota for soldiers the Confederate government, now based in Richmond, deemed necessary.

Conscription immediately drew the ire of poor and middle-class South Carolinians. Those who could afford it were allowed to hire someone to serve in their place. Nearly 800 South Carolinians did just that. Planters who owned twenty or more slaves were exempt entirely from the draft, as were their overseers. The draft also angered constitutionalists, who claimed that the Confederate government had no legitimate authority to enforce compulsory military service and doing so only mirrored the abuse of power exercised by Washington. As much as South Carolina valued states' rights, it also valued the rights of the individual. Still others complained that "true" South Carolinians would volunteer for military service, and conscription indirectly questioned the honor, integrity, and loyalty of Palmetto State citizens. Whether in response to these arguments or simply because they did not wish to fight in the current war, several thousand draft dodgers eluded the reach of South Carolina's armies. Opposition to the draft was so intense that in some districts conscription officials refused to press the issue, much less prosecute draft resisters. Many draft dodgers slipped deep into the forests of Horry, Marion, Pickens, Greenville, and Spartanburg Counties and survived the best they could. Others, often operating in small, armed squads, periodically raided outlying farms for food, clothing, and similar necessities.

The question of the council's power and the turmoil over conscription soon paled in the face of Union military and naval operations along the South Carolina coast. In early 1862 Georgetown's defenses were evacuated, and the Confederate garrison was shipped to Charleston to supplement that city's fortifications. Union warships moved into Georgetown Harbor, and white residents fled inland, taking as many slaves as they could reasonably control. Federal troops formed a strong perimeter around the coastal town to secure it from a Confederate counterattack, and gunboats moved more than 30 miles up the Waccamaw River seeking rebel encampments along its shores. In June, 6,000 Federal troops landed on James Island outside Charleston. Confederate defenders ultimately repulsed the Federal forces but lost almost half of their 600-man garrison in the battle.

By autumn 1862, along South Carolina's coast only Charleston remained free of Federal control. Sixty northern missionaries and teachers ventured into the narrow region to begin the process of preparing blacks for life as free citizens. At the same time, the War Department reluctantly authorized the enlistment of blacks into the United States Army. Most Northerners saw the war as one fought for the preservation of the Union, not the abolition of slavery, and few accepted the racial equality of blacks. But the enlistment and training of black troops was a wartime measure by the Lincoln administration to placate abolitionists. It also had a dual military advantage, the president believed. First, the additional manpower would greatly benefit the North's war effort. Second, the image of former slaves armed and dressed in Union blue would serve as a form of psychological warfare against the Confederacy. In 1862, a segregated army was established, the United States Colored Troops. On November 7, the First Regiment of South Carolina Volunteers was formed and added to the USCT, and one year later a second regiment was established. Of the 180,000 black soldiers who served in the Union army, nearly 5,500 were former South Carolina slaves.

Federal forces met defeat after defeat in the peninsula campaign in Virginia, and the North's efforts to conquer the Confederate capital in Richmond proved disastrous. New Orleans did fall to Union invaders in 1862, but Federal authorities soon discovered that controlling the city was far more problematic than taking it. In Tennessee, Union troops commanded by Ulysses S. Grant did secure victories at Fort Donnelson and Shiloh and quickly moved southward toward Corinth and to Vicksburg on the Mississippi River,

Confederate soldier

but those gains required horrendous losses in Federal manpower and supplies. Many in the North questioned which army had actually won the battles. Along the South Carolina coast, only the city of Charleston remained free of Union control, but little traffic successfully exited its harbor and slipped through the awaiting blockade. Rice plantations and cotton fields in the Lowcountry fell into Federal hands, and thousands of slaves found themselves freed. On September 22, Lincoln issued the Emancipation Proclamation, to take effect on January 1, 1863. The decree emancipated slaves in rebel states (the four slaveholding states that had not joined the Confederacy were exempt). While the proclamation was unenforceable outside Federal occupied territories, it nonetheless signaled to South Carolinians that the president wanted more than preservation of the Union; to them he clearly desired the complete destruction of the South. The spirit of independence still pervaded most of the white population, but that spirit would be further tested over the next 28 months.

The Fall of Confederate South Carolina

The War Department was determined to take Charleston in 1863 and use it as a staging base for operations against South Carolina's interior communities and eventually Columbia itself. In April, Union naval forces battered Fort Sumter but were soundly driven off. Confederate gunners claimed they fired 2,200 rounds and made 520 hits in one afternoon. Admiral S. F. DuPont, who commanded the Union navy, confessed the attack was nothing less than a total disaster for his ships and sailors.

Three months later, in July, as Vicksburg fell to Grant, and General Robert E. Lee's Confederate forces were driven from the Pennsylvania countryside surrounding Gettysburg, Federal troops struck Fort Wagner on Morris Island, just outside Charleston. Rebel defenders easily brushed aside the first attack on the 10th and another assault days later. But on July 18, Wagner's 1,000-man Confederate garrison faced a sight it had not expected—a frontal attack led by the 54th Massachusetts Regiment, an all-black Union force. Having earlier learned of the North's founding of the USCT, the Confederate government ordered "no mercy" be shown to black soldiers and their white officers. Small engagements

CSS H. L. Hunley

Technological developments made the American Civil War the nation's first truly modern conflict. Among the wartime innovations was a submarine responsible for the first successful attack on an enemy vessel. *H. L. Hunley* was constructed at Mobile, Alabama in 1863 from plans drawn by James R. McClintock and Baxter Watson, and financed by Horace Lawson Hunley. A hand-powered, direct-drive shaft propelled the 40-foot-long *Hunley*; nine seamen and one officer manned the vessel. A harpoon torpedo was attached to its bow, intended to ram the side of a wooden ship, be released, and detonate once the submarine had reversed course and reached a safe distance. In August 1863, *Hunley* was transported to Charleston, South Carolina to help defend the city's harbor against the Union blockade. The submarine sank and drowned its crew twice before it was proclaimed operational, Horace Hunley himself going down with the vessel in the second accident in October. On February 17, 1864 *Hunley* made her maiden attack against USS *Housatonic*, successfully ramming her torpedo into the Union ship's hull and retreating before the explosion ripped through the ship, sinking it within minutes. *Hunley*, however, never returned to port and was presumed lost with her entire crew.

In 1972 a group of historians, archaeologists, and others financed by private and university funding commenced the search for *Hunley*, finally locating her wreckage off Sullivan's Island near Charleston in May 1995. With the help of the Naval Historical Department, *Hunley* was raised to the surface on August 8, 2000 and taken to the Lasch Conservation Center, located at the former Charleston Naval Base, where it was restored and is now open for public viewing.

with black soldiers had been fought in Mississippi, but never before had Confederate troops encountered such a massive wave of black troops. The 54th assembled on the shoreline late in the afternoon and launched its assault at dusk. Wagner's defenders rained artillery fire on the attackers.

The Union troops faltered but quickly regained their composure and pressed the battle. As darkness fell over the island, the Confederate garrison rallied and drove away the 54th, but not before it had breeched the fort's walls. Union and Confederate losses were nauseatingly heavy. The Union didn't attempt another frontal strike, but its army and navy commenced a 50-day siege that eventually forced the evacuation of Fort Wagner on September 7.

About 22,000 Federal troops occupied Morris Island and neighboring Folly Island and erected a battery of heavy cannon that effectively halted all ship movement in Charleston Harbor and turned Fort Sumter into a shattered pile of brick and timber. On August 22 Union guns shelled the city of Charleston itself and terrorized the local population. Homes, stores, churches, the local orphanage, and banks all came under cannon fire. On Christmas night 1863, more than 130 shells fell in the city. Businessmen moved their operations inland or north to Wilmington, North Carolina. Residents fled inland as well, leaving Charleston a ghost town whose spirit was protected by a weakening Confederate army. The battery fired on the city daily until Charleston's surrender in February 1865.

Civilian and military morale dropped as the fate of the South became increasingly clear in 1863. Desertions from the army increased, totaling 3,615 South Carolinians by war's end. As the war progressed, Confederate soldiers came to label the conflict as a "rich man's war" fought by the "poor man." Adding to the soldiers' frustration was both a reduction in monthly pay and spiraling inflation that made their earnings virtually worthless. The carnage of battle, exacerbated by grossly unsanitary field hospitals, convinced many soldiers that death awaited them all. Only the grave offered a reprieve from hell on earth.

Shortages of cloth, thread, paper, salt, sugar, eggs, meat, and a host of other items forced South Carolinians to take extreme measures. Women accustomed to the finer fashions learned to recycle material and sew their own garments. Meat packers dug into the hard-packed earthen floors of smokehouses to retrieve salt used in the curing process. Beef, if available at all, was rationed, and sugar and flour were completely absent in Columbia. Across South Carolina, local churches and benevolent societies provided what goods they had to those in most desperate circumstances. By December 1863, nearly 55,000 South Carolinians statewide were officially listed as "destitute." Tens of thousands more barely subsisted. To meet military demands, church bells were removed from their steeples, melted, and recast into cannons. Gunpowder production commenced on the grounds of the State Hospital for the Insane in Columbia, and most workshops in the state were converted to the manufacture of muskets and handguns.

The war also depleted the state of its physicians. Of the 1,000 doctors who claimed South Carolina as home in 1860, 70 percent enlisted their services with the Confederate army and other wartime agencies. With Charleston's hospital and clinics within Union range and shelled repeatedly, temporary facilities were erected just outside the city, and makeshift facilities were hastily erected outside the city and throughout the state. An emergency medical facility was set up at the state fairgrounds in Columbia, and buildings at South Carolina College were refitted for the care of wounded soldiers. Aid stations were placed at railroad depots, in order to treat more quickly wounded soldiers removed from combat areas. With so many physicians gone to the war, the burden of emergency medical care fell on volunteering women, who worked in shifts around the clock, performing what had traditionally been male jobs. Indeed, the demands of war forced the blurring of long-accepted gender lines.

With rice and cotton lands devastated by Union military operations, and coastal plantations within range of naval guns, many planters abandoned their lands. In some cases, they simply turned loose their slaves, accepting in advance the visible outcome of the war. Slaveholders farther inland, however, increasingly confronted slave rebellions, especially in Anderson, Chesterfield, Darlington, Sumter, and as far west as Lancaster. Where uprisings did not develop, planters raged about the absence of civil authority to enforce slave laws and regulations, and throughout South Carolina slaveholders complained that their slaves were increasingly "insolent," "disrespectful," and "disobedient."

Conditions in South Carolina only deteriorated in 1864.

Must-See Sites: National Cemetery, Beaufort

The National Cemetery was established by President Abraham Lincoln for the burial of Civil War soldiers. More than 7,500 soldiers are buried here, Confederate and Union alike. Among the Union graves are the remains of 4,000 unidentified bodies. The site is located at 1601 Boundary Street.

Telegrams and newspapers reported the absurdly high battlefield death rates. Few families in the Palmetto State went untouched by the war. In December, General William Tecumseh Sherman's Union army sat in Savannah after having made Georgia "howl," as he had promised Lincoln he would. On February 1, 1865, Sherman moved his 60,000-man force north. The Confederate defenders, commanded by General P. G. T. Beauregard, included only 20,000 men, many of whom were between fifteen and seventeen years old or over fifty. Beauregard fully believed Charleston to be Sherman's primary objective, but he also knew the Union army would want to take Columbia, the state capital. Unsure of where to concentrate his defenses, Beauregard committed his army to a most undesirable course of action—he divided his forces, placing a contingent in Charleston, a second force in Columbia, and a smaller garrison in Augusta. He hoped to consolidate all forces once it became clear which path Sherman would take.

Charleston, Sherman figured, was but a shell of a city in early 1865. Union guns controlled its streets, and its ability to prolong the war was nonexistent. He therefore chose to send only a small portion of his army to the city where secession began but move the main body inland to the state's capital. Sherman marched just west of Beaufort with his army in parallel columns ranging 10 to 25 miles apart, pushing through Branchville, Orangeburg, and converging on Columbia. The Union troops laid the state to waste, leaving a swath of total destruction in their wake. Sherman's only serious impediment was not the

Confederate army but the nasty winter weather, unusually bitter for South Carolina.

Columbia was in complete chaos as Sherman's army approached. The city's population of 8,000 in 1860 had mushroomed during the war years to 24,000, many of whom were refugees from the coast. Fearing the brunt of Union force would be at Charleston, many residents of the once-pristine city had shipped their most valuable possessions to Columbia for safekeeping. As the Union army drew closer, its artillery shells arched over the statehouse, destroying homes, churches, banks, warehouses, and bridges. Thousands poured out of the city, most gathering what few possessions they could carry and fleeing north toward Charlotte, North Carolina, 100 miles away. Not only were Federal forces destroying Columbia, local looters smashed storefront windows and broke down doors to steal whatever goods they could get. The terror that gripped Columbia and the wholesale destruction of the city crushed what little secessionist spirit remained in South Carolina. General Beauregard ordered the burning of all cotton in the city's warehouses and then evacuated his remaining troops on the morning of February 17. As the last of the Confederate soldiers stumbled out of Columbia, Mayor Thomas Jefferson Goodwyn saddled his horse, rode out to meet General Sherman, and surrendered the city. The same day, Charleston tendered its official surrender.

The bluecoats entered Columbia before nightfall. Soldiers guzzled whiskey taken from civilian homes and stores, and in their drunken condition harassed and abused local residents. Fire, probably from the torching of cotton earlier in the day, was whipped by wind gusts and burned more than 30 square blocks of the city before morning. Fortunately, the nighttime melee took no lives. By his own admission, Sherman "never shed any tears over the event," but he demanded his officers restore order, and 370 of his soldiers were arrested. The destruction wreaked on Charleston, however, resulted in the death of more than 100 civilians.

Sherman's army left Columbia on February 20, this time with four parallel columns moving toward North Carolina. En route, Federal troops passed through Winnsboro, Camden, Chester, Cheraw, and Florence and left a path of destruction almost comparable to their approach to Columbia. Once in North Carolina, Sherman's forces consolidated their attack on Fayetteville and then Goldsboro to the northeast, completing their mission before learning of Robert E. Lee's surrender to General Grant at Appomattox Courthouse, Virginia, and consequently the end of the war, on April 9.

It has been estimated that 60,000 South Carolinians fought in the Civil War, most of whom served in Palmetto regiments, but some in North Carolina units that paid higher enlistment bonuses. Moreover, South Carolina troops fought in every major battle of the war, distinguishing themselves at Bull Run, Antietam, Fredericksburg, Gettysburg, Cold Harbor, Chickamauga, and the Wilderness Campaign. They were present at General Robert E. Lee's surrender at Appomattox and General Johnston's surrender days later in Durham, North Carolina. South Carolinians paid dearly in the Civil War. The state ended the war with a debt of $2.6 million ($24 million in 1998 dollars) and for white citizens the loss of nearly $300 million ($5.5 billion) in money invested in human property—slaves. The commercial districts of Columbia and Charleston lay in ash, and many residential areas were now in rubble. Bridges, telegraph lines, railway lines, ports, plantation houses, and farm animals had been destroyed by advancing Union troops under Sherman. Lewis P. Jones, in his study of South Carolina, quoted one traveler to Charleston in 1865 who described the city as one of "vacant houses, of widowed women, of rotting wharves, of deserted warehouses, of weed-wild gardens, of miles of grass-grown streets, of acres of pitiful and voiceless barrenness." Materially, South Carolina experienced greater loss than any other Southern state. The human result of war was equally catastrophic. Families were dislocated, and some were shredded by divided wartime loyalties. Records indicate that nearly 20,000 of South Carolina's white soldiers and sailors perished in the war, or about 30 percent of all those who served. Four years of war had laid South Carolina bare, destroyed its long-cherished traditions, and left its survivors facing an uncertain future. Of immediate concern to whites and blacks alike, what would be the postwar status of former slaves in a state heretofore defined by race and slave labor? South Carolina's former leaders in turn were left wondering whether the state's political motives in 1861 had been pure enough to justify such loss—could any perceived offense to its honor ever justify the death and destruction its defense had cost? Was slavery so prized, so fundamental to South Carolina's wealth in 1861, despite all signs pointing to its natural demise, that war had truly been the Palmetto State's only recourse?

Ruins of home in Charleston and another house in background. Photograph by Haas and Peale, taken between 1863–65.

9

Reconstruction

A numbing silence draped South Carolina in spring 1865. The state remained under martial law, which served as a constant reminder of the South's fall to Union military power. Poverty haunted cities and countryside. Merchants and bankers were bankrupt, and the rice and cotton plantations had collapsed from absent labor, depressed market values, and demolished ports. Hunger was a constant companion for many people. Local churches provided what relief they could, but food was in short supply. People wandered city streets in search of any type of job, regardless of pay and in many cases regardless of their prewar social standing in their community. Thousands were homeless and dispossessed of their land, wondering where they might find temporary shelter. The legacy of death and destruction scarred the hearts and dulled the senses of most everyone. Questions loomed large. Who would rebuild the roads, bridges, houses, and churches? From where would the money come to resurrect a sound economic base? And what would frame the new economy? What role would freed slaves have in the postwar social order of the state? There were no easy answers to these questions, and no one was sure what the future would hold.

A Persistent Defiance

Despite the widespread misery that pervaded the state, there remained a certain resentment and air of defiance among South Carolinians. Armies may have demobilized, navies may have returned to port, and guns may have fallen silent, but another kind of war definitely continued. South Carolina refused to relinquish entirely all it held dear and was determined to preserve as much of the past as possible. Diehard traditional South Carolinians felt they would simply need patience and new tactics.

President Andrew Johnson named Greenville's Benjamin Perry the provisional governor for South Carolina on June 30, 1865. Governor Perry's principal duty was to ready the state for readmission to the Union, and toward that end he called a constitutional convention to meet in Columbia. District elections followed, and in September delegates assembled at First Baptist Church. Hardly a man or woman in South Carolina was surprised to see the antebellum elite returned to power, most of whom had breathed the fire of secession only four years earlier.

Under orders from Washington, southern governments were to renounce secession as a legitimate right of the state and accept the abolition of slavery. Rather than "renounce" it, the delegates defied the president's order and instead "repealed" the Ordinance of Secession. A matter of semantics, one might think, but South Carolina's new governing body consciously selected the term to signify that it retained what it believed was a fundamental, inherent right of state government. Delegates then voted to sanction the eradication of slavery in the state; the measure passed, but eight men voted "no" on the issue. South Carolina may have been conquered in war, but some refused to acknowledge defeat.

The convention did draft a slightly more democratic constitution. It acknowledged the abolition of slavery, abandoned property-owning requirements for office holders, granted the governor veto power, and permitted the general voting population to elect the state's chief executive.

President Johnson approved the state's new constitution. Elections soon followed, and James L. Orr of Anderson was elected governor. Orr's postwar General Assembly convened in a special session in October 1865 on the South Carolina College campus, where it ratified the thirteenth amendment to the United States Constitution, which banned slavery. The regular session that opened in December, however, proved a harbinger of coming political battles between the state's Republican government and its Democratic conservatives.

Although initiatives were desperately needed to rebuild the state's economy, the December meeting concentrated principally on defining the position of freed blacks in South Carolina society. The General Assembly produced a series of laws collectively known as "Black Codes" to restrict the movement, behavior, and rights of African-American residents, a step also taken in every former Confederate state. Blacks were legally entitled to purchase land, files suits in courts of law, and enter into binding contracts—a modicum of economic equality. Social and political equality, however, was expressly prohibited. The new laws forbade interracial marriages, restricted personal travel between cities and towns, denied blacks the right to own firearms, required segregated housing and public facilities, prevented the congregation of blacks on public streets, and enforced a nighttime curfew on African Americans living in cities.

In the United States Congress, Radical Republicans, an extremist minority element within the Republican Party, were enraged over the Black Codes. Most Radicals were themselves former abolitionists who promoted full racial equality and saw these laws as the South's open defiance of Republican reconstruction. The Republican-controlled Congress declared the Black Codes invalid acts of the states, and Radicals immediately introduced, passed, and in March overrode President Johnson's veto of a bill that ensured federal protection of equal rights for blacks, the Civil Rights Act of 1866. In June, Radicals and moderate Republicans joined forces in Congress to pass the Fourteenth Amendment to the Constitution, which made blacks legal citizens of the United States and prohibited states from depriving any individual his rights because of race. Congress sent the amendment to the states for ratification, informing southern states that its approval was a prerequisite for full readmission to the Union.

The Radicals' influence grew. Because the prewar elite who had carried the South into secession once more commanded state legislatures, Congress in 1867 dissolved southern state governments, placed the entire region under federal military authority, and disenfranchised former Confederate political leaders and military officers. Voting privileges and seats in the reconstructed state assemblies were opened to blacks. Congress further insisted each state hold a convention and draft a new constitution. In South Carolina, the General Assembly called for a convention, but voters had to approve its establishment at the polls and then select local delegates to attend it. Of the 128,000 citizens registered to vote in South Carolina's November 1867 election, 56,000 voters, mostly white, chose not to participate in the proceedings. The existing system, they contended, reflected the will of South Carolinians; they condemned plans for a new constitutional convention as the product of evil Radicals who wished to complete the final destruction of the state. Because most registered black voters went to the polls, the call for a convention passed and black men for the first time served the state as elected officials.

The convention opened in January 1868 in Charleston with 124 delegates, of whom 73 were black and 51 were white—all but four delegates were Republican, the product of block voting by African Americans. Building on the democratic direction embedded in the 1865 constitution, delegates granted the franchise to all men and required the state to provide a system of universal education, both without regard for race. They intended to create a political and social order fundamentally different from the prewar governing system and that reflected the Radical Republicans' altruistic vision of equal opportunity for all persons.

A statewide public school system had long been desired by white citizens and would certainly have provided their children with far greater opportunities, but white South Carolinians denounced the 1868 constitution. They condemned the new government for its inclusion of blacks and the Republican Party dominance that allowed for the "Africanization" of the state. That blacks were permitted to vote, to hold seats of government, to introduce legislation, and to enjoy all the rights previously reserved for whites threatened the historical value of white supremacy in South Carolina. Neither the document nor the composition of the convention represented majority opinion in the state. In short, the majority of South Carolinians felt that the 1868 constitution overturned the values they had defended for four years on the battlefield and for which so many lives had been lost.

Another boycott by eligible white Democratic Party voters allowed easy Republican ratification of the constitution and netted Republican control of the General Assembly in the elections that soon followed. In the lower chamber of the General Assembly, 109 of the 124 elected

HARPER'S WEEKLY.
A JOURNAL OF CIVILIZATION

Vol. XI.—No. 568.] NEW YORK, SATURDAY, NOVEMBER 16, 1867.

"THE FIRST VOTE."—Drawn by A. R. Waud.—[See first Page.]

Wood engraving by A.R. Waud, "The First Vote" as appeared in *Harper's Weekly*, November 16, 1867 representatives were Republican and of these 75 were black. In the state senate, Republicans took 25 of the 32 seats; of these, 10 were black. With their newfound political clout backed by the Republican Party, the status of South Carolina's African Americans improved substantially. Six African Americans were elected to the United States House of Representatives, and others blacks served as lieutenant governor, secretary of state, state treasurer, and state supreme court justice. African Americans comprised 61 percent of the membership in the General Assembly by 1872, and they chaired the majority of committees. From their position in the state legislature, black and white Republicans passed public equality laws that provided access to public facilities such as restaurants, bars, theaters, retail stores, and restrooms—access denied to free blacks before the war. The University of South Carolina (as South Carolina College was renamed in 1865) was opened to black enrollment in 1868 and employed black professors. But, as black enrollment increased, the university witnessed an exodus of white professors to colleges in other southern states that still refused admission to African-American students and by 1875 the student body was 90 percent black. Although the university received appro-priations annually from the General Assembly, the loss of white students and professors collapsed most private contributions USC had enjoyed before the war, forcing many academic programs to be sidelined.

Most African Americans, however, saw little change in their lives under Republican rule. Although public equality laws were erected and in cities some blacks exercised their newly gained right to move freely where earlier they were not permitted, the majority of South Carolina's African-American population remained tied to the land. Without the cash required to purchase their own property and without the skills that allowed them to gain employment in urban settings, many had little choice but to accept sharecropping as their livelihood. Planters needed laborers to cultivate the fields and produce crops for sale at market. Without slavery, they could either hire day hands, a potentially expensive proposition, or encourage former slaves to remain on the land as semi-independent farmers. Sharecroppers resided on a portion of the former plantation where they could construct a house and live with their family. They were to grow their own food, raise their own sources of meat, and market for their own profit whatever crops they produced. In return, they were also to grow the cash crop preferred by the landowner and provide him with a portion, or share, of the harvest. To ensure the rights of both planter and sharecropper, legally binding contracts were drawn and signed. The system, in theory, appeared sound.

On the surface, it appeared that South Carolina was witnessing the dawn of a new age, particularly regarding opportunities for blacks; however, a darker reality swirled just underneath the image of progress. Historians agree that the ten years following the Civil War were notorious for bribery, widespread corruption, and graft involving politicians of both races. Government contracts to private businesses frequently included kickbacks, and appropriation bills often were inflated to cover the pilfering of the treasury. During one session of the General Assembly, more money was spent on whiskey and wine for legislators than on public schools. Furniture purchased for the State House was diverted to the private homes of legislators. What little money the state took in was being grossly wasted, Democrats complained. Rather than rebuild South Carolina's economy, legislators used the advantage of elected office to line their own pockets. Moreover, they added, the Republican government in Columbia was more interested in destroying the state's social structure by granting blacks rights which they were not qualified to exercise than they were interested in promoting and defending the values held by white citizenry. The level of corruption in state government brought waves of charges from Democrats and served as a point around which the general population rallied and used to attack the Reconstruction government in general elections.

Carpetbaggers and scalawags further alienated South Carolinians from Reconstruction efforts. Carpetbaggers, Northerners who ventured into the state to exploit the postwar turmoil for their own financial and political benefit, took ownership of property held by families for generations simply by paying back taxes. No concern or compassion did they offer evicted families; they were interested only in profit. They established businesses in urban communities that generated profits, but earnings were not plied back into the economy for community

Must-See Sites: Governor's Mansion, Columbia

The South Carolina governor's mansion is open to the public for first-floor tours. Guests walk through the state dining room, library, and small dining areas. The governor and his family occupy the upper floors of the mansion. Built in 1855, it became the governor's residence in 1868. The home includes exquisite furniture dating to the Antebellum era and paintings of the state's chief executives in the Hall of Governors. Located at 800 Richland Street, the mansion is open Tuesday, Wednesday, and Thursday. Call (803) 737-1710 to book a guided tour.

development. They claimed residency status, voted Republicans into office, and occasionally were elected to political seats themselves. With their property holding, net wealth, and political influence, the carpetbaggers attempted a wholesale makeover of South Carolina's society and institutions for their own advantage. Scalawags, native South Carolinians who aligned themselves with carpetbaggers, were despised even more. They exploited their longtime neighbors for personal gain, truly dishonorable behavior. Together, the activities of carpetbaggers and scalawags inflamed South Carolinians and helped build the foundation from which a Democratic rebellion would rise.

When South Carolinians surveyed the immediate postwar period, they were horrified at the changes wrought by Reconstruction. The presence of a state government controlled by black and white Republicans rather than the traditional Democratic Party elite, a new constitution that turned the social structure of South Carolina on its head, a level of public equality that countered longstanding norms, and "outsiders" profiting from the state's misery altogether gelled a determination in the hearts of Democrats to purge the state of its current ills and recapture the old order.

The Counterattack against Republican Rule

The drive to retrieve prewar traditions first manifested itself in violence. The Ku Klux Klan surfaced in Tennessee in 1866 and within two years spread throughout the South, folding into itself dozens of similar but smaller local organizations. In South Carolina, the KKK operated principally in the upstate section, from Columbia west to the mountains, and intimidated and assaulted Republicans, carpetbaggers, and scalawags in its bid to chase from South Carolina what they believed were the sources of most trouble. Local businessmen were forced to dissolve contracts with "outsiders," judges and jurors were "encouraged" to render decisions in favor of white South Carolinians who valued the traditional structures, and bankers were told not to issue credit or loans to "undesirable residents." Klansmen burned the homes of carpetbaggers and scalawags, and those who championed public equality of the races were warned in no uncertain terms that their lives were in jeopardy. State legislators were beaten, and three were murdered in 1868.

As for African Americans, the Klan's object was not to hasten a black exodus but rather compel their subservience to white, Democratic authority, force them to assume a status akin to their prewar role as a cost-efficient labor force for white landowners, and strip blacks of the rights granted by what the Klan saw as an illegitimate state government. Cloaked Klansmen promised to destroy the businesses, crops, livestock, and even homes of blacks who did not separate themselves from politics and white society. The KKK did not deny blacks their right to cast a ballot, but they were determined to make sure blacks voted for Democratic Party contenders. Nighttime visits to African-American homes on the eve of election day terrorized families, and Klansmen promised vengeance on any African-American man who voted for Republican candidates. Election officials were bribed to prepare lists of black voters who cast ballots for Republicans, and, as promised, the KKK inflicted serious injury, and sometimes death, to those men whose names were recorded. In short, the Klan waged terrorism against African Americans. Because they concealed their own physical identity and that of their horses under sheets, pledged themselves to silence, and represented the sentiments of most white citizens in their communities, few specific charges were ever filed against individual Klansmen.

So widespread was the violence that the governor in 1869 established a new state militia to restore order in the state. Whites not affiliated with the Klan believed their participation would signify support for a corrupt Republican government and the newfound status of blacks; therefore, white South Carolinians refused to enlist. Blacks, on the other hand, hoped a militia could afford protection against the rising violence being directed against them. By 1871, the militia numbered about 70,000 men, almost entirely black.

Rather than shrink from the militia's power, the Klan and its supporters intensified their statewide rampage. Across South Carolina, Klansmen torched the homes of local Republican officials, burned African-American churches, destroyed black schools, whipped hundreds of persons supportive of the Reconstruction government, warned hundreds more to flee the state or suffer brutal punishment, and ravaged stores owned by African Americans and Republicans. All the more horrifying, the Klan and white mobs murdered dozens of African Americans, government officials, and sympathizers of Reconstruction.

In October 1871, President Ulysses Grant moved Federal troops into nine upstate counties and declared a state of martial law. York County, the site of the most violence and most widespread Klan activities, was pronounced to be in a state of rebellion and received the greatest number of soldiers. Troops were also posted in the counties of Union, Spartanburg, Laurens, Chester, Chesterfield, Fairfield, Lancaster, and Newberry. Federal prosecutors compiled a list of 1,300 names of men suspected to be involved with the Klan or to be Klan sympathizers and filed charges against them. But, a year later, the courts had heard only 150 cases and won conviction in only 90.

The trials briefly slowed the KKK, but, as the courts proceeded with their hearings, Klansmen in 1873 resumed in force their aggressive campaign. Along with the Klan, whites rioted across the state against the Reconstruction regime. Laurens, Abbeville, and Charleston all erupted in violence and in Aiken dozens of blacks were murdered. Governor Daniel Chamberlain requested Washington deploy more troops, and Grant responded with 1,100 fresh soldiers; the additional soldiers, however, could not stem the tide of rebellion against the Republican and black state government.

Redemption

Emerging as an opposition candidate to Republican control was Wade Hampton. A solid member of South Carolina's prewar elite and ardent defender of state interests, he held the respect of Sandlappers. Hampton was a voice of moderation and cautioned the state against secession in 1861, but when war broke out he committed himself to the defense of South Carolina. After April 1865, he encouraged white Democrats to work within the legal system, permit African Americans their newfound constitutional rights, and so earn their votes. With African-American support, Republicans could be driven from South Carolina and the state would be freed of external influence. In 1868, Hampton's appeal to the KKK for nonviolence secured a brief respite in violence, and in the 1870s he openly denounced the extent of Klan brutality directed against Republicans and blacks. Hampton envisioned a point in the near future when South Carolina would be freed from what he believed was the oppression of Washington, and the traditions of the state, minus slavery, would once again reign supreme.

In 1876 Hampton challenged Daniel Chamberlain's reelection bid for governor, and the Democratic Party promoted him as South Carolina's savior. Hampton collected 1,000 votes more than Chamberlain on Election Day. The incumbent, however, claimed Democrats had rigged the ballot returns and forced the General Assembly to decide the election. Republicans still dominated the statehouse and secured Chamberlain's victory, protected in their duty by Federal troops stationed around the building. Mobs descended on Columbia and threatened to battle past the soldiers and take down by force what they believed was a fraudulent Republican government. Hampton intervened, restored a measure of calm, and advised the crowd to go home. The Democrat, however, had another plan.

While Chamberlain was being inaugurated on December 7, Hampton spoke before a gathering of his

followers elsewhere in Columbia and announced that he himself was the legal governor of South Carolina by popular vote. The following week, Hampton's supporters swore him into office; from December 1876 until April 1877 South Carolina had two governors and two legislatures, each proclaiming itself legitimate. The matter was resolved in April by the new president of the United States, Rutherford B. Hayes, a Republican who had himself won a narrow and hotly contested election. Hayes interviewed both Chamberlain and Hampton, studied developments in South Carolina over the previous decade, and decided Hampton held the real power in the state. On April 3, rather than risk further violence and perhaps open warfare in South Carolina, the president officially ended the period of Reconstruction and withdrew all Federal troops. Without the protection of Washington, Chamberlain understood he could not stay in Columbia and relinquished the governor's office to Hampton on April 11. Reconstruction in South Carolina was over; the old prewar power base once more controlled the state.

To South Carolinians, the election of Wade Hampton and a host of other Democrats to public office marked the state's redemption from the corruption spawned by Radical Republicans who spewed their contrary values of racial equality and the supremacy of federal authority over states' rights. Hampton's immediate ring of advisors and elected officials were former Confederate military officers and politicians, the prewar landed elite who embodied the essence of antebellum South Carolina. Controlling the state's executive office and both houses of the General Assembly, the Redeemers quickly moved to purge Republicans from office, dismantle Reconstruction programs, and strip from the books most of the statutes passed under Republican rule.

In matters of race, the Redeemers proved themselves surprisingly tolerant, in part because blacks still were the majority in the state's population and their political support would be required for Democrats to fulfill their agenda, and in part because Hampton himself accepted the premise of fundamental rights for free blacks. African Americans were

Wade Hampton. Photo taken between 1860 and 1870.

encouraged to join the Democratic Party, and nearly 100 of those who did were appointed to selected administrative posts. Under Hampton, the funding of black schools was equal to that of white institutions, truly a rare feature of South Carolina's educational system before the 1960s.

Race and the Conservative Regime, 1876–1890

Wade Hampton ran unopposed in his bid for reelection in November 1878; the following month, the General Assembly elected him to represent South Carolina in the United States Senate. By South Carolina's standards, Hampton was a moderate, and the state's Redeemers believed his presence in Washington would garner a modicum of respect for the Palmetto State that had been absent in Congress for decades. But there was another current moving in political circles. As admired as the governor was statewide, many South Carolinians hoped to tighten control over the state's black population; if Hampton's direct influence from Columbia were removed, antebellum-styled Conservatives might be able to manipulate his support base statewide and return South Carolina more fully to the antebellum center.

Because black politicians in the Reconstruction Era had been rather successful in legislating public equality measures, the Conservatives' first target was South Carolina's African Americans, who still comprised 60 percent of the total state population. Limit black voting opportunities, they reasoned, and African American political power would vanish. Toward this end, Conservatives introduced and pressed through the General Assembly over the opposition of Hampton's moderates a series of laws that, by 1890, effectively disenfranchised the black population. An 1882 statute contained several key measures. Voters were required to pass a literacy test. This provision alone was expected to purge the overwhelming majority of African Americans from the ranks of voters in South Carolina. Those who had been registered voters in the Reconstruction era and passed the exam were to re-register by June 1, 1882 or forfeit forever their right to vote. African Americans who resided on isolated farms, as most did, found it difficult to leave their fields and travel to distant registration sites; many never even learned of the provision. Those who completed each of these first two steps received a card entitling them entry to the polls; however, should the voter change his residency, as often occurred in the years following the war, he was required to pay a substantial fee for the transfer of his name to a new polling precinct, generally an expense few black South Carolinians could afford. Should an elections official deny anyone registration for any reason, they could appeal, but the appeals process was made elaborate and time-consuming in order to frustrate the under-educated.

The 1882 measures yanked voting privileges from about 77,000 African Americans, reducing the number of eligible black voters from 91,000 in 1876 to 14,000 in 1888. African Americans had no legal recourse. The Fifteenth Amendment stated that the right to vote would not be denied to anyone on the basis of race. The 1882 statutes did not violate the amendment; the requirements were applied to blacks and whites alike. Estimates placed the loss of white registered voters at twenty percent, generally the poorest and least educated whites in the state. Democrats considered their absence from the elections process a minimal sacrifice to attain their ultimate objective, the removal of black voters. Neither was the Fourteenth Amendment violated. It prohibited any state from erecting any law that denied any right to anyone on the basis of race. Again, blacks were entitled to vote in South Carolina, provided they meet the same qualifications whites faced.

Within the Democratic Party, blacks confronted other restrictions. County by county, local party units denied African Americans the right to vote in primary elections. This measure tested the boundary of constitutional law; however, since blacks retained the right to vote in general elections and the matter was confined within the party, no violation technically existed.

Race remained a pivotal, fundamental issue in South Carolina well beyond the collapse of the post-Reconstruction Conservative period, but between 1876 and 1890 other matters also claimed widespread attention.

Economic Patterns to 1890

Agriculture rooted South Carolina's economy in the Reconstruction and post-Reconstruction periods as it had before the Civil War. Cotton production reclaimed its antebellum place of primacy and actually expanded well beyond prewar levels. South Carolina's farmers produced 350,000 bales of the fiber in 1860 but 750,000 bales in 1890. Marginal lands were cultivated, and farmers committed more of their acreage to cotton than to basic food crops, all in hopes of cashing in on an apparent skyrocketing global demand for the fiber caused by rising population growth and new consumer demands. With this startling production came an unwelcome response—falling market prices. Not only were South Carolinians growing more cotton, so were farmers across the South. Added to the total amount was a corresponding rise in cotton production elsewhere in the world. In short, excess cotton glutted the national and global markets, driving down farmers' earnings. In 1873, notes historian Walter Edgar, cotton sold for fourteen cents per pound, but in 1880 it brought only ten cents a pound. The trend persisted well into the twentieth century. As terrible as declining prices were for farmers, they never lost faith in a prosperous future for cotton and, consequently, clung tenaciously to the crop.

But other enterprises added to the state's income. Phosphate fertilizer production prospered and contributed to increased productivity in truck farming (vegetables and fruit) for farmers who refused to stake their livelihood on cotton. Some farmers experimented with planting tobacco and found a ready market for their harvest in Durham, North Carolina. Tobacco generated little wealth for South Carolinians in the 1880s, but would emerge as a dominant crop in the twentieth century. The manufacture of Edgefield pottery also generated substantial profits. Noted for the greenish hue that derived from the iron in upstate clay, factories wheeled out an array of pots annually and distributed them to markets along the East Coast. Lumber mills, always present in the state, increased production following the Civil War, and by the late 1880s South Carolina supplied nearly fourteen percent of the nation's lumber needs. Adding weight to an economy beginning to diversify was railroad expansion. Between 1870 and 1890, track mileage almost doubled. State tax breaks and low-interest state-backed loans attracted railroad companies to the Palmetto State. By 1890, major cities in North Carolina and Georgia were connected with rail lines stretching through South Carolina, such as the connector between Charlotte and Atlanta. The introduction of textile mills also added to the South Carolina economy. In 1880, fourteen mills employing 2,053 workers in Anderson, Greenville, and Spartanburg Counties converted raw, cleaned cotton into finished goods. Although the rise of textile manufacturing was minimal before 1890, it portended a significant redirection of the state's economy as South Carolina entered the twentieth century.

Education under the Conservative Regime

The Reconstruction government established the state's public school system, a service maintained by the Conservative regime that succeeded the Republican era. Neither government, however, developed educational services significantly. South Carolina had 3,200 public schools in 1882 but only 3,400 teachers. Needless to say, the preponderance of schools were single-room, multi-grade structures. But South Carolina's school system going into the final decade of the century exhibited certain features that would continue into the post–World War II period, among them per-pupil expenditures. The General Assembly in 1890 spent an average of $3.38 per child per year, four dollars less than the South Atlantic average and fourteen dollars below the national average. Per-pupil appropriations in 1890 for black children were about fifty cents less than that provided to white children (between 1890 and 1940 the unequal funding actually widened significantly).

Appropriations were never adequate. Per-pupil expenditures barely covered the cost of instruction, providing largely the salaries of teachers and administrators. Because teachers in the state earned far less than their northern counterparts, South Carolina consistently lost trained and experienced teachers to states offering higher salaries or supplemental benefits, also a trend common to the state into the post–World War II period. As a result, many of the state's 3,200 schools were served by instructors barely out of high school themselves.

African American girls walking single file outside school, Charleston, 1891.

Most schools also lacked essential equipment. Blackboards and chalk, desks, maps, and even stoves for the winter were either nonexistent or purchased through donations given individual schools by local churches or town fundraising projects. Students purchased their textbooks and at year's end passed them on to younger brothers and sisters.

Hugh S. Thompson served the state as superintendent of education from 1877 to 1882 and as governor from 1882 to 1886. Under his tenure in both seats, Thompson tried to improve the quality of schools. He secured state financing for summer institutes that prepared teachers for the classroom. In 1886 he oversaw the founding of Winthrop College in Rock Hill for the professional training of teachers, who received official state certification upon graduation. Thompson also made repeated calls on the General Assembly to raise state appropriations for education and worked to make the citizenry more supportive of the public school system. Despite his sincere efforts to elevate the quality of education in the state for both races, Thompson actually accomplished little. Although South Carolinians and their elected representatives all championed "good schools," illiteracy rates hovered at 75 percent for black children and 20 percent for whites in the 1880s.

Higher education also struggled. The University of South Carolina closed its doors for three years following Reconstruction. When it reopened, African Americans were denied admission, and the university was appropriated the paltry sum of $2,500. Its nearly nonexistent budget allowed for only 185 students in 1882. Inadequate funding prevented the rebuilding of prewar academic programs, and nationally recognized professors refused to accept positions with meager salaries. The Citadel remained closed until 1882, but being the state's military academy, its funding more nearly matched its financial needs. Private, church-supported colleges such as Furman and Wofford fared better, their operational costs provided by their Protestant benefactors. Black colleges also faced uncertainty. The Reconstruction government established South Carolina Agricultural and Mechanics Institute in Orangeburg for black students in 1872 and received supplemental funding directly from the federal government under an 1862 law that promoted the founding of such schools. Claflin College, next door to South Carolina A & T, was sustained by northern Methodists; Benedict, founded in 1871 by the American Baptist Church, and Allen College, chartered the same year by the African Methodist Episcopal Church (both in Columbia), were also financed principally by sources outside South Carolina.

South Carolinians had rebelled against Reconstruction, returned the prewar elite to government, and purged African Americans from the political process. To be sure, the Reconstruction government and moderate Democrats in the 1880s ushered in some positive changes, but South Carolina in 1890 closely resembled its predecessor of 30 years earlier.

10

Tillmanism, Progress, and War: 1890–1918

Farmer Discontent

Between 1860 and 1890 more land was placed under cultivation nationwide than in the 250 years from the founding of Jamestown to the Civil War. New farm machinery promised greater productivity from fewer man-hours and with less cost, and the introduction of manufactured chemical fertilizers ensured the quality of soil. In addition, the nation's population nearly tripled in those years, from about 32 million to almost 90 million Americans, giving rise to what appeared to be an insatiable demand for food crops, cotton, and tobacco. At first glance, one would presume a windfall of opportunity and prosperity for America's farmers, but the reality was far different. The price of new machinery well exceeded the farmers' reach, and transportation costs for the shipment of crops to distant markets were prohibitive. The advent of agribusiness (corporate-financed farming) only compounded the farmers' difficulties. Market prices became depressed as southern and Midwestern farmers produced surplus harvests, and by 1900 farmer income was half what it had been in 1860.

Farmers solicited help from their state governments and from Washington, but aid never materialized. With government aid denied to them, farmers established organizations for mutual support and political action, among them the Grange. In South Carolina, 342 local Grange chapters formed in the early 1870s, a movement principally the product of D. Wyatt Aiken from Cokesbury, who traveled the state extensively calling on farmers to unite. Despite widespread support, the Grange accomplished little beyond the founding of the Agricultural Bureau in 1879.

The Farmers' Alliance replaced the Grange in the mid-1880s, claiming 60,000 white and black members in the Palmetto State and 6 million nationwide. The Alliance, nationally and locally, called for government regulation of railroads, the addition of silver to the monetary system, government-backed loans to individual farmers at one percent interest, government storage of crops to force a rise in market values, and a federal personal income tax to finance government aid to farmers. At the time, Alliance proposals were viewed as revolutionary and a direct attack on the free enterprise system.

In 1892, the Farmers' Alliance formed a separate political party, the Populist Party, held a national convention, and ran its own candidates for all state offices, Congress, and the presidency itself. Alliance farmers naturally flocked to the movement, and they netted support from northeastern factory workers whose concerns were included in the party's campaign planks. Populists lost the race for the White House, but some were sent to Congress and many won seats in state legislatures.

Despite the efforts of the Grange and Alliance, South Carolina's farmers confronted deteriorating conditions. The number of acres under cultivation remained constant, but by 1890 eight percent of the state's farmers had been driven from their lands because they could not pay their taxes. Many resorted to selling portions of their property to cover debts, but this further reduced family income. The loss of income required many Palmetto farmers to tie themselves into the dreaded crop-lien system: to finance his work for the coming season or to pay taxes, the farmer mortgaged his crop to the local merchant. The merchant held the lien on the yet-to-be planted and harvested crop, allowing the farmer to purchase seed, fertilizer, tools, feed, and other necessary supplies. Merchants' profits soared as they typically added 20 to 50 percent to the cash price of goods purchased on credit. By 1880, fully two-thirds of South Carolina farmers found themselves bound in debt to local merchants and unable to see any avenue for escape. The Conservatives, or "Redeemers," who governed the state following Reconstruction offered no comfort; they were the large landowners, lawyers, and businessmen who profited from the crop-lien system and cheap farm labor. But in 1885, a new voice for reform echoed across the state.

Benjamin Ryan Tillman

Benjamin Ryan Tillman was not a veteran of the Civil War, unlike most of the men who directed the affairs of South Carolina. He had not attended college, nor was he an established member of the state's elite. But Tillman was certainly not a common farmer. On the eve of civil war, his Edgefield County family owned 100 slaves and anticipated acceptance into the state's ruling class. He himself held 2,200 acres in 1881 and employed 30 day laborers. Nonetheless, Tillman in the 1880s claimed to understand the farmers' discontent, after having been battered by a series of droughts and crop failures. He conceded that an ignorance of profitable farming techniques contributed to farmers' problems in South Carolina, but the Conservative businessmen and lawyers of the legislature did not understand farmers' frustrations and did not care to comprehend what farmers faced, he argued.

Benjamin Ryan Tillman circa 1905
© G.V. Buck

Tillman spoke before the State Agriculture and Mechanical Society in Bennettsville in 1885 and instantly shocked both farmers and Conservatives. Conservatives, he shouted, "hoodwinked the people," making them believe government worked for the welfare of the people when in practice they lined their own pockets with money that rightly belonged to farmers; the legislature was utterly corrupted by wealthy men, intent on appropriating funds to institutions and public services that netted themselves financial gain and further bolstered the Conservative grip on South Carolina. The vilest term he could use against professional legislators in Columbia was "politician," a term frequently spoken with a slithering drawl through curled lips and accentuated with an obvious look of disgust. Turning on farmers, he blamed them for much of their own misfortune. Their refusal to band together and apply sufficient pressure on state government for action could not be excused. Remaining fixed to outmoded and failed farming techniques only ensured continued poverty. Indebtedness to merchants devolved the farmer to the status of slave. Crop diversification and education, he thundered, were the two pillars of farm success. Tillman's speech popularized his nickname "Pitchfork," a moniker he gained possibly because he represented farming interests, perhaps because Conservatives suddenly believed the Devil himself stood in their midst, or because he threatened to "pitchfork" his opponents—all explanations farmers attributed to Tillman's assumed title.

In 1886, Pitchfork Ben Tillman and his closest friends founded the Farmers' Association to seek solutions to Conservative rule and farmers' ills. Any white man who supported fundamental reform in government was welcome as a member, whether farmer or businessman. Tillman was cultivating a political movement, with himself at the helm. Among the most immediate needs, the association believed, was an agricultural college. The following year, Thomas G. Clemson died, and his will specified his expansive estate and $80,000 were to be used to found an agricultural college. After much wrangling in the General Assembly, including intense pressure from the Farmers' Association, the legislature in 1889 finally acquiesced and founded Clemson College, its main building named in honor of Benjamin Tillman, who had led the crusade for the school's establishment.

"Tillmania" swept the state, and in 1890 the Farmers' Association struck once more at the Conservative regime in a publicly read document calling Conservatives the enemy of the people who had "bamboozled and debauched" honest legislators, forcing them to conform to aristocratic goals or fall victim to Conservative political power. Conservatives, the document continued, were antebellum South Carolinians who inhibited the state's modernization and progress.

The Farmers' Association met again in a March 1890 convention to draft potential candidates for the Democratic Party slate. Through rather shady methods, Tillmanites controlled whose names the organization would support and then moved to capture the Democratic Party itself by nominating Tillman as the convention's candidate for governor. Before the summer party convention, Tillman's candidates conducted "stump meetings" in each county, local face-to-face, personal campaign presentations and speeches to voters (a system continued today in many small communities, such as Gallivants Ferry on the Little Pee Dee River just inside Horry County). More committed to rallying the voters than to intelligent debate of critical issues, the "stumps" garnered an enthusiasm heretofore absent among small farmers and working-class South Carolinians. Pitchfork Ben himself breathed unrelenting fire against the Conservatives and their institutions. He derided Charleston as the "greedy old City" of the state's elite and the University of South Carolina as the producer of Conservative aristocrats. He condemned Conservatives for their backward-looking rather than forward-looking perspective and blamed them for low cotton prices, farmers' land loss, and profiting from the farmers' troubles. Tillmanites trounced Conservatives in the convention, and with South Carolina essentially a one-party state, Tillman carried the November general elections. Perceived as a reformer, Tillman reaped the endorsement of the national Farmers' Alliance.

As governor from 1890 to 1894, Tillman ushered in not a revolution but instead "changes." He oversaw the construction of Clemson College, which opened in 1893 with 400 students, toned down his hostile rhetoric toward

The Lost Cause

Edward A. Pollard's 1866 book, *The Lost Cause,* was a literary exposition of the South's defeat in the Civil War, but the title soon entered southern vocabulary as a phrase that captured the South's understanding of itself as a region and culture and defined the very essence of Southerners until recent years. The "Lost Cause" embodied everything dear to Southerners—antebellum values of honor, deference, and propriety; defense of states' rights and the legitimacy of secession; and pride in the region's culture. It cast a sense of glory—almost a holy veil—over the Civil War, vaunted the courage and mettle of the Confederacy's military commanders and ordinary soldiers, and ascribed defeat to the South's exhaustion of resources rather than loss of will. It presented the North as mechanical and inhuman and the perpetual exploiter of the South. In short, the Lost Cause spirit defined truth from a purely southern perspective and shaped the collective memory of the war and its aftermath. It held the South to be the bastion of godliness and simplicity, the defender of the common man, and the advocate of true democracy and equality. Southern politics in practice was anything but democratic and the region viciously maintained that white supremacy and race segregation mattered little. The image of the South cast in Lost Cause terms united the region against the perceived corruptive and dehumanizing power of the North, which was responsible for the war, the South's destruction, and the region's postwar economic and social deterioration.

Following the period of Reconstruction (1865–1877), the Lost Cause rooted itself deeply into southern communities. Cities, towns, and villages all erected statues of war heroes and monuments honoring the glorious war. Iron figures of solitary Confederate soldiers stood on courthouse grounds and college campuses, always facing north. Organizations were founded such as the Sons of Confederate Veterans and Daughters of the Confederacy. Many southern states abandoned any celebration of Independence Day for the annual Confederate Memorial Day, a calendar date still marked in South Carolina and until quite recently honored with a day off work, while President's Day went unheeded. The Lost Cause found expression in two classic Hollywood films, *Birth of a Nation* and *Gone with the Wind*. Southern universities developed an extensive curriculum focused on southern history, literature, and culture, programs that in the 1920s and 1930s pressed the Lost Cause myth as reality and expunged the Confederacy of guilt in the Civil War. Although the content of these programs have changed substantially, to present the war and the antebellum South in a far more objective light similar college courses continue to flourish and attract native Southerners.

Symbols of the Old Confederacy surfaced during the Civil Rights Movement of the 1960s. The Confederate battle flag was hoisted above South Carolina's statehouse and there it remained until 2002. The song "Dixie" echoed through high school and college football stadiums, and frequently was heard the statement "The South is going to rise again!" Civil War museums appeared in many southern communities and invariably gave greater and more positive attention to Confederate memorabilia than to any symbol or artifact of the Union. In tourist communities such as Myrtle Beach, the Confederate flag was emblazoned on ocean floats, beach blankets, and bathing suits. Tours of war-era plantation homes, Fort Sumter, the Battery, and the Slave Market all became popular attractions in Charleston. The Lost Cause mentality pervaded South Carolina and the larger South, giving its proponents a sense of belonging, an identity, and greater meaning.

As the twentieth century approached its end, the spirit of the Lost Cause waned in South Carolina. The state's population was becoming much more diverse, a product of "outsiders" moving into the Palmetto State and diluting the emotional base that sustained the myth. Moreover, the nation's population became more transient, breaking regional identity. Television, music, motion pictures, and the internet all pulled younger Americans into a national consciousness. And, sadly, public schools across the United States, including school systems in South Carolina, reduced student academic requirements in history and social studies coursework. Time and modernity have contributed to a diminished awareness of and feeling for the Lost Cause; despite this, the myth has not died completely.

"The Lost Cause" lithograph published by Currier & Ives, New York , c1872

USC and encouraged financial support for the university, and kept open the Citadel, though he questioned its continued service to the state. The Tillman administration failed to pass railroad reform bills, and from his seat in Columbia he never attacked the crop-lien system that so indebted farmers. In his first term, which ended in 1892, Pitchfork Ben not only accomplished little for South Carolina farmers but expended little effort on their behalf.

The governor's 1892 campaign adopted much of the Farmers' Alliance platform, including coinage of silver, control over railroads, and low-interest government loans to farmers. Following his reelection, Tillman pushed through the General Assembly legislation establishing a state railroad commission that was empowered to govern freight rates and an additional law that limited textile mill workers to a 60-hour week. As the General Assembly approached the end of the 1892 session, Pitchfork Ben slipped a rider onto a rather innocuous bill stating that the sale of liquor would be directly governed by the state and profits from the sale of alcohol would go to the state. In their rush to leave Columbia for the Christmas holiday season, few legislators read the rider and ignorantly passed Tillman's measure into law. The bill created the State Dispensary, giving the state exclusive rights to sell liquor, open liquor stores, and regulate the industry.

In matters of race, Tillman never hesitated to state unequivocally that white supremacy would always be enforced statewide. White South Carolinians, he shouted, "never recognized the right of the Negro to govern white men" and never would acknowledge black governance. Although he promised to remove from office sheriffs who allowed lynchings to go unpunished, Tillman openly supported the lynching of African Americans for the crime of rape and said repeatedly he would himself lead the mob in such a situation. Five lynchings occurred during his first term as governor and thirteen in his second term. Tillman's words appealed to farmers throughout the Palmetto State, and his rabid racism expanded his base of popular support.

Tillman clearly exploited the issue of race. The Eight Box Law had effectively stripped voting rights from thousands of black men; in a rewrite of the state constitution in 1895, poll taxes were added as a requirement for voting under the presumption that most blacks would not be able to afford the cost. Moreover, to enter the polling place, a voter who had paid his tax was required to present his receipt; Tillmanites believed few blacks would retain the slip of paper after paying their taxes. To get around the literacy test that in practice removed many uneducated whites from the polls, the Tillman administration added an "understanding" clause to the constitution. If an illiterate man understood the state constitution when read to him, he could vote. African Americans would have a very difficult time convincing white elections officials of their "understanding." The governor's tactics effectively derailed the Fifteenth Amendment and removed virtually all black influence in state government.

Tillman's tenure as governor ended with the 1894 elections, but he continued to wield influence in the state constitutional convention of 1895. Determined as ever to restrict the rights of African Americans and to protect white supremacy in the state, Tillman and his supporters pressed into the constitution a provision that defined as "black" anyone who had "one eighth or more negro [*sic*] blood." The new constitution further stipulated that the two races were to have separate public schools and colleges.

The Rise of Jim Crow

Neither Tillman nor South Carolina was unique in legalizing segregation; indeed, throughout the South and eventually in many northern states, segregation laws were erected and sternly enforced. Collectively and generically termed Jim Crow Laws, these laws required racial segregation in all public facilities. The United States Supreme Court ruling in *Plessy v. Ferguson* in 1896 gave official sanction to the racist measures, provided separate facilities assured equal opportunity. The doctrine "separate but equal" became the base of race relations nationwide.

With the court's decision, segregation became the domain of local communities and state government alike—common ground among South Carolina's whites. Segregation laws separated the races on trolley cars, railroad passenger cars, public restrooms, restaurants, water fountains, theaters, retail stores, public parks, hospitals, textile mills, and any place where the two races might encounter each other in public. "White Only" and "Colored Only" signs soon littered public establishments in every community in the state. The only time in which the two races were permitted by law and social custom to interact in public was in black service to whites—nursemaids to white children, "errand boys" to white businessmen, and custodians in the white workplace. Additional customs were also maintained. Blacks were to address whites as Mr., Miss, or Mrs. although whites addressed African Americans by their first names. It was not acceptable for blacks to look squarely into the eyes of whites when answering or asking questions. In all matters, blacks were to demonstrate deference to whites. The age of Jim Crow had descended on the state, as it had on the nation, and would remain entrenched for another 60 to 70 years.

Agricultural Developments, 1900–1920

Although truck farming and livestock production gained numerous converts in the early years of the twentieth century, cotton remained South Carolina's principal cash crop, despite its low market value of thirteen cents per pound in 1913. War in Europe collapsed many of the state's overseas markets, and as a result, domestic buyers were swamped with surplus fiber. Prices plummeted to six cents a pound in October 1914. The state government responded, restricting the number of acres on which cotton could be planted. Reduced supply along with mill production of war-related items for sale to English and French military forces reversed the downward spiral and drove prices upward, a pattern that continued throughout World War I and shortly thereafter, with cotton ultimately reaching 40 cents per pound in 1920.

Another crop that was acquiring greater importance in South Carolina agriculture was tobacco. Some farmers in the colonial era had experimented with the plant, but rice production proved far more profitable. In the late 1700s and early 1800s, tobacco was once more harvested, but depressed market prices for the plant along with the rising profitability of cotton again reduced interest in tobacco. This particular pattern, however, reversed following the Civil War. As postwar cotton values plummeted, Bright Leaf tobacco was developed and offered smokers a flavor milder than earlier blends. Sales soared, and cigarette rolling and packaging machines invented in the 1870s further stimulated sales as consumers no longer had to roll their own cigarettes. By 1890, South Carolina had a second cash crop to plant, and farmers hoped it would generate a prosperity that cotton no longer offered.

Tobacco farming was largely centered in the Pee Dee region, and the plant, once harvested and cured, was hauled to local warehouses and auctioned to manufacturers such as the American Tobacco Company in Durham, North Carolina. Between 1890 and 1900, harvests rose from 223,000 pounds to 20 million pounds. Demand soared, and farmers' profits rose to $154 per acre, in glaring contrast to the $10 per acre profit gleaned from cotton. But the lure of rising income drove farmers to overproduce, and tobacco profits plunged to $54 per acre in 1910. Despite the substantial drop in profits, tobacco still generated far higher proceeds for farmers than cotton. South Carolinians had discovered another cash crop that would, in decades to follow, displace cotton from its long-held throne.

Industrialization

Under the Conservative regime following Reconstruction, South Carolinians hoped to diversify the state's economy and toward that end took steps to enlarge the textile industry. Expansion proceeded at a rather rapid rate. In 1880 there were only fourteen textile mills in the state; in 1900 there were 115, and 165 ten years later. Not only did the number of mills increase, they also became much larger operations. Two thousand men and women were employed in the business in 1880, but by 1910 nearly 40,000 South Carolinians were fully engaged in textile manufacturing. Capital investment also rose during the same period, from $3 million to $85 million. The Poe Manufacturing Company in Greenville operated 60,000 spindles, and John Woodside's mills, also in Greenville, had 1,000,000 spindles. By 1910, only Massachusetts's textile industry produced more goods than South Carolina.

The wealth generated by textile production, however, was largely concentrated in the hands of mill owners. Mill workers were almost exclusively poor white farmers who sought a financial security the land could not provide, but wages were low. More often than not, several members of a single family held jobs in the mill to provide sufficient income for the family's survival. Owners compensated for the poor pay by providing company housing for employees, but houses were poorly constructed four- or five-room structures and generally rented for 50 cents per room per month, the equivalent of one week's wages. Roads in the mill villages were unpaved, and few modern conveniences such as indoor plumbing existed. By the early 1900s, however, some mill towns included a community recreation center and a school for village children. The system, however, cultivated a workforce almost entirely dependent on the mill owner.

Textile manufacturing commanded South Carolina industry into the post–World War II years, but there were other efforts to diversify the economy. Lumber mills opened upstate where hardwood trees were plentiful, and the Lowcountry's pine forests supplied soft wood for the manufacture of paper. The production of naval stores carved a niche in the state's emerging industrial base, principally the manufacture of turpentine. Along the coast, commercial fishing assumed greater importance supplying shrimp and crab to markets the length of the Atlantic seaboard.

Modernization of Society

The rising standard of living washing across America's burgeoning middle class by 1900 encouraged families to leave the confines of northern urban communities for short visits to other, more "colorful" locales. The modern "vacation" gave rise to South Carolina's tourist industry, today a centerpiece of the state's economy. The romantic ideas of pre–Civil War Charleston once more lured Northerners to the city. Aiken and Camden drew thousands to the annual horse races, steeplechases, polo matches, and foxhunts. A few vacationers escaped the heat of New York City to relax in the cool air of South Carolina's mountains or lounge on the long, lonely, desolate strips of beach that today are the Grand Strand. Others ventured deep into the state's backwoods to hunt wild game or to fish in the network of streams and rivers that etched their way through the midlands to the coast. Tourists brought their wallets to the Palmetto State, and the state became a little richer from their visits.

In Columbia and Charleston, theaters opened featuring amateur performances—similar to the vaudeville stages found in northern communities. Many towns built public parks, and a few constructed baseball fields to tap into the rising popularity of intercity competition. Collegiate football gained popularity across the United States in the late 1890s and early 1900s, and in the Palmetto State a rivalry quickly emerged between Clemson and the University of South Carolina. The teams met yearly at Columbia's state fairgrounds. The State Fair as well as county fairs attracted thousands of South Carolinians each autumn and provided entertainment affordable to the general population.

Wealthier South Carolinians in the early 1900s purchased automobiles, clearly a status symbol for the rich at the time. Cars sold for about $1,000 in 1904, a price that did not include optional and costly accessories such as a windshield. That year, 50 automobiles puttered the streets of Columbia, the "automobile town" of South Carolina. Traffic lights were nonexistent in the city until 1922, and collisions attracted curious spectators and made good copy in the local newspaper. In 1909, the introduction of the $500 Maxwell, a two-cylinder, twelve-horsepower competitor, drove auto prices downward, making them affordable to more residents, but the horse and carriage continued to dominate city streets into the early 1920s.

Persistent Problems

The importance of agriculture in South Carolina meant that children living on small and mid-size farms were long accustomed to helping parents in the fields. Rare was the boy or girl before the turn of the century who enjoyed the opportunity of attending school instead of spending the entire day tending crops and livestock. Even in the years leading up to World War II, most farm families expected their sons and daughters to rise before dawn, start the morning fire in the home's wood-burning stove, gather additional wood, and handle other essential chores before leaving for school. Upon their return home in the afternoon, their labor was again needed, plowing fields, caring for farm animals, making repairs to the house or barn, mending fences, and a myriad of other tasks.

Child labor also extended into textile mills. Youngsters generally worked in the spinning room, mending snapped yarn and replacing full bobbins with empty ones. Others swept floors, ran errands, emptied garbage cans, removed lint from machinery, or boxed manufactured goods. Children fourteen years and older occasionally operated machinery in the cutting room. Wages were as small as the children—thirty cents for a twelve-hour shift, six days a week. By 1900, fully 25 percent of textile employees were children under the age of 16. School was not an option for young workers. Illiteracy served mill owners quite well, assuring the factory of a steady supply of adult workers in years to come.

In the late 1890s, reformers vented concerns for the children's safety and lack of education. N. G. Gonzales, editor of Columbia's newspaper *The State*, and Governor Miles B. McSweeney initiated an effort to purge industry of child labor, a movement concurrently pressed in most states nationwide. Gonzales and McSweeney were supported in their endeavor by the American Federation of Labor and the recently formed South Carolina Child Labor Committee. Progress came slowly. In 1903 the General Assembly passed a law that banned the employment of children under twelve years of age. This left 9,000 children between twelve and sixteen years old in the workplace, or 24 percent of the total work force in 1905, and those youngsters continued their standard 60-hour work week. No further restriction surfaced until 1917 when the minimum work age was raised to fourteen.

Reform efforts in South Carolina seldom addressed the treatment of convicted criminals. Prisons were intended as punishment, not as rehabilitation centers. Facilities were inhuman; little light, stale air, filthy toilets, limited bathing service, insufficient and poor-quality food, and a dampness that pervaded cells and hallways altogether made prisons truly punishing detention centers. Abusive guards further dehumanized prisoners. Persons convicted of less serious offenses spent time in local jails, and these varied in quality according to the community's willingness and ability to provide suitable facilities.

The state permitted the use of chain-gang labor. Under this system, prisoners were outfitted with heavy, striped uniforms, shackled around the ankle, chained to each other, and assigned to public works projects such as road repair, ditch digging, and swamp clearance. Armed guards stood watch over the prisoners and were authorized to "shoot-to-kill" those who attempted escape. Chain gangs frequently were camped at the work site until their assignment was completed. At night, prisoners were exposed to mosquitoes, rain or high humidity, uncomfortably cool evenings, minimal food, and physical abuse. Many became ill, and many died. The chain-gang system, so common in South Carolina, did come under attack by reformers in the 1920s and 1930s, but it persisted well into the 1950s.

A Reactionary Moment

As one historian phrased it, after 1900 "Senator Pitchfork Ben Tillman was still the big frog in the political pond," but his Washington residency as United States senator substantially lessened his direct influence in South Carolina. A modicum of calm descended on the state following Tillman's departure and lasted until 1910. In that year the governor's seat went to Newberry resident Coleman Blease. Since 1890 Blease had bounced in and out of the General Assembly and adopted many of the political tactics employed by Tillman, but his coarseness, fanaticism, and borderline demagoguery compelled even "Pitchfork Ben" to denounce him.

Governor Blease proclaimed himself a friend of the poor, capitalizing on the growing sense of frustration and alienation the white lower socioeconomic class felt. He lashed out at the holders of wealth who buttressed an economic system beneficial to themselves but which saddled the working class with debt and few opportunities. He criticized the temperance movement's insistence that alcoholic beverages be outlawed, the one comfort poor men could afford. Blease praised the fortitude, the loyalty, the work ethic, and the spiritual base of the common man and did so in a language they fully understood.

Blease used his two terms as governor (1911–1915) to attack what he saw as the two enemies of the state's working class. He held the opinion that the state's institutions of higher education only turned out more members of the exploitative elitist class in the state and insisted that the General Assembly sharply reduce appropriations for South Carolina's colleges. He also despised the idea of African Americans attending school, believing blacks were naturally inferior to whites and better suited to a life as subservient laborers. Unable to purge the state constitution's provision that authorized funding for black schools, Blease demanded that allocations to those schools not exceed the taxes paid by African Americans. Had the General Assembly conformed to the governor's demand, black educational institutions would have nearly vanished across the state. Blease further tried to censor newspapers that challenged his views, repeatedly terming news reporters and editors "liars," "slime," and "scurrilous blackguards." The governor also battled the legislature's social agenda, which included further restrictions on child labor and efforts to implement compulsory school attendance laws, factory inspection laws, and medical examinations for school children—all measures that were being widely adopted throughout the nation under the reform banner "Progressivism." The governor believed the workingman in South Carolina wanted to be free of all forms of government regulation; social legislation only placed the government deeper into family and personal affairs. Although the frequency of lynching had noticeably declined in South Carolina, Blease offered pardons to those convicted of the crime. When confronted by his counterparts at a southern governors' conference in Richmond, who flatly denounced the practice as illegal, Blease retorted "to hell with the Constitution."

Blease's support came from South Carolina's white working poor. The state's dispossessed white citizens felt shackled in a form of economic slavery governed by a corporate aristocracy that reaped profits from the sweat of laborers. Families saw greater benefit from the income their children could bring home rather than the long-term rewards of educating their sons and daughters. And, poor whites despised any progress blacks might attain, a feeling predicated on the fear of losing their jobs to African Americans willing to work for lower wages and on the presumption that, despite their poverty, being white still meant they were "better" than someone else.

Progressivism: The Return to Reform

The reactionary moment embodied in the governorship of Cole Blease dissipated as poor South Carolinians realized he was more mouth than substance. In 1914 voters sent Richard I. Manning to Columbia as their new governor. Manning, generally regarded as a Progressive reformer, albeit a conservative one, promised to raise South Carolina's economy, modernize the state, and elevate the standard of living for all citizens. He politically placed himself in the camp of President Woodrow Wilson, the first postwar Southerner to occupy the White House and an outspoken proponent of social, economic, and political reform based on the spirit of Christian morality.

South Carolina in 1914 held the embarrassing position of being ranked 47th among 48 states in its level of statewide illiteracy. During his four years in office, Manning doubled state appropriations to public schools. His fight for a compulsory attendance law failed, but he did manage a "local option" provision that permitted each community to enact a local ordinance regarding school attendance. Manning convinced the General Assembly to establish a state tax commission that was charged with the responsibility of assessing property values statewide and collecting taxes on that property, money that would be spent partially on public education. He and his supporters believed government should accept some responsibility for human problems and public services and toward that end his administration modernized the state hospital for the mentally ill and laid the groundwork for a second facility in Clinton. He was instrumental in creating the State Highway Commission and the State Highway Department, both founded in 1917, to plan the expansion of roads and oversee their construction. With the power of Progressives behind him, he raised the minimum work age from twelve to fourteen, removing 2,400 children from factories across the state. The legislature adopted a workmen's compensation law, and the governor further advocated the right of workers to organize labor unions.

The Progressive spirit that sifted through the state during Manning's years as governor also embraced African Americans, but rather than seeking direct aid from the General Assembly, blacks initiated "self help" programs. Taylor Lane Hospital opened in Columbia to serve black patients with trained black nurses. A Negro Health Association was established that sought to educate African Americans in home sanitation, the preparation of nutritional meals, personal hygiene, and community health. A Colored Civic League was founded in Charleston, and similar organizations surfaced in other cities and towns. The South Carolina Federation of Colored Women built the Fairwold Home near Columbia for the care of orphaned, abused, and delinquent young girls.

The changes brought to South Carolina by the Manning administration mirrored national trends and seemed to place the state on a track toward modernization. Manning was not a political liberal; perhaps more than anything, he was guided by a sense of Christian duty to work for the welfare of his fellow man.

The Great War

On April 6, 1917 Europe's war finally snagged the United States as President Woodrow Wilson declared war on Germany, and South Carolina immediately committed its resources and manpower to the nation's war effort. Across the state, Sandlappers rejoiced in the noble crusade to "end all war" and to "make the world safe for democracy." Parades rolled down Main Street in most every community, replete with marching bands, local militia units, flags, waves of red, white, and blue streamers, and civic leaders riding in automobiles and trucks calling on citizens to enlist their time and money in home front duties. Enlistment posters and announcements to purchase war bonds covered storefront windows and lined city sidewalks. Army and navy recruiting stations multiplied in each county, beckoning young men to don the nation's uniform and defeat the Hun. More than 200 community leaders formed a speakers' bureau in South Carolina and offered themselves as patriotic promotional speakers at rallies, blood drives, school assemblies, and anywhere else their presence was desired. War bond sales totaled $100 million in South Carolina during the war, which when figured on a per capita basis made the Palmetto State one of the largest financial contributors to the war effort. The patriotic fervor that gripped the state also manifested itself in the most innocent features of daily life. Anything German was immediately suspect, including those things that sounded German. In true patriotic fashion, Dachshunds became "liberty pups," German Shepherds were now "liberty Shepherds," and sauerkraut "liberty cabbage." Most telling of statewide sentiment, South Carolina celebrated the Fourth of July for the first time since the Civil War.

The nation and state that now pressed war in Europe for the preservation and ultimate expansion of democracy, however, exhibited some rather undemocratic behavior. The State Council of Defense in April clearly and succinctly stated in its *Handbook on the War* that South Carolinians would support the war effort or be branded traitors. Opposition was not tolerated. Antiwar rallies in Lexington, Orangeburg, Newberry, and Charleston counties confronted angry mobs; newspapermen who challenged the president's decision were jailed, and publications that opposed the war were banned. State leaders who questioned the war and its motives found their political careers shattered. The aggressiveness of war supporters in the Palmetto State mirrored the sentiment and behavior of Americans nationwide.

Although South Carolinians rallied behind the flag, Jim Crow nonetheless required racial segregation in all war-related activities such as bond drives and volunteer work for the American Red Cross. Blood donated by citizens for the medical care of servicemen was also segregated by the race of its contributors. This was not unique to South Carolina and the practice persisted into the early months of World War II. Both the War Department and Department of the Navy strictly enforced the segregation of its soldiers and sailors in training, unit assignment, and deployment.

During the war, 307,000 South Carolinians registered with the military draft; 54,000 were drafted, but thousands more volunteered. Most served in the 30th Infantry Division, nicknamed "the Old Hickory Division" in commemoration of South Carolina's native son and icon Andrew Jackson. Following their training at Camp Jackson in Columbia, one of three army training posts erected in the state during the war years, the 30th was shipped to France and immediately engaged German troops on the dreaded Hindenburg Line. The 93rd Infantry Regiment of the Old Hickory Division was made up of African-American troops and was attached to French combat forces for most of its tenure in France. In battle, the regiment distinguished itself immensely, earning more combat medals than most white American units in the entire United States Army. Among those soldiers was Fred

Stowers of Sandy Springs, who received the Congressional Medal of Honor (CMH), the only African American awarded the distinction in World War I. A white soldier of the 30th Infantry Division, James Dozier from Rock Hill, was the only other South Carolinian to receive the CMH for service in France. Following the war, Dozier became the state's adjutant general and was central in the creation and preparation of South Carolina's Home Guard Units and domestic defense programs in World War II.

The war provided the Palmetto State with unanticipated opportunities to draw a greater cash flow into its economy. Army training posts were established at three locations—Camp Jackson in Columbia, Camp Wadsworth in Spartanburg, and Camp Sevier in Greenville. Within weeks of their founding, servicemen at each camp nearly equaled in number the civilian population of the surrounding cities. With the troops and military installations came federal dollars to local companies to build army facilities and construct roads to serve the military's needs. Paychecks directly benefited local retail stores, banks, grocery stores, and a host of other area businesses. Although both the Marine Corps training base at Parris Island near Beaufort and the Charleston Navy Yard had been founded years before the war, the financial windfall on their parent communities was likewise impressive.

Americans nationwide certainly worried for their sons in uniform who fought in France, but they were equally concerned for their welfare while in training stateside. So many American servicemen, like most from South Carolina, had never ventured very far from home prior to April 1917. They were, for the most part, innocent to the ways of the world. Americans feared that military life and the availability of certain forms of vice typically associated with training centers would potentially corrupt the moral integrity of their sons. To reduce the likelihood of young men being serviced by prostitutes or falling victim to the Devil's brew, "sin-free zones" were erected around the nation's military posts and bases. In Greenville, Spartanburg, Columbia, Beaufort, and Charleston, brothels and bars were closed in areas immediately adjacent to training camps and were declared off-limits to servicemen elsewhere in the cities. Despite this national and state campaign, the French proved far less puritanical and the song's refrain "How are you goin' to keep 'em down on the farm now that they've seen Paree" carried special meaning to South Carolina's rural boys.

In November 1918, the guns of war fell silent along the western front in Europe. Over the next four months, ships packed with American soldiers inched from docks and moved toward the open sea. As the men of the American Expeditionary Force steamed from France, they scanned the coast, recalling in vivid detail the hell of Belleau Wood, Chateau-Tierry, and the Argonne Forest and remembered their friends and comrades who would remain in Europe, forever young. Ahead of them were victory parades, the open arms of loving families, and the trappings of civilian life. Their war was over, and they now wondered what lay ahead in the postwar years.

From the rise of Ben Tillman to the end of the Great War, South Carolina teetered between reformism and reactionary movements. The economy witnessed some diversification, giving rise to tobacco farming and the expansion of textile manufacturing, but cotton still ruled the state. Although the urban landscape of the Palmetto State became increasingly modernized, with increased railroad service, automobiles, paved roads, city parks, trolley cars, and annual expositions, nearly 90 percent of blacks and 60 percent of whites continued a rural existence similar to that of their fathers and grandfathers. Clemson was founded as an agricultural college, the University of South Carolina became the state's liberal arts institution, schools opened for the training of professional teachers, and more local public schools opened their doors to meet the needs of a growing population. South Carolina's illiteracy rate, however, remained abysmally high and state appropriations were well below regional and national averages. Many politicians clung desperately to the values and temperament of the antebellum South; others tried to lead the state into the twentieth century. Perhaps the only consistency in South Carolina in those 30 years was the continued, undying effort to dispossess blacks of all the rights and opportunities provided to them by the post–Civil War Reconstruction government. Year after year, state laws whittled down the number of African Americans eligible to vote, reducing the number to a few thousand in 1920, and Jim Crow laws confined blacks to a separate existence.

Between the Wars

"It was the best of times, it was the worst of times; it was the age of wisdom, it was the age of foolishness" wrote Charles Dickens in *A Tale of Two Cities*. Although the novel centered on characters and issues in England and France in the late eighteenth century, the first sentence in the 1859 masterpiece might have just as easily have applied to the Palmetto State from 1920 to 1940. In those twenty years, the South Carolina's economic base increasingly diversified and promised greater prosperity for the state, but South Carolina nonetheless plunged to the dismal depths of depression. The physical symbols of contemporary America reached into South Carolina, yet much of the population lived lives of quiet desperation untouched by modernity. The out-migration of Sandlappers increased at the very point in time that fundamental, constructive change emerged in the state. A body of sincere, civic-minded reformers led the Palmetto State toward a brighter future, but antiquated values were still sung by a vocal Old Guard. That contrary patterns defined South Carolina was nothing new, but never before had the state and its citizens confronted such unparalleled opportunity for redirection.

Controlling Society

Many South Carolinians believed morality itself was under attack in the 1920s, a perception seemingly validated by the exuberance of youthful rebellion spreading through the nation's urban centers. Indeed, a "modernist impulse" invaded urban communities in the 1920s, born recently in the trenches of France and carried home by veterans of the Great War to an America also wearied and horrified by the utter destruction of Europe and the loss of so many men in a "war to end all wars." More intensely aware of life's brevity, former soldiers and young people in the general population held little patience for the "old order of society" and believed long-accepted social constraints inhibited the fuller enjoyment of one's brief existence.

"Flappers" and young men in cities across the state, region, and nation exuded a spirit of personal independence that sharply deviated from long-cherished norms. Young women wore face powder, rouge, and lipstick; hemlines rose almost to the knee, and necklines dropped to unacceptable depths. Short hairstyles for women were in vogue for the first time, and cigarette smoking became commonplace among women. The most popular song and dance of the decade bore Charleston's name and was condemned by church congregations statewide as sexually provocative and an instigator of sinful behavior. One priest claimed the dance's performance was best suited to certain houses that have "fortunately been closed by law." Young couples found a previously unimagined freedom with the automobile, and "parking" at "passion pits" carried unwelcome implications for conservative society. Popular literature and published reports from university research projects on human sexuality only exacerbated parents' fears. Demands to rescind the state's Blue Laws threatened the sanctity of the Sabbath. The rising secularism, the advocacy of liberal school curricula, and the "live for today" attitude of so many young men and women altogether conveyed the impression that conventional behavioral patterns were on verge of collapse.

Clearly, there existed a current of rebellion among the South Carolina's youth as well as a real loosening of social constraints, but the appearance of wholesale perversity and morality's demise belied reality. The overwhelming majority of young South Carolinians still pursued established patterns of employment, land ownership, marriage, child rearing, church attendance, obedience to the law, and conservative values. But, images carried greater weight and resulted in a societal effort to regulate morality and personal behavior.

To preserve and protect the moral order of the state, South Carolina's law enforcement offices effectively curtailed gambling, and Blue Laws that required all businesses to be closed on Sunday were strictly enforced. Persons involved in public displays of affection, such as kissing, faced a choice of steep fines or 30 days in jail. Christian fundamentalists launched a crusade to ban the teaching of Darwin's theory of evolution, which contradicted biblical creationism. Although their effort failed in the wake of the Scopes "Monkey Trial" in Tennessee in 1925, teachers in small, rural schools were nonetheless duly warned to avoid teaching Darwin's heathen theory. In all these efforts and in many more, church leaders called for the return of morality in the state. Governors, legislators, town councilmen, mayors, and officials at all levels of government answered the call to action.

Even the Ku Klux Klan entered the "battle against immorality." The "new" Klan certainly continued its rousting of African Americans, but it also proclaimed Jews and Catholics as co-corrupters of Protestant morality. Rarely did someone of either religious group receive a fair trial when brought to court in districts dominated by the KKK; in cities and towns alike, non-Protestants were "encouraged" to conform to Klan-approved moral codes or be driven from the state. The KKK officially championed complete adherence to Blue Laws, Prohibition, sexual abstinence, and all laws that would make the Palmetto State the earthly manifestation of godly behavior. That its treatment of African Americans, immigrants, Jews, Catholics, and political liberals, along with its own private defiance of proper moral behavior, was hypocritical of its avowed stance apparently mattered little. Defense of South Carolina warranted whatever action was deemed necessary.

Contradictory, too, was the state's response to Prohibition. The Eighteenth Amendment to the US Constitution banned the manufacture, sale, possession, or consumption of alcohol in an effort to elevate moral virtue nationwide, and South Carolina's General Assembly cast its vote for ratification. In spite of the moral "high ground" taken by the legislature, liquor flowed with little restriction outside South Carolina's smallest and most fundamentalist communities. Not only did young adults flaunt their drinking in the era of Prohibition, few older South Carolinians conformed to the law. Policemen, attorneys, and judges in Columbia and Charleston often accepted bribes not to prosecute suppliers of demon rum. Notes Walter Edgar, "somewhere between twenty-five and forty thousand

Must-See Sites: Brookgreen Gardens, Murrells Inlet

Brookgreen Gardens is a 9,000-acre natural wildlife and botanical preserve and includes a 300-acre garden of local and exotic plants. The grounds once belonged to Archer and Ana Hyat Huntington, who opened the garden in 1931 as a display site for sculptures. More than 500 pieces are spread throughout the garden. Brookgreen Gardens offers guided tours, programs for local public schools, and activities for the general community. The preserve and garden is a National Historic Landmark and is located at 1931 Brookgreen Drive, just off Highway 17S in Murrells Inlet. For more information, call (843) 235-6000, email info@brookgreen.org or visit www.southcarolinaparks.com.

Image of Murrells Inlet © Ron Chapple Studios

Carolinians made a living as bootleggers, moonshiners, and rumrunners." Pints of the "devil's drink," "home brew," and "bathtub gin" sold for as much as $2.50 per pint ($22 in 1998 dollars). Cities were awash in alcohol slipped into the state by motorboats transporting crates of liquor from ships anchored in international waters just three miles from shore. Some distilleries actually continued manufacturing whiskey, conducting their operations in basements, in remote buildings in the countryside, or on the premise that their product was for medicinal use only. Prohibition was a total failure in South Carolina.

The Klan continued to exert control over African Americans, who were forced to conclude that any change for the better would have to come from themselves. The National Association for the Advancement of Colored People (NAACP) established local chapters in South Carolina in the 1920s, although whites in some communities, such as Greenville, successfully blocked the founding of local chapters until 1930. In Columbia and Charleston, the NAACP succeeded in planting a Young Women's Christian Association (YWCA) branch and a public library for black patrons, and in Charleston black teachers replaced white instructors in African-American schools. Given the unquestioned dominance of white supremacy and the strict enforcement of Jim Crow laws, white South Carolinians felt no threat from the NAACP and believed the few changes and services it was responsible for actually enhanced racial segregation in public facilities.

Economic Patterns

As the state's economy weakened in the 1920s, South Carolina's cities and towns actively sought a source of income apart from farming and textile mills. Tourism had never generated much prosperity for the state. Although Charleston, Aiken, and Camden had all turned a slight profit from northerners traveling through the South in the 1880s, native-born South Carolinians were always suspicious of "outsiders" and did not desire an influx of strangers lingering in the state. Nonetheless, the fractured economy required attention.

In 1923, Governor Thomas McLeod organized a conference of civic leaders from across the state for the expressed purpose of promoting tourism. His "Boost South Carolina" initiative failed to elicit widespread support at the convention, but several cities and towns accepted McLeod's idea and established their own local booster clubs to lure visitors from outside the state. Aiken and Camden both promoted their annual horse races, steeplechase, and horse show; Columbia organized a yearly automobile convention; numerous towns commenced seasonal beauty pageants and harvest festivals; and Beaufort opened its more elegant homes for tours.

Charleston capitalized on its image as a "must-see" antebellum southern city. To reclaim the attention of tourists, and in so doing capture some of their money, the city government founded an aggressive booster club to promote Charleston's local attractions and beauty. It also donated land at the Battery (the location where the first shots of the Civil War were fired) for the construction of the Fort Sumter Hotel in 1923. Streets were repaired, historic buildings and homes refurbished, community gardens beautified, museums expanded, and theaters founded. The city also commenced a campaign to clear back lots and drives of standing pools of water and eradicate the ever-growing rat population that infested Charleston. As hoped, tourists flooded Charleston; by 1929 nearly 47,000 guests spent $4 million yearly in the rejuvenated city; on the eve of World War II, the city attracted nearly 300,000 visitors annually. Charleston's rise as a modern tourist destination rested on its historical significance and long-recognized elegance, but life was being breathed into a community 100 miles up the coast that would ultimately challenge Charleston's dominance of the tourist trade.

Throughout much of the 1920s, Florida grabbed national headlines as the new vacation Mecca. Hundreds of millions of dollars poured into the "Florida Land Boom." Railroad lines soon edged the peninsula, connecting cities that seemingly rose from sandy soil and swamps overnight. John T. Woods, a Greenville, South Carolina entrepreneur, believed he could tap into the southbound travelers' wealth by providing them with a stopover point en route to the Sunshine State. He built Ocean Forest Hotel on Horry County's coastline in 1926 and plotted streets for the town of Myrtle Beach. The Ocean Forest proved such a welcome rest for vacationers headed to Florida and a windfall profit to both Woods and the fledgling community that before the decade ended Garden City Beach and Edisto Island each were incorporated and followed Myrtle Beach's lead. Pawley's Island advertised its salt marshes, natural wildlife, general serenity, and closeness to a simpler, quieter era. The campaign attracted the interest of Anna Huntington, who built a magnificent vacation home and established an expansive, beautiful garden in the area (today's Huntington Beach State Park and Brookgreen Gardens). Barnard Barauch, who later served the Franklin D. Roosevelt administration, purchased hundreds of acres along the coast between Pawley's Island and Georgetown and was a frequent guest in the region.

Most beneficial to the burgeoning tourist industry was the improvement of state roads. The State Highway Department had been erected in 1917, and among its first actions was the creation of a two-cent-per-gallon tax on gasoline with the revenue earmarked for the repair of existing roads and the construction of new highways. The measure contained three fundamental problems. First, few South Carolinians could afford automobiles, and consequently gasoline sales remained pitifully low. In 1917, there were only 40,000 cars in the entire state, or one automobile for every 41 people. Second, the tax rate was so minimal that revenue never met the expected costs for road projects. And, finally, the state's determination to have a balanced budget meant that all funds for road projects be banked before construction began. With each passing year, inflation cut into the reserved money. As late as 1925 there were only 300 miles of paved roads in South Carolina and few bridges over rivers for auto traffic. In 1929, however, the state attempted a different tactic—floating $65 million in road bonds to "build now and pay later." The department also raised the tax rate to six cents per gallon, and as car prices dropped in the 1920s, sales rose. A sound network of highways remained many years in the future, but in the postwar decade the Palmetto State was at least on the correct road to progress, and tourism had gotten a "jump start."

As tourism showed signs of promise, cotton and tobacco prices both fell. During the war years and for a

Mary McLeod Bethune

The fifteenth of seventeen children, Mary Jane McLeod was born on a Mayesville cotton farm on July 10, 1875. Her family's stories of slavery horrified Mary, but within those recollections she found hope for a better life.

Mary saw education as the only means to escape poverty. Beginning at age eleven, she walked four miles daily to the nearest schoolhouse for black children, the Mission Board School of the Presbyterian Church. Mary excelled in school, earning a scholarship to Scotia Seminary in North Carolina and another for advanced study at Moody Bible Institute in Chicago, where she was the only African-American student.

Her academic training complete, Mary returned to Mayesville to teach at the Mission School. The Presbyterian mission soon transferred her to Haines Institute in Augusta, Georgia and in 1896 to Kendall Institute in Sumter, South Carolina, where she met and married Albertus Bethune in 1898.

Committed fully to her "calling," she and her newborn son in 1899 moved to Palatka, Florida to manage the Presbyterian Mission School and to work with prisoners in the county jail, teaching them to read and helping overturn convictions for those she believed were innocent. Her husband reluctantly followed her to Palatka, but his job netted little money. To compensate, Mary sold life insurance after school hours until moving to Daytona in 1904. Albertus refused to relocate again, and the two separated on friendly terms.

With boxes for chairs, packing crates for tables, and used rugs on the floor, Bethune opened Daytona Educational and Industrial Training School for young African-American women. Students paid $2 each month and received instruction in the standard curriculum of reading, writing, and mathematics, along with courses in cooking, nutrition, home budgets, sewing, and childcare. Mary supplemented the school's finances by working odd jobs. Under her guidance, the school expanded to include a 30-acre campus, eventually becoming Bethune-Cookman College.

Politically active, she joined the Equal Suffrage League of the National Association of Colored Women in 1912 and lobbied for women's voting rights. Despite passage of the Nineteenth Amendment, poll taxes and literacy requirements remained obstacles for potential black voters. In autumn 1920, Bethune bicycled from house to house, soliciting donations to cover the expense of poll taxes imposed on otherwise eligible voters, and teaching African-American men and women enough to pass state literacy tests. Her efforts angered the local Ku Klux Klan, 80 members of whom "visited" her home one evening and "requested" she cease her work. Mary ignored their threats and by Election Day she had prepared 100 African Americans for the electoral process and personally led voters to the polls.

Her defiance of the KKK brought Bethune national attention and garnered her a seat on the National Urban League's executive board. She founded a home for wayward black girls, and twice in the 1920s served as president of the National Association of Colored Women, which had more than 200,000 members. She directed the National Association of Teachers in Colored Schools, sat on the Interracial Council of America, and founded the National Council of Negro Women in the 1930s. President Calvin Coolidge in 1928 appointed her to the Child Welfare Conference, and President Hoover sent her to the White House Conference on Child Health in 1930. President Franklin D. Roosevelt made Bethune his special advisor on minority affairs and director of the Negro division of the National Youth Administration from 1936 to 1944, making her the first African-American woman to direct a federal agency. She regularly attended White House functions, enjoyed a close relationship with First Lady Eleanor Roosevelt, and spent the World War II years campaigning for equal opportunities for black women in the armed forces, winning for African-American women the opportunity to become commissioned officers in the Women's Army Auxiliary Corps.

Bethune earned many honors for her selfless work. In 1932, journalist and muckraker Ida Tarbell listed her as one of the 50 greatest American women, and she was the first African American to receive an honorary Ph.D. from any white southern college, being granted the degree by Rollins College in 1949. Mary was also awarded the Thomas Jefferson Medal for Leadership in 1942, among many other national and international honors. She died on May 18, 1955. On July 10, 1974, what would have been her 99th birthday, a statue honoring her was unveiled in Washington, D.C.'s Lincoln Park. In South Carolina's statehouse today hangs an oil painting of the state's respected daughter.

brief period thereafter, farmers produced for both domestic and European markets. By 1920, however, Europeans had rebuilt their commercial fleets sufficiently to rely less on American imports and once more trade with suppliers worldwide. Added to Europe's rebound was another equally disastrous development. In the 1920s, notes one historian, cotton farmers confronted an "invader" every bit as destructive as General William T. Sherman in the Civil War—the boll weevil. The insect, which feeds on cotton, first entered South Carolina in 1917, migrating from Mexico, and by 1921 totally destroyed sea-island cotton. Between 1920 and 1922 the pest infested the entire state, and cotton production fell 70 percent. Williamsburg County alone suffered a production collapse from 35,000 to 2,500 pounds, and statistics collected by state agents revealed similar patterns in all cotton-producing counties in South Carolina. The boll weevil drove thousands of farmers into abject poverty, weakened banks that served rural depositors and issued small loans, crippled farm-supply warehouses, and threatened the survival of country stores. Farmers confronted several options: battle the insect with insecticides, surrender farming for millwork, or relocate outside South Carolina. Insecticides were expensive and farmers would have to dip deeply into their already limited income to buy them; textile mills in the early '20s were no longer expanding and therefore did not require additional employees. Although most white farmers chose to remain on the land, 24 of the state's 46 counties in the 1920s experienced a decrease in its white population. Far more African Americans emigrated from South Carolina, as they had little investment in the state to lose. In that single decade, 207,000 African Americans, or eight percent of the black population, exited the Palmetto State in search of opportunities elsewhere.

If the boll weevil was not destructive enough, the increased erosion of the soil and the concurrent depletion of its fertility added further misery to farmers. Again, rather than sell their property and abandon South Carolina, many opted to purchase fertilizer, buying 660,000 tons in 1940, while Iowa farmers consumed only 16,000 tons. A series of droughts further damned farmers. Altogether, cotton production fell nearly 60 percent in the 1920s.

The Great Depression

Unpaid loans, poor investments, and a souring economy compelled dozens of banks to close their doors in the late 1920s. Overproduction of manufactured goods in America's manufacturing sector, overextended business expansion, indebtedness, and deteriorating market conditions forced thousands of businesses into bankruptcy; those that continued operation had to scale back operations and lay off employees. The collapse of the stock market may have signaled the beginning of depression, but the nation's economy was shattered long before October 1929. Depression blanketed the state. In December 1931, People's Bank closed its 44 satellite offices statewide, taking with it the entire city payroll of Charleston. Per capita income in South Carolina sat at $150.

Tens of thousands of Sandlappers lost their jobs and teetered on the brink of hunger. Government, however, chose not to intervene and directly aid the citizenry. Instead, help came from people in less desperate conditions. Charities in Columbia supplied nearly 500,000 free meals to persons "down on their luck" in 1931 and another 715,000 the following year. The Salvation Army, Community Chest, and Travelers' Aid Society offered what little comfort they could provide. Churches raised money to feed, clothe, and temporarily shelter unfortunate members of their congregations. Even the Ku Klux Klan chipped in, delivering food baskets to the rural white poor. Unemployment skyrocketed between 1929 and 1932, reaching a national average of 25 percent. The only positive feature for South Carolina was that so many Sandlappers remained on farms and so were able to feed themselves, unless banks called in their mortgage notes. But, in summer 1932, a glimmer of hope surfaced.

South Carolinians, with few exceptions, rejoiced in the candidacy of Franklin Delano Roosevelt in 1932. FDR promised to remember "the forgotten man" if elected to the presidency and work for the common good. He slashed the incumbent, Herbert Hoover, for doing too little too late to ease the suffering of Americans and for not accepting the new reality that government does have an obligation to aid its citizens in times as desperate as the current crisis. He blasted big business for perpetuating disreputable business practices

African American convicts working with axes, Reed Camp, South Carolina, December 1934

and for contributing directly to the economic calamity that gripped the United States. In the November elections, fully 98 percent of South Carolina's votes were cast for Roosevelt, his greatest margin of victory in any state.

The president's inaugural address on March 4, 1933 convinced South Carolinians that they had made a sound choice in the recent elections. FDR promised a "new deal" for Americans, aggressive federal government intervention in the nation's economy for the defense of its citizens, much like how as commander-in-chief he would act against an invading enemy. He pledged to create policies and programs that would provide immediate relief in the form of government-sponsored jobs or money payments to persons in greatest need; programs to affect the recovery of business and stabilize the economy; and reforms that would prevent future depressions from occurring. Underpinning the New Deal was FDR's conviction that government has a responsibility to regulate the economy when necessary for the benefit of all citizens.

Franklin Delano Roosevelt's arrival in the White House did not immediately translate into a new day for South Carolinians. It took time to erect the myriad of agencies and programs that would transform the state, and more time for those agencies and programs to organize, staff, and shake out their bugs. In the meantime, depression continued its death grip on the state. By summer 1933, day laborers on farms earned 50 cents, among the lowest wages nationally. Nearly 320 banks were no longer open in the Palmetto State, and the value of crops stood at $63 million in contrast to $166 million in 1913. Per capita income dropped to $150, down from $261 in 1929. Cotton prices also continued their plunge, hitting less than five cents per pound, its lowest value since the middle 1890s. In Columbia, 24 percent of working-age residents were aggressively seeking jobs.

The New Deal

Among the first New Deal programs to provide direct aid was the Federal Emergency Relief Administration (FERA), founded in May 1933. FERA's principal purpose was to provide food, clothing, and federally funded jobs to those individuals and families in greatest need. It also established a school lunch program. More than 400,000 South Carolinians received federal aid under FERA, and, as one historian has noted, it "literally saved thousands of Carolinians from starvation."

The Civilian Conservation Corps (CCC) was another of FDR's earliest New Deal agencies. It enlisted men 18 to 25 years of age for a period of six months, clothed them in khaki shirts and pants, and sent them to perform conservation work at one of the 30 CCC camps in South Carolina. Men were provided with three hot meals daily, educational programs in evening hours, and a $30 per month paycheck, of which $22 was detoured to their families back home. Enlistees planted trees and sewed grass where needed, built ranger towers in forests, implemented soil erosion programs, fought forest fires and erected firebreaks, constructed roads deep into wilderness areas, and established state parks at Hunting Island, Paris Mountain, and Myrtle Beach. Almost 50,000 South Carolinians were enrolled in the CCC between 1933 and 1939.

The Works Progress Administration (WPA) and Public Works Administration (PWA) hired men to construct a variety of public-use structures, generally in more populated areas of the state. WPA workers built Conway's two-lane, arched bridge over the Waccamaw River and a highway connecting the county seat to Myrtle Beach fifteen miles to the southeast (today's Highway 544). The WPA built public theaters such as the Dock Street Theater in Charleston while the PWA improved and expanded the Charleston Navy Yard. Both agencies constructed public housing projects, roads, schools, airports, libraries, museums, college dormitories, and a host of state and local government buildings in cities and towns statewide. The WPA ran a historical project that collected and reprinted government records and distributed copies to repositories in each state, generally at the flagship university (USC in the Palmetto State). Its personnel also conducted interviews of Native Americans, immigrants to the United States, and former slaves, and the WPA published historical and travelers' "guides" to each state of the Union.

FDR's Rural Electrification Administration (REA) carried electrical service into the most isolated reaches of South Carolina. In 1924, only 1,000 rural families statewide boasted electrical service; ten years later only two percent of South Carolina's farms were electrified. With federal loans channeled through the REA, communities formed electric cooperative companies, such as the Horry County Electric Cooperative, and ran power lines throughout the town and into nearby rural areas. In 1940, nearly 15 percent of the state's farms had electrical service; in 1944, the number reached 50 percent of the state's farming families.

The largest New Deal program in South Carolina was the Santee Cooper Project. Approved by the Roosevelt

Must-See Sites: Hobcaw Barony, Georgetown

This 17,000-acre estate was originally a gift issued to John, Lord Carteret by King George I in 1718 and evolved into a very prosperous rice plantation. In 1905 it was purchased by South Carolina native, Wall Street millionaire, and presidential advisor Bernard Baruch, who used the land as a winter hunting retreat. At the 13,500-square-foot mansion Baruch entertained President Franklin Delano Roosevelt, Prime Minister Winston Churchill, and other prominent figures. Today, Hobcaw Barony is used as a research center for the colleges and universities of South Carolina. Tours are available for the house and the rice plantation. Admission is free to the visitors' center, which is open Monday through Friday. The Barony is located at 22 Hobcaw Road just off Highway 17S. Call the office at (843) 546-4623 for more details or email the Barony at hobcaw@baruch.sc.edu.

White House in 1935, the plan refaced much of the state and provided electrical power to tens of thousands of South Carolinians. Work commenced in May 1939, and within three years the project was completed under budget. More than 170,000 acres of land were cleared, 200 million feet of timber were cut (much of which was sold to the state's paper mills), millions of cubic feet of earth were excavated, and 3 million cubic yards of concrete were poured. Dams were built, swampland filled in for development, hydroelectric power plants constructed, inland waters were made more navigable, flooding along the Santee River ended, and public lakes for community enjoyment were created. The Santee Project blessed much of the state, employing 9,000 men at a time when jobs were most needed. Over the following decades, the Santee system expanded, and by 1985 it alone provided electrical service to half the state.

The Great Depression nearly destroyed South Carolina's agricultural base. Farm income in 1932 was only

39 percent of the 1920 level. Roosevelt's Agricultural Adjustment Act (AAA) was designed to create demand for crops and in so doing elevate farmer income. Farmers who opted into the program agreed to produce fewer crops on their land, a practice that generated shortages but increased market values. Participating farmers plowed under crops already in the fields or sectioned off the agreed-upon acreage to lay idle, and received government money to compensate them for the value of the crops normally harvested on the now-unused property. In short, farmers were allotted a certain expanse of land on which to produce their crops. In 1933, once the AAA was inaugurated, cotton farmers rushed to enlist in the program and plowed under 500,000 acres of the plant. Tobacco farmers also joined the AAA but with less determination. As expected, prices for cotton and tobacco rose, bringing farmers income levels not enjoyed since World War I.

Textile mills also suffered early in the Great Depression. Staggeringly high unemployment in the state and nation yanked consumer demand from the industry, families choosing to mend and patch garments and then pass them down to younger children rather than spend what little money they had on new clothes. Market prices for finished goods tumbled, and many mills were ultimately driven into bankruptcy. Roosevelt's National Recovery Act (NRA) moved to recover the nation's businesses. It raised workers' pay through a minimum-wage provision, regulated company profits by fixing a price range for marketed goods, banned child labor completely, and protected labor's right to bargain. It also reduced the workweek to 40 hours for individual employees and limited mill production to 80 hours per week, steps that compelled the affected companies to hire additional workers to cover the weekly period of production and thus to drive down unemployment levels. Stores, shops, and companies that voluntarily joined the NRA placed posters or stickers bearing the image of a blue eagle in storefront windows to identify themselves as participants, and the Roosevelt White House strongly encouraged Americans to patronize only those businesses displaying the NRA symbol.

Columbia and Greenville both held parades in August 1933 to publicize the NRA and, as FDR did from the Oval

Office, to solicit community support for local businesses affiliated with the New Deal agency. Most businesses in South Carolina joined the NRA and witnessed renewed consumer confidence, employee satisfaction, and recovery. The National Recovery Act was directed at every industry and business in the nation, and it did bring direct, immediate, and positive benefits to South Carolina's textile mills. One mill in Easley, for example, reduced its working hours from 128 to the required 80, but its profits turned upward.

Other New Deal agencies also served as a safety net in South Carolina. The Federal Deposit Insurance Corporation (FDIC) guaranteed bank deposits and convinced citizens to return their money to local bank accounts, deposits that then could be distributed as small business loans in the community. The Civil Works Administration (CWA) hired individuals from relief rosters and unemployment rolls to refurbish public schools, lay sewer systems, and upgrade roads and bridges. The Social Security Administration provided an employment service and established a system of income for the elderly. The National Youth Administration (NYA) trained high-school students in a variety of job-related skills and provided them with part-time work opportunities to gain experience in addition to needed income. With New Deal blessings and supplemental funds, Wil Lou Gray organized adult education programs in South Carolina's upstate region, bringing students a curriculum based on individual needs, teaching some to read, others domestic skills, and still others the fundamentals of securing off-farm employment. A network of New Deal agencies and bureaus in Charleston launched a coordinated effort to rid the city of its rats, purify drinking water, improve street drainage, and eradicate malaria—all initiatives that never received sufficient funding or interest in the 1920s but under the New Deal made remarkable gains. In Orangeburg, long noted for its intense poverty, community recreation centers were built and educational programs were organized for the town's poor, black majority. Roosevelt's programs put money into the hands of those who most needed it and returned people regardless of race to the ranks of the employed, stabilized the state's economic structure, raised personal income and business profits, and erected a safety net of governmental services that aided citizens. Across the state, South Carolinians applauded the president's boldness and determination to end the economic crisis and directly help Americans.

Perhaps the most visible evidence of appreciation emanated from the state's black population. Since 1865, African Americans had stood firmly in the Republican Party camp—the party of Lincoln, the party of emancipation; South Carolina's Democratic Party had historically defended the institution of slavery, circumvented postwar laws and constitutional amendments granting rights to blacks, erected Jim Crow legislation, and openly denounced any threat to white supremacy. But in the 1936 presidential election, the state's African Americans almost unanimously threw their collective support behind Roosevelt and joined the very party that for so long had been their antagonist. FDR's New Deal included African Americans. It funneled work and employment programs, educational opportunities, health-care services, and community development programs into black neighborhoods. Nationally, more than 100 African Americans were appointed to administrative posts in the federal executive branch of government. From South Carolina, Mary McLeod Bethune commanded the ear of First Lady Eleanor Roosevelt and became the first African-American woman to have direct influence in the White House. No president or political party, not even Abraham Lincoln and the Republicans, had ever accomplished so much for African Americans.

There were, to be sure, complaints directed against Roosevelt and his economic program. FDR's agencies often held overlapping responsibilities and were occasionally complicated by poor administration. Citizens sometimes complained that WPA wasted entirely too much money and the agency's progress in local projects was too slow, a charge that found its most popular expression in referring to the WPA as "We Poke Along." South Carolinians sometimes expressed their frustration that the CCC limited an enrollee to six months of service with no opportunity for another period of enlistment. But the loudest and most derisive sounds emanated from the state's fire-breathing conservatives and die-hard proponents of states' rights. The

New Deal erected a large bureaucracy that spread its reach deep into state and local affairs previously immune to federal intervention. Federal dollars and programs, they contended, increasingly made the state dependent on Washington—a variation on colonialism, they seethed. Increased federal authority smacked of socialism, cried Roosevelt's critics, and the New Deal's inclusion of blacks threatened white supremacy in the state.

Among FDR's most vicious opponents in the Palmetto State was Ellison D. "Cotton Ed" Smith, United States senator from 1908 to 1944 and unfaltering devotee to cotton as the state's continued economic base. His spellbinding orations and vicious harangues on the stump captivated listeners, and his tirades became more virulent with each passing year. He blasted the administration's efforts to regulate the nation's industries, preferring the marketplace cure its own ills. Smith ridiculed work-relief agencies, criticizing them as inefficient and costly. He warned that Washington's programs were collectively creating a climate of dependency among the nation's laborers and, consequently, destroying the work ethic that historically had driven America forward. And, Smith cautioned, Roosevelt's New Deal intended to corrupt the independence of states, making them subservient to federal authority. South Carolinians appreciated his promotion of states' rights and the protection of the state from federal intrusion, but the extent of poverty citizens had endured and the promise of recovery under the New Deal convinced most residents that some help from Washington was necessary. So supportive of FDR's recovery program were South Carolinians that the president took all but 1,600 votes in the state in his 1936 reelection race. Roosevelt held little affection for South Carolina's senior senator. "Cotton Ed" and his "colorful" ranting was frequently the butt of private jokes in the White House, and his condemnation of the New Deal was seldom considered serious.

Smith's dogged defense of white supremacy, however, reflected the genuine sentiment of his white constituents. No liberal or progressive politician in the state dared challenge "Cotton Ed" or attack Jim Crow in public. Smith's unbridled racism and devotion to white supremacy were ever-present thorns for the president, who needed the state's Democratic vote. Notes historian Lewis Jones, *Time* magazine described "Cotton Ed" as a "conscientious objector" of the twentieth century and "the last of the spittoon senators" from South Carolina.

In sharp contrast to Smith were South Carolina's rising stars in the Democratic Party, men who vaunted New Deal programs and modernization of the state. Olin D. Johnston, twice-elected governor of South Carolina in the 1930s, pushed through the legislature reform measures enacted in most other states of the nation decades earlier. Through his efforts came a compulsory education law, workers' compensation, and an eight-month school year. More money filtered into public education, and he championed greater economic diversification. Passage of the Social Security system, the NRA, WPA, CCC, and AAA all received Governor Johnston's enthusiastic endorsement. Burnet Maybank, a Charlestonian who also served as governor and senator during FDR's tenure in the White House, supported New Deal measures as fully as Johnston. He was instrumental in securing federal funds for further expansion of the Charleston Navy Yard and the Charleston Dry Dock Company, and he called for increased spending on public health programs and adult education for both whites and blacks.

Of all New Deal politicians in South Carolina, none commanded as much influence as James F. Byrnes. Elected to the United States Senate in 1930, he proved central in securing Roosevelt's nomination as the Democratic Party contender against Republican Herbert Hoover in 1932, and he quickly aligned himself with the Roosevelt agenda once FDR was elected in November. It was Byrnes who, with Maybank's support, pressed the Santee Cooper hydroelectric project in Washington and won congressional approval. Byrnes was South Carolina's "point man" in Washington, and through his efforts the reform programs of Johnston and Maybank met little resistance statewide or in the halls of Congress. He was also instrumental in 1940 in convincing South Carolinians to support a third term for FDR in the White House, and 95 percent of the vote went to Roosevelt. As war in Europe threatened England's survival in 1940, Senator Byrnes unequivocally endorsed America's defense readiness, backed passage of the

Selective Training and Service Act, and attracted War Department and Department of the Navy funds to the Palmetto State that opened training posts, airfields, and additional ship construction. In 1941, South Carolina's senator carried FDR's Lend-Lease Bill through the Senate. Roosevelt admired Byrnes' intellect, his commitment to the New Deal nationally and inside South Carolina, and his unabashed determination to prepare the United States for war. In return, FDR in June 1941 nominated Byrnes to the United States Supreme Court. As evidence of the respect given to him by his colleagues, the senate took less than ten minutes to approve Byrnes as the new justice.

The reformist spirit of the New Deal swept the Palmetto State with a fresh air of hope; indeed, Roosevelt's programs collectively amounted to a watershed in the course of South Carolina's development. The New Deal pumped funds into the state, rescuing the economy and laying the foundations for South Carolina's modernization. Although many problems persisted as the New Deal drew to its close with the advent of war, Palmetto State residents had witnessed a fundamental redirection and entered the twentieth century.

12

The Palmetto State in World War II

A crisp air and sunlit skies welcomed early-risers from Greenville to Charleston on Sunday, December 7, 1941. Across South Carolina, most families made their way to church services as they did every Sunday; others settled themselves in front of the family radio to enjoy the music of Glenn Miller, Tommy Dorsey, and other popular performers while they scanned the morning newspaper and sipped their coffee. Christmas advertising and reports of local preparations for the coming holidays dwarfed analyses of the stalled Japanese-American negotiations and stories of Britain's continued heroic defense of the isles against German air attacks. Results of Saturday's Shrine Bowl game between high-school football stars of the two Carolinas played just across the state line in Charlotte, North Carolina made the front pages of many upstate newspapers, and updates on the progress of the Santee-Cooper hydroelectric power plant's construction near Charleston commanded similar space in Lowcountry papers. This particular Sunday morning began like most others; little did anyone suspect that their lives would be irrevocably altered by midday.

News broadcasts of Japan's strike on Pearl Harbor first aired just before 2:00PM. Many families, already gathered around their dinner tables for their traditional after-church midday meals, moved into living rooms and stood or sat around their radios to listen more carefully to the information coming stateside from Hawaii. Bewildered motorists pulled off the road, adjusted their radio dials, and sat motionless as they tried to comprehend the reality of the moment. Local theater managers stopped their movies and personally informed their audiences, and window-shoppers strolling city streets in Columbia and Charleston learned of the Japanese attack from policemen who used their megaphones to tell soldiers and sailors to return to their bases immediately.

South Carolinians, like Americans nationwide, were initially numbed by the reality that war had come to the United States so suddenly, so viciously. An often unspoken fear coursed through state residents. Fathers who were veterans of the Great War remembered the indescribable horror of modern warfare and now realized their own sons would most likely face a conflict far more brutal than that of 1918. Small children often stood silent, stunned to witness for the first time tears in their fathers' eyes or to hear their parents spew improper words and racial epithets. Fear, however, was soon joined by anger, and the call for vengeance dominated editorials printed in newspapers by late Sunday afternoon and over the following week. "Wipe the Japs off the map!" cried one journalist; a "foul attack by a foul nation," proclaimed another. Editorialists, area politicians, and the ordinary man-on-the-street termed Japan's strike "unprovoked," "unwarranted," "appalling," and "dastardly." Many described the Japanese as "assassins" and "members of an unholy alliance... seeking world domination by brutal force." "This is the kind of thing that Americans may expect from the Japanese," thundered a writer for Charleston's *News and Courier*. "Their government is destitute of the conception of truth and honor that Americans have," stormed the writer. Noted an editorial in Columbia's newspaper, the *State*, "it takes no skill to double-cross.... Cruel, beastly, highly mechanized force is their only god." South Carolinians united behind the demand for the total destruction of Japan. "I hope that when the war is over the empire of Japan will be as nearly free of Japanese as the Sahara is of oases," cried one South Carolina judge. The United States must "unsheathe [its] swords and vow that they will not rest in the scabbards again until decency has been restored among the peoples of the earth," demanded a writer for Florence's *Morning News*. "We enter the war on the side of right," he continued, "and for no other purpose than the task of crushing the evil forces which are seeking to shackle the freedoms and decencies fundamental to a stable world order." "By the grace of God and of all good humanity," roared the editor of Conway's *Horry Herald*, "we will show the Japs where they made the greatest mistake in their history.... Japan fired the first shot. A united America will see to it that Japan does not fire the last."

The rage exhibited by South Carolinians was not directed solely at Japan; most residents believed Hitler was ultimately responsible for Japanese militarization and aggression. "It is too obvious that Adolf Hitler encouraged this warlike gesture of a helpless oriental puppet. This unwarranted and unheralded bombing today is but the final plunge of the world's final defender of democracy into a cauldron stirred by the crazed Adolf Hitler," wrote one Southerner. Said another, "The attack on Hawaii is just as surely an attack by Hitler as if German bombers instead of Japanese had done the job." "What airplane, what tank, what battleship, air bomber, or gun that Japan has was a Japanese invention?" wrote the editor of the *News and Courier*. Most South Carolinians argued that without the direct, conspiratorial involvement of Germany, Japan would not have been capable of waging modern war; without the safety net of German military might, Japan would not have committed itself to war with the United States. War with Nazi Germany, then, was not only expected but championed by the state's residents before nightfall on Sunday, December 7, 1941.

The State Mobilizes for War

Within hours of Japan's attack on Hawaii, Governor Joseph Emile Harley activated South Carolina's Home Guard, a defense force organized one year earlier on the assumption that America's entry into the global war would require the federalization of National Guard units and, therefore, leave the state essentially defenseless. The state's 6,200 members, who ranged in age from 16 to 60, stood guard at predetermined sites by nightfall. Armed with shotguns and pistols, men controlled traffic flow across bridges both small and large, such as that which linked Conway to Myrtle Beach and the recently constructed frame that connected Mount Pleasant to downtown Charleston; they patrolled riverbanks and waterways such as the Little Pee Dee River at Gallavant's Ferry and points of entry into the

Rising Profitability of Tobacco

Pounds Grown (1000s)

1940	1941	1942	1943
87,550	69,660	96,750	86,480

Cents per Pound

1940	1941	1942	1943
14.6	24.8	37.4	38.9

Source: Eldred E. Prince, Jr., *Long Green: The Rise and Fall of Tobacco in South Carolina* (Athens: University of Georgia Press, 2000), p. 203.

Intracoastal Waterway; they carefully watched all movement around the Santee-Cooper hydroelectric power plant; and they stopped vehicles attempting to enter airports. Despite cold weather and frequent rain, Home Guard units remained on their assigned posts well into January 1942 and thereafter regularly received supplemental training at military posts across the South and conducted small-scale maneuvers at various points within the state. As the war progressed, younger members eventually entered the armed forces.

Even before President Roosevelt's heated message and request for a declaration of war by Congress on December 8, army and navy recruiting stations across the state were inundated with volunteers. "Filled with vinegar," as South Carolinians often describe enthused and energetic youths, young men from every social and economic class rushed to enlist in the armed forces. Outside the navy recruiting office in Charleston stood 30 applicants who had waited anxiously since daybreak for the doors to open. The navy's Florence office found itself busier on December 8 than on any single day since 1917 and extended its hours of operation from the customary 4:00PM closing to midnight simply to accommodate demand. "They all seem to want to get at the Japs," said the officer in charge. One former sailor personally delivered two of his sons to the recruiter. "Here they are," he announced, "and I've got two more at home under seventeen *in South Carolina, 1940–1948*

1945	1946	1947	1948
139,520	171,825	155,495	131,560
43.9	48.7	41.8	50.3

years of age. If you can use them, I'll go back and get them." One hundred Greenville men volunteered for naval duty by December 9. Two hundred men rushed to the army recruiting office in Columbia before noon that same day, and the response across the state proved similar. In Conway, Aiken, Spartanburg, and dozens of other communities, thousands of young men offered themselves for military service in the wake of Pearl Harbor. By war's end, more than 200,000 South Carolinians served in the nation's armed forces; were it not for a rejection rate that surpassed the national average—largely the result of poor physical health or illiteracy—many more Sandlappers would have willingly and enthusiastically served.

Over the next few days, local and state officials activated civil defense measures. Airplane-spotting observation towers were manned, and air raid sirens were tested. Citizens volunteered for community preparedness work as auxiliary firemen and policemen, demolition experts, road and bridge builders, and traffic supervisors—all necessary jobs in the event of an enemy attack on the state. Charleston's Roper Hospital registered 375 men and women to manufacture surgical dressings, and dozens more did the same at hospitals and clinics in Conway, Loris, Columbia, Sumter, Greenville, Aiken, and Spartanburg. South Carolinian support for the nation's war effort was immediate and almost unanimous.

Marine recruits in training at Parris Island Marine Recruit Center, May, 1942

War Comes to South Carolina

Japan's strike on Hawaii proved that an enemy could reach the United States, and residents of all coastal states realized they were vulnerable to enemy attack. Camden's civil defense coordinator warned of a possible German air assault on the East Coast and possibly against Newfoundland. Charleston's officials considered a Nazi strike on the city's naval yard and inland military training centers more likely from aircraft carriers just beyond the horizon or from bases in the Caribbean. Mayor Henry Lockwood ordered sandbags be stacked around the community's hospitals and city offices. Throughout spring and summer 1942, air-raid drills were held along the coast in Beaufort, Charleston, Georgetown, and Myrtle Beach as well as in the interior communities of Columbia, Sumter, Camden, Aiken, and Greenville. In many of these drills, the United States Army Air Corps provided a squadron of bombers to play the role of Nazi attackers in order to test fully the state's air observation and warning system.

The real threat to America's coast, however, came not from warplanes but from German submarines, or U-boats. From January 1942 through August 1943 the war for the Western Atlantic raged, U-boats sinking hundreds of Allied cargo ships and tankers from Massachusetts to the mouth of the Mississippi River, sending 171 to the ocean floor by June 1942 alone. The greatest German activity was centered along the Carolinas, American sailors terming the stretch "torpedo junction." Sixth Naval District Commander Admiral Jules Jones, based in Charleston, confirmed 150 U-boat contacts on the Carolina coast by war's end in 1945, one-third of these spotted between Georgetown and Savannah. Nazi submarines were both successful and brazen. In July 1942, U-751 slipped into Charleston Harbor and laid twelve mines, and on September 18 U-455 dropped another dozen into the harbor.

Part of the U-boat success against Allied shipping resulted from the behavior of coastal residents themselves. Homes, businesses, and amusement parks along the shore remained lighted at night when not blacked-out by air-raid drills and, consequently, served as beacons for German submarines. Coastal lights also silhouetted ships at sea and made them visible targets. In mid-March 1942, Admiral William White of the Sixth Naval District fired a letter to the new South Carolina governor, Richard Manning Jefferies, advising him of the problem of ship silhouetting and recommending that at the minimum he order a mandatory dim-out from Beaufort to Myrtle Beach. The governor urged seaboard businesses to comply with the Navy's request, and many did so grudgingly and expressed their concerns that "tourist season would be ruined." The owner of the pavilion at Folly Beach outside Charleston agreed to implement a dim-out "if such action becomes necessary." By April, however, every city and town on the South Carolina coast adopted navy-recommended blackout guidelines—use of parking lights only when driving at night, no exterior lighting after dusk, and blackout curtains in oceanfront homes.

To help locate enemy submarines, the navy employed the Civil Air Patrol organized shortly before Pearl Harbor. South Carolina's CAP was based at James Island just outside Charleston and flew eight missions daily, four to the

Barrage balloons are raised into the air near Beaufort, serving as navigation obstacles against possible enemy bombing raids along coastal South Carolina, May 1942.

north and four to the south. Should they spot a U-boat, they were to radio its position to the Coast Guard and keep it under surveillance until warships arrived. CAP work proved indispensable in ridding the coast of enemy submarines.

Federal and state officials also considered extensive use of the Intracoastal Waterway to secure Allied shipping. Barges could easily navigate the twelve- to fifteen-foot-deep channel that extended from Florida to Maine. The only problem was the lack of barges. Georgetown and Charleston officials concluded that their local shipbuilders could quickly manufacture a sufficient number of barges to handle general cargo and oil shipments for the war effort and concurrently bring newfound profits to their communities. In the United States Senate, South Carolina's Burnet Maybank introduced a bill to construct a canal across northern Florida to link the Gulf Coast Intracoastal Waterway system to that of the East Coast and in so doing provide inland transportation from Texas to Maine. The measure passed both houses of Congress and Roosevelt signed the bill into law in summer 1943; however, by that time the U-boat menace had evaporated and the waterway connector was no longer needed.

South Carolinians Settle into War

World War II transformed South Carolina, in part as a result of the nation's military and naval presence in the state. Since November 1941, the 56th Interceptor Squadron based in Charlotte, North Carolina used the small Myrtle Beach Army Air Base as its temporary home from which it flew gunnery practice missions in the waters off Georgetown and Murrell's Inlet. During the war, the base was substantially enlarged and became a permanent coastal air defense post, an assignment that continued until military cutbacks forced its closure in the early 1990s. Just three days after Pearl Harbor, Washington committed $12 million to construct a pilot training base at Greenville that would house 400 pilots, 4,500 enlisted men, and 130 bombers. Spartanburg Municipal Airport became home to the Navy Air Transport Service that ferried recently manufactured aircraft from eastern factories to the West Coast. A new air base was constructed at Walterboro for the search and pursuit of German U-boats, and smaller training fields were established at Bennettsville, Camden, Sumter, Aiken, Beaufort, Florence, Spartanburg, Chester, Anderson, Barnwell, Georgetown, Johns Island, Hartsville, Greenwood, and Columbia. All of the expanded airfields and those newly built by the War Department remained in service following the war, some as permanent military air stations and others as civilian fields.

In addition to pilot training, several of the new or expanded air bases trained pilots in the use of live ammunition before deployment to overseas posts. Columbia Air Base in May 1942 warned the public to remain clear of the southern side of Lake Murray, where warplanes regularly practiced with live rounds. The army and navy both cautioned coastal fishermen who trawled along Murrell's Inlet, Pawley's Island, and Georgetown to be on the watch for American aircraft, and restricted the waters to military use only during certain hours of the day. The military also required large tracts for bombing ranges. In Horry County, the War Department designated 54,000 acres of the Red Hill District north of Conway and a 6,400-acre stretch between the Intracoastal Waterway and the ocean as bombing ranges for pilots stationed at the Myrtle Beach Air Base. More than 37,000 acres in the Carver Bay section of Georgetown County were also earmarked as a bombing range. In late December 1941, the War Department ordered Red Hill's three hundred families to vacate the area, their property to be purchased by Washington at fair market value. By March 1942, the War Department held title to the needed land and soon afterward commenced bombing practice missions in the region. As late as 2008, the Army Corps of Engineers still required its personnel to search for undetonated bombs before new neighborhoods were constructed in the area.

Upstate, Sandlappers were invaded by the United States Army in July 1942. The War Department needed to train its infantry for European warfare and selected six counties bordering North Carolina along with ten counties in the Tarheel State for field maneuvers. Plans were laid long before Pearl Harbor to give Washington sufficient time to secure the necessary legal permits from landowners; by April 15, 1942, every Sandlapper in the affected counties had waived all trespass rights to the army. Between July and September, mock battles raged across the region at no small sacrifice to local farmers and businessmen.

Fort Jackson in Columbia received 40,000 new recruits for basic training in spring 1942, and throughout the war years it was one of the largest army training facilities in the nation. The air bases in Greenville, Spartanburg, Myrtle Beach, Charleston, and nearly one dozen other communities also brought thousands of servicemen into South Carolina. The naval base in Charleston expanded to become the second largest facility on the East Coast, second only to the naval station at Norfolk, Virginia. The presence of so many servicemen strained local community services. The influx of so many servicemen and military families forced towns and cities to build recreation halls and public parks to serve military personnel in their off-duty hours, parks and recreation centers that remained open to the general public following the war. In February 1942 Aiken residents donated chairs, tables, lamps, books, and writing paper for soldiers who used the town's servicemen's recreation center, and local funds supplied the facility with a ping-pong table, balls, and paddles. One unidentified resident paid in full the first year's rent on the building. In Columbia, 21 fully supplied recreation centers tended to the needs of both civilians and soldiers, providing tennis courts, a lighted softball field, a boxing ring, and gardens.

The expansion of army and navy training facilities brought a massive wave of federal dollars into the state. Prewar airport development statewide totaled $10 million; Greenville alone received $12 million in 1942, and another $6 million went to smaller fields that same year. Larger airfields also witnessed expansion of civilian use. Eastern Airlines used Columbia's facility for air travel between Miami and New York, and Delta routed traffic through the city for flights running from Charleston to Dallas, Texas. Airports at Spartanburg, Greenville, and Charleston all reaped the financial windfall of wartime civilian air travel. So lucrative was civilian use that the South Carolina Aeronautics Commission requested and received $4 million from Washington for further development of air service in the state. Millions more were appropriated by Congress for the expansion of port facilities in Charleston and Georgetown, the building of army bases statewide, the construction of roads leading to military posts and the widening of highways for military traffic, and the extension of electrical and water service for army and navy bases. The war also demanded maximum production of cotton, tobacco, textile goods, and food crops. South Carolina's farmers netted windfall profits, as did the state's manufacturing sector. Wages for factory and mill workers also rose to record levels, giving Sandlappers a purchasing power unmatched in the state's history. Unfortunately, wartime rationing left little to buy, and most money sat in savings accounts until the war ended.

As the war progressed, South Carolinians contributed more of their time and money to the war effort. Thousands volunteered their services to the American Red Cross (ARC), the majority producing a steady supply of surgical dressings needed by both the army and navy. Marion volunteers alone produced more than 68,000 bandages by summer 1943. Other volunteers aided nurses in hospitals, read to recuperating patients, wrote letters for servicemen unable to pen their own words, cleaned bedpans, delivered ice and water to each room, and changed bed linens. Still others worked as typists, filing clerks, publicists, printers, and general errand runners. Even those who did not

Must-See Sites: McLeod Farms Antique Museum and Roadside Market, McBee

Four miles south of the little town of McBee on Hwy 151 sits McLeod Farms, a rest stop heavily visited by travelers to and from Myrtle Beach. Inside the rustic-looking museum sit more than twenty antique automobiles, among them a collection of Model T's and Model A's, a 1930 Lincoln, and a "woody." A 1968 Chevrolet Camaro, a Nash Rambler, and other cars manufactured in the '60s also are housed in the museum. Visitors can also examine antique farm equipment and tractors, record players, outdated drink machines, and a wide array of memorabilia. A roadside market next door sells fruits and vegetables produced on McLeod Farms, freshly picked strawberries and peaches being the most popular. In October each year, visitors can take a wagon ride into the fields and pick their own pumpkin. The market also sells fresh-baked pies and cakes and homemade ice cream. Admission to the museum is free, and both the museum and market are open daily except on holidays.

contribute time to the ARC nonetheless donated their blood for Red Cross distribution to hospitals stateside and to aid stations in combat zones. In June 1945, 620 Columbia women contributed 8,300 hours of their free time to the city's Red Cross office. The pattern was replicated in towns and cities statewide throughout the war years. The ARC also desperately needed money to cover its operational costs, to purchase supplies in demand by army and navy units, and to help families dislocated by the war. Throughout the war, the Red Cross held a series of fundraising campaigns, each town and city assigned a financial quota to meet. South Carolina's communities organized golf tournaments and sponsored dances and town picnics to raise money for the Red Cross. Spartanburg County residents contributed $130,000 in the ARC's spring 1944 fund drive, $34,000 over its quota. Even children participated. Four Aiken schoolgirls organized a dog show and netted $117 for the ARC.

South Carolinians gave their time to many organizations in addition to the Red Cross. The Travelers' Aid Society opened offices throughout the Palmetto State to attend to the needs of servicemen and their families. Spartanburg, for example, staffed four full-time volunteers and by August 1944 had aided 4,902 people. Local community efforts to support area servicemen also surfaced. Marion's Junior Chamber of Commerce collected enough money from town residents to purchase 550 cartons of cigarettes to send to soldiers from the county stationed overseas. Churches conducted special services for military personnel and members of the congregations invited soldiers and sailors into their homes for Sunday dinner. Schools held assemblies for students to promote patriotism, and students crafted checkerboards, stationery, crossword puzzles, and even furniture for the soldiers' use in local military recreation halls.

War and Race

In May 1942, in a personal letter to Major Corbett Carmichael, a native-born South Carolinian serving at Maxwell Army Air Base in Alabama, Governor R. M. Jefferies noted that "the race problem is becoming more and more serious in the State and I do not know what will be the final outcome." The governor's comment proved prophetic. Many South Carolinians viewed President Roosevelt's inclusion of African Americans in the New Deal, particularly his appointment of blacks to administrative posts, as evidence of FDR's plan to smash Jim Crow race segregation. The National Association for the Advancement of Colored People (NAACP) had also pressured the president into creating the Fair Employment Commission, which established something akin to present-day affirmative action. War industries throughout South Carolina were now required to employ black workers in the same jobs and at the same wages held by whites. Thousands of African Americans rushed to the better employment opportunities generated by war manufacturing demands. Also, the United States Army accepted African-Americans for pilot training, and the ranks of black officers in all arms of the service bulged as America entered World War II. With such advances, many white South Carolinians worried that African Americans would use the crisis of war to press their own civil rights agenda and ultimately destroy the longstanding system of segregation in the state. What surfaced between 1942 and 1945 was a visible "white backlash" against a perceived attack on white supremacy in South Carolina.

Much of the backlash was violent. In Spartanburg County in June 1942, 65-year-old Louis Nesbitt, a black employee of Turner Wholesale Company, was allegedly overheard telling friends that blacks should not fight "a white man's war." That evening, masked white men approached Nesbitt's home in Greer, abducted him, carried him to a remote location, and severely beat the elderly man. On August 8, a crowd of white men rampaged through Greenwood's business district slapping, punching, and beating all blacks they encountered. In Charleston on September 6, a car bearing North Carolina license plates and occupied by four African Americans innocently drove through the Dorchester community. Suspicious as ever of "outsiders," but particularly blacks, and swept by the pervading fear of black agitators for civil rights while the nation waged war, local whites gave chase and fired birdshot at the car's passengers, wounding all occupants.

Rumors filtered through the state of an impending race war. One hinted that African-American women were buying ice picks to use against whites during nighttime air-raid drills. Another claimed that blacks intended to designate one day each week as "bump day," during which African Americans on city streets would purposely collide with white pedestrians. The most popular rumor centered on "Eleanor Clubs," purportedly a South-wide movement among black domestic workers to walk off the job, leaving white women to tend to their own household chores, and possibly directing violence against their white employers. Word of all these allegations spread statewide, from Beaufort to Greenville, and so raised the specter among whites of a black rebellion in South Carolina.

To ensure public safety and reassure whites that African Americans were not plotting rebellion, Governor Jefferies instructed the State Law Enforcement Division (SLED) to survey the sale of weapons and ammunition in South Carolina to determine if any surge in gun purchases was evident. SLED's chief, S. J. Pratt, reported on September 10 that there appeared no unusual activity in the towns he checked, among them Gaffney, Florence, Winnsboro, Chester, and Bennettsville. White fears continued throughout the war years, but no rumor of a black conspiracy was ever confirmed.

To the contrary, South Carolina's black population enthusiastically embraced the war as their own, as Americans. Of the 200,000 South Carolinians in uniform, nearly one-third were African Americans. Thousands more African Americans secured jobs in defense plants, donated blood, bought war bonds, and volunteered for defense work. To be sure, within the civilian community, black wartime activities remained racially segregated. Thousands more emigrated from the state seeking high-paying jobs in the North and on the West Coast.

City Congestion and Wartime Economics

War required expanded production of ships at the Charleston Navy Yard and its neighboring Charleston Dry Dock Company; expansion required the employment of additional workers. As a result, thousands of men and women flocked to Charleston in search of high-paying jobs. The navy yard hired 6,000 new workers in 1941 and another 22,000 by summer 1943. Outside the naval facilities, another 72,000 people secured employment in the city and county. Many came from within South Carolina, many from outside the state. So attractive were the high-paying jobs, teenagers quit school to seek employment. In 1941, there were 100,000 children enrolled in junior and senior high schools statewide, and 11,149 South Carolina students received diplomas. In 1944, however, only 54,000 youngsters attended the state's secondary schools, and 9,700 graduated high school. Many of the children relocated with their parents to other states during the war, and older teens bailed out of school for military service. Most, however, left school for jobs. South Carolina enjoyed full employment and respectable wages for the first time in its lengthy history, but at what expense to the state?

Employment opportunities during the war raised the population of Charleston County 41 percent, and with that sudden growth came heightened demands for city and county services, along with a degree of wartime profiteering. Rents skyrocketed, and retail stores and marketplaces boosted prices. Cars and buses packed city streets. Bars, nightclubs, theaters, churches, restaurants, all were jammed with men and women, uniformed and civilian alike. Charleston was so overcrowded and expensive, and yet the earning potential so high, that some workers at the Charleston Navy Yard lived as much as 50 miles from the city and commuted daily to their jobs. Washington listed Charleston as one of the nation's eight most congested cities during the war years.

The war directly affected public school services. Statewide, teachers were in short supply. Many educators, both men and women, answered the nation's call and entered the armed forces. Others abandoned the profession, long noted for its sub-par pay and paltry benefits, for much better salaries in defense plants and private industry. In addition, South Carolina suffered a loss of teachers to nearby states; educators who wished to remain in the profession were promised a far better salary and benefits package in North Carolina and Georgia than the Palmetto State offered. In September 1941, white teachers earned $765 per year in contrast to the national average of $1,500. During the war, teacher salaries did rise, reaching $1,152 annually in 1945; still, the national average stood at $2,000 at war's end, with North Carolina at $1,600 and Florida at $1,700. African-American teachers continued to earn salaries far less than their white counterparts. Most schools compensated for the loss by increasing their class student-to-teacher ratios and hiring the untrained wives of naval officers and plant supervisors in the city. These "emergency teachers," however, seldom stayed in the classroom very long. The workload drained their energy, many found better-paying jobs outside the classroom, and others followed their husbands to naval postings or jobs elsewhere in the nation.

Not only did schools find it difficult to retain teachers and provide a reasonable student-to-teacher ratio, per-pupil expenditures proved dismally insufficient. In 1945, South Carolina provided $88 per year per white child and only $36 annually for each African-American child. In contrast, New York spent more than $200 annually on every child,

Must-See Sites: Patriot's Point Naval and Maritime Museum, Mt. Pleasant

In 1975, the aircraft carrier USS *Yorktown* was berthed in Charleston Harbor and in October opened as a public museum at Patriot's Point, located in Mt. Pleasant. Within a few years, the United States Navy destroyer USS *Laffey* and submarine *Clamagore* and the Coast Guard cutter *Ingham* were placed alongside Yorktown. Located on the carrier's hangar deck and on the flight deck is a large collection of warplanes dating from World War II to the present, among them the famed F4U Corsair, B-25 Mitchell, A-4 Skyhawk, F-4 Phantom, the F-14 Tomcat, and a variety of military and naval helicopters. Recently opened to visitors is the Medal of Honor Museum, which includes interactive exhibits highlighting the history of the award and honoring some of its army, navy, and air force recipients. Also housed at the Patriot's Point Museum is a replica of a Vietnam War naval support base that features a patrol boat used in the Mekong Delta, a Huey helicopter, and artifacts from the war. The Cold War Submarine Memorial nearby traces the role of America's navy from 1947 to 1989, paying particular tribute to the submarine fleet. Around the central plaza are seven educational stations and a full-sized replica of a Benjamin Franklin Class Fleet Ballistic Missile submarine. The Patriot's Point Naval and Maritime Museum is among the largest of its kind in the world.

Patriot's Point is open daily, except on Christmas Day. For more information, telephone (866) 831-1720 or visit www.patriotspoint.org.

regardless of race. The disparity in appropriations assured the continued inferiority of black schools and consequently the continued relegation of African Americans to the lowest paying jobs in the state. The unequal distribution of funds protected white supremacy, despite the wartime goals of freedom and equality espoused by Americans nationally.

Like Charleston, Columbia was swamped with a sudden population growth and confronted its own congestion, but the state capital's overcrowding was never as severe as the coastal city's. The overwhelming majority of new arrivals to the Columbia were soldiers, shipped to Fort Jackson for basic military training and quickly deployed to advanced training centers elsewhere in the United States or to overseas duty posts. Fort Jackson was more like a revolving door, Charleston more like a rest and refitting station. Civilian employment also rose in Columbia, but Columbia's available jobs were principally centered in construction and the service industries rather than defense production. Greenville and Spartanburg, each with moderately-sized military posts, followed the same pattern as Columbia.

Forty counties in South Carolina actually witnessed population decline during the war. Residents migrated to Charleston, Columbia, Greenville, and Spartanburg for job opportunities. Textile mills hummed 24 hours daily, supplying the armed forces with military wear and supplies. Concrete plants in the state shipped their product throughout the South for road construction projects and military base development, paper mills churned out millions of reams of paper, and plywood factories produced building material for military posts. Fishermen along the coast increased their haul of shrimp and crab for sale to both the armed forces and local civilian markets. Construction companies begged for laborers, and large farming operations never had enough hands to harvest the crops or pick the fruit. Many South Carolinians left the state entirely to shipbuilding plants, aircraft factories, and a variety of defense factories in states as far north as Michigan and west to California. At no point in South Carolina's history had in-migration or out-migration been so great as it was during World War II.

Overcrowded cities bred a serious problem—vice. Charleston, Columbia, and Greenville had the highest concentration of sailors and soldiers in the state, and in these communities gambling, drinking, and prostitution flourished during the war. Bars lined city streets, "juke joints" were numerous, and houses of prostitution increased in proportion to the number of servicemen stationed in the cities. Where these existed, so, too, did rising violent crime rates—servicemen swindled of their money, assaulted and robbed. The environment contributed to hundreds of fistfights nightly among service personnel and compelled police forces to hire more officers at the very time when qualified men were in short supply. A June 1942 article in *PM* magazine titled "Sailors Beware of Charleston, SC" described the city as the most corrupt and dangerous naval port in the nation. Sailors were targeted for exploitation, alcohol flowed too freely, "reefers" were too widely available, violence against servicemen entirely too frequent, and "entertaining women" far too numerous.

Indeed, infection rates for syphilis and gonorrhea staggered the imagination. Of every 1,000 men examined for military service in South Carolina in 1942, 156 were infected with a "social" disease. Statewide, estimates placed the civilian infection rate for syphilis at 140,000 and gonorrhea at 300,000 that year; rather than being reduced, by 1944 the number of civilians infected were 225,000 and 900,000 respectively. South Carolina ranked second in the nation in its level of infection in 1942, barely above Florida.

What worried the navy most was the incidence of venereal disease among sailors. No one was certain just how many prostitutes worked the city of Charleston, but most blamed these women rather than the men for the unbelievably high VD infection rate in the city and state. Admiral William Allen argued that in Charleston alone enough sailors each year were sidelined by syphilis to man an aircraft carrier and its smaller support ships. The disease, he said repeatedly, reduced the navy's fighting capability and consequently benefited the enemy.

Steps were taken beginning in 1942 to deal with venereal diseases. Admiral Allen declared 25 of the more notorious Charleston night spots off limits to sailors; within six months he added another eleven establishments to the list. Local businesses that served sailors quickly understood the point: either clean up their establishments or lose profits. The city, which had traditionally focused on the diagnosis and treatment of infected women and men, now concentrated on the enforcement of anti-prostitution laws. This accomplished little. Prior to Pearl Harbor, prostitution, though not legal, was tolerated and confined to a "red light district" where police and social workers could exert some influence over the trade. But wartime enforcement of the law only scattered the women and girls throughout the city, from dark alleys to dozens of hotels and bars. Many women became mobile, plying their trade in taxicabs. Adequate enforcement had hardly any chance of success.

In March 1942, the state legislature passed into law new penalties for violating the anti-prostitution statute. Fines for first offenders amounted to $100 and 30 days in jail; repeat offenders faced up to $1,000 and three years in prison. Even this failed to slow the business. Once convicted of their first offense, women simply changed their names and operated under a new identity. Moreover, the law only addressed the prostitutes; there was no prosecution of the men who solicited prostitution or those who profited from the trade. The State Board of Health did initiate treatment programs that detained infected women in abandoned Civilian Conservation Corps camps, such as the Pontiac Camp just east of Columbia. There, the women received medical care and education before being released back into the general population. The Board of Health, however, never received sufficient funds nor adequate facilities and equipment to make the program very effective. In addition, the board only quarantined women, not infected men.

Returning to Peace

As it became increasingly evident in late 1944 that an American victory in World War II was but months away, South Carolinians began to redirect their attention to domestic issues. That year, the United States Supreme Court ruled that African Americans could not be prevented from voting in the Democratic Party primary elections. South Carolina responded by passing 147 laws and a state constitutional amendment declaring political parties to be private organizations and therefore free of federal regulation. These measures effectively barred African Americans from primary elections, sidestepping the court's ruling.

To prepare for America's demobilization, the state's Research, Planning, and Development Board conducted a blind survey of 65,000 South Carolinians in uniform to determine their postwar intentions. Fully 90 percent indicated that they planned to return home to South Carolina. Most of these men expressed their desire to acquire a job in a field different from their prewar employment. And, African Americans openly stated their determination to press for equal rights and equal opportunity, both in quantity and quality.

The state planning board realized demobilization and the substantial reduction of defense production would likely spawn a postwar recession. In Washington, South Carolina's representatives and senators voted in favor of the Servicemen's Readjustment Act (GI Bill) in September, hoping its provisions would soften the economic and social blow that awaited the state once peace returned. The act's allotment of money for tuition, textbooks, and living costs while in school proved quite attractive to veterans. College enrollment jumped once the war ended; the University of South Carolina, for example, enrolled 2,244 in 1945 but 4,078 just three years later, the majority of whom were war veterans. Clemson experienced similar growth, as did private colleges from the coast to the mountains. The bill also granted low interest rate small business loans; thousands of veterans took advantage of the provision and formed their own businesses. The Servicemen's Readjustment Act further provided "no money down" home mortgages for veterans at a one percent interest rate. Combined, these measures cushioned the impact of demobilization in South Carolina. With so many veterans attending college and technical schools, many of those dismissed from their home front defense jobs at war's end were able to find other work; construction companies needed laborers to build more dormitories, classrooms, and homes. Farmers produced record crops to feed veterans and their new families. Retail stores hired thousands of displaced defense workers as the end of rationing unleashed a purchasing power based on wartime savings. Recession did descend on the state but not with the viciousness anticipated in 1944.

Returning veterans were also determined to effect political reforms. In the 1946 race for governor was a decorated airborne infantry war hero, J. Strom Thurmond. Thurmond publicly condemned the Old Guard control of South Carolina politics and called for a fundamental redirection in state affairs. He won the election and during his tenure in Columbia pushed through the General Assembly a number of reforms. Thurmond extended the school year from eight months to nine months and added a twelfth grade to high school. The poll tax was repealed, the State Port Authority was given sufficient funds to expand and modernize the port at Charleston, divorce was legalized, and aid was granted to dependent children under eighteen who remained in school. In addition, Thurmond took a bold stand in 1947 demanding the full prosecution of 21 white men who kidnapped and brutally murdered a black man who himself was accused of killing a white taxicab driver. The defendants were found not guilty, but the nation had witnessed a governor of a southern state defying the white majority's acceptance of lynching. African Americans applauded Governor Thurmond's courage.

World War II brought unparalleled prosperity to South Carolina. It stimulated industrial development, reinvigorated the old economic base, poured federal dollars into cities and towns, built airbases and highways, and brought outsiders into the state in record numbers, who themselves breathed new ideas into a state previously locked in its past. South Carolina in the wake of war stood at the proverbial crossroads—one path returning the state to its past and one leading in a new direction. Many wondered which path the state would follow once it readjusted fully to peace.

13

Joining the Union

War joined South Carolina to the rest of the nation. Federal dollars enlarged the state's infrastructure, the immigration of men and women from every corner of the United States diluted the power of antebellum values, and the Axis peril had given Sandlappers a common interest with the rest of the nation. With the return of peace, the Old Guard intended to restore prewar norms, but instead it found a people and a state at the proverbial crossroads of retrenchment and progress, pulled simultaneously in both directions. For the next 25 years South Carolinians stood at the "intersection" and grappled with a choice as pivotal as secession in 1860.

The Persistent Issues of Race and States' Rights

The United States Supreme Court's 1944 ruling that opened Democratic Party primary elections to African Americans was not well received in South Carolina. In the minds of many Sandlappers, it was a clear federal violation of states' rights. That year, the legislature convened, considered, and passed into law 147 bills to reshape party structure and elections. Collectively, the laws redefined the Democratic Party in the state as a private organization, it and its primary election process free of federal authority. White South Carolinians believed they had successfully sidestepped the federal government's interference in state matters.

But the legislature's move to secure white supremacy at the ballot box and so to retrench itself in prewar norms confronted a wall of opposition that had not existed before Pearl Harbor. The war had created opportunities for African Americans to an extent only imagined before 1941—jobs, federal protection in the workplace, equal work and pay in defense factories, educational programs, administrative positions in government, and movement into the officer corps in the armed forces. The very goals for which the United States had waged war—democracy and equality—were the goals African Americans were determined to acquire for themselves in the postwar period. They had defended the nation overseas and on the home front and were not about to remain second-class citizens. Within the black population, a determined spirit arose. In South Carolina alone, black membership in the National Association for the Advancement of Colored People (NAACP) rose from 800 in 1939 to 14,000 in 1948, ready to challenge in state and federal courts race segregation and undemocratic policies.

A segment of white society readily offered its support to African Americans in challenging retrenchment. More than 200,000 South Carolinians had served in the armed forces, and many took President Roosevelt's wartime goals to heart—freedom from fear and want, freedom of religion and speech, and the protection of democracy for all. In their encounters with men from diverse walks of life, religions, and ethnic groups, the state's white soldiers were exposed to ideas far different from those they had accepted before the war. Many witnessed black servicemen in action; others relied on the work of African Americans who kept supplies running to the front lines. Combat taught soldiers that a man's worth was determined by his courage, loyalty, and integrity and not by the color of his skin. The war left a profound imprint on many white veterans. Moreover, whites that remained on the home front themselves questioned the logic of defending democracy and freedom while concurrently depriving African Americans of both. Interracial conferences were held throughout much of the South during the war to address the status of African Americans in white society, and these attracted the attention and understanding of many whites. Books and articles printed in nationally distributed magazines championed the equality of all men, and Hollywood's wartime productions highlighted the interdependency of all Americans regardless of race, ethnicity, and religion. By war's end, white society had been inundated with the message of a new "Americanism," one that ideologically embraced all persons.

Must-See Sites: Greenville County Museum of Art, Greenville

This museum offers visitors a rich sampling of the very best in American art, with pieces from the colonial era to the present. Its Southern Collection is nationally respected, with work created by southern artists or focused on southern culture. The Andrew Wyeth Collection includes 32 paintings, representing every period of his career. The museum houses works by Georgia O'Keefe, Thomas Hart Benton, Andy Warhol, and Jasper Johns, among others. The museum is located at 420 College Street. For more information, call (864) 271-7570, email info@greenvillemuseum.org, or visit www.greenvillemuseum.org.

In summer 1947, opposition surfaced among many white South Carolinians to the legislature's efforts to protect the Democratic Party. Party officials in Richland and Marlboro Counties denounced the legislature's reactionary move. In Charleston, Judge J. Waties Waring struck down the party's new oath that required all voters to uphold racial segregation. Waring's move opened the polls to 35,000 black voters in the August 1948 primary elections. Within the Democratic Party itself and from the bench, the Old Guard confronted white opposition to retrenchment and the denial of wartime values to African Americans.

South Carolina's Democratic Party also found itself at odds with the national organization. President Harry S. Truman's special committee on race in 1948 issued its statement "To Secure These Rights," a lengthy denunciation of the second-class citizenship of black Americans and a long list of suggested federal actions to ameliorate the disparity between whites and blacks. Separately, the president desegregated the nation's armed forces. Truman advocated the full extension of equal rights to all Americans, regardless of race, as a fulfillment of the nation's constitutional obligation. Additionally, he understood that the votes of white, southern Democrats were no longer essential to the party's national success and consequently he was freed from bowing to their demands.

South Carolina's Old Guard viewed the president's direction as an attack on states' rights and Jim Crow segregation. In response, the southern wing of the Democratic Party bolted from the 1948 national convention, reassembled in Birmingham, formed the States' Rights Democratic Party (Dixiecrats), and nominated South Carolina's Governor Strom Thurmond as the party's presidential contender. Thurmond repeatedly voiced the dominant sentiment of white Southerners and white South Carolinians—opposition to direct federal intervention into the affairs of individual states, including matters regarding race and civil rights. In November, Thurmond won 1 million votes and 39 Electoral College votes from the South; he carried all but two counties in South Carolina.

Retrenchment was especially virulent in rural South Carolina. In rural Clarendon County, the school system provided bus service only to white children, although there were nearly three times as many black youngsters enrolled in the county's schools. African-American children were forced to walk miles to the nearest racially segregated schoolhouse, facilities that were heated with woodstoves and had no indoor plumbing or electric lights. The white-controlled school board consistently rebuffed all requests by the black community for better school buildings and for school bus service, often in the harshest and most derogatory terms. African Americans in one remote district of Clarendon County met with NAACP attorney Thurgood Marshall in Columbia and, on December 20, 1950 (exactly 90 years to the day after South Carolina had seceded from the Union), filed suit against the school district in *Briggs v. Elliott*. The case intended a direct attack on the constitutionality of Jim Crow, which had been sanctioned by the United States Supreme Court in *Plessy v. Ferguson* (1896), and was the first challenge of school segregation in the twentieth-century South. In Charleston's federal district court in May 1951, the panel of three judges ruled 2–1 against the plaintiffs but in their ruling stated clearly that race segregation has never and would never provide equality. Marshall appealed the court's decision to the United States Supreme Court, adding it to four other pending cases under the banner *Brown v. the Board of Education of Topeka, Kansas*.

As the court deliberated over the next two years, South Carolina moved to improve its national image on race and give evidence that segregated schools could, indeed, be equal. James Byrnes, former United States senator, New Dealer, and White House insider under FDR, was elected in 1950 as the state's new governor, Thurmond being elected to the Senate where he would remain for the next 50 years. Byrnes, like his predecessor, championed states' rights, but he encouraged the legislature to equalize the quality of education in the state's segregated schools. The General Assembly responded favorably, raising the state's sales tax rate to cover the cost of improvements in public schools. Over the following five years, South Carolina appropriated $124 million to the school budget, two-thirds of which was spent on black schools.

In May 1954, the Supreme Court issued its ruling in the *Brown* case, stating that racially segregated schools did not provide equal opportunity and calling for desegregation. South Carolina was enraged by the court's decision. Throughout the state, retrenchment-oriented whites fumed that the ruling amounted to a real threat to state sovereignty and insisted South Carolina would not obey the court. Governor Byrnes himself called on the state to commit itself to total resistance against the intrusion of federal authority inside the Palmetto State, and local citizens' councils held public rallies and pressured all those who wished to or who attempted to implement the *Brown* decision in South Carolina. In May 1955, on the anniversary of its historic, landmark ruling, the court issued a follow-up statement commonly referred to as *Brown II* that demanded the desegregation of public schools "with all deliberate speed." The court's statement only fueled the rage of South Carolinians and led the legislature to repeal the state's compulsory school attendance law, as a means of assuring white parents that their children would not have to attend classes with black youngsters. A referendum was also put before voters to change the state constitution's requirement that a public school system be provided; fortunately, the

South Carolina Tobacco,

Pounds Grown (1000s)

1950	1955	1960	1965
150,480	197,200	147,600	134,808

Cents per Pound

54.3	54.5	61.5	53.3

Source: Eldred E. Prince, Jr. *Long Green: The Rise and Fall of Tobacco in South Carolina* (Athens: University of Georgia Press, 2000), pp. 203–204.

referendum failed. Senator Strom Thurmond in March 1956 co-authored the "Declaration of Southern Principles" (also known as the Southern Manifesto), which viciously attacked the audacity of the court in declaring segregated schools unconstitutional and called on southern states to prevent racial integration using any legal means necessary. One hundred and one southern congressmen and senators signed the document. Thurmond also warned that he and his southern colleagues would adamantly oppose any civil rights bill that came to the Senate floor.

Thurmond, Byrnes, and white legislators in the General Assembly represented the old South Carolina; many World War II veterans, the NAACP, and newcomers to the state championed a new direction. Private institutions began to desegregate voluntarily and peacefully, among the largest the Lutheran Theological Seminary in Columbia in 1954. The yearly statewide conference of Methodists denounced the state's reactionary position, and from their pulpits many white ministers of many denominations advocated racial equality. The South Carolina Christian Action Council, an interdenominational organization, openly associated racial equality with biblical teachings and decried the unchristian behavior of reactionary white Carolinians. In 1957 Congress passed a civil rights bill into law over South Carolina's official objection, but the measure received the endorsement of the progressive element within the state.

Postwar Production and Value

1975	1980	1985	1990
189,000	125,450	98,900	109,905
99.5	139.5	172.7	158.6

The Civil Rights Movement was in full stride by 1960, led by the NAACP and the Southern Christian Leadership Conference (SCLC). While the NAACP pressed for African-American equality through the courts, the SCLC employed peaceful public demonstrations based on a prescription first advocated by India's Mahatma Gandhi—"passive resistance." Given a demonstration of its effectiveness in a lunch-counter sit-in in Greensboro, North Carolina in February 1960, African Americans across South Carolina embraced the tactic. Peaceful protests and sit-ins were held in Greenville, Spartanburg, Columbia, Rock Hill, Charleston, and a dozen other communities and continued for the next ten years wherever African Americans confronted race segregation and a denial of their civil rights. Police and state troopers were expected to maintain order; however, in some communities, law-enforcement officers unleashed tear gas, fire hoses, and clubs on marchers and jailed hundreds more in an effort to break up the rallies. Occasionally, police looked the other way while white gangs tore into black demonstrators.

So much violence was directed against African Americans engaged in passive resistance that South Carolina's business community worried that outside investments might vanish in those cities and towns hardest hit. Prominent business and civic leaders of Greenville met in 1961 and agreed that the violence and general confrontation had to cease. In the name of business growth and prosperity, they called on city residents to accept desegregation. Given their status and influence in the community, the Chamber of Commerce in 1962 founded a biracial committee to coordinate desegregation of Greenville and to convince the public to accept the new direction. The state legislature, however, was not so accommodating. That year, the General Assembly gave legal sanction to the flying of the Confederate battle flag on the statehouse dome as a visible symbol of South Carolina's position on states' rights.

In conflict with the legislature's move, the chief executive clearly understood the national current on the race issue. By proclamation in January 1963, out-going Governor Ernest "Fritz" Hollings announced his acceptance of racial integration as he turned the executive branch over to Donald S. Russell, and Governor Russell endorsed Hollings' pronouncement, inviting everyone, of all races, to his inaugural address and to the barbeque that followed at the governor's mansion. From the executive mansion, South Carolina relinquished its heritage of segregation and white supremacy, but long-cherished values were not yet dead in the general population. Jim Crow still governed the hearts and minds of many private citizens, and local ordinances requiring racial segregation were still enforced.

In June 1963, the NAACP announced plans for demonstrations in key cities statewide unless Jim Crow was buried on the local level. The sluggish response of city councils resulted in a series of demonstrations that summer, mostly in Columbia. But by year's end, the capital city had forced local merchants to remove their "whites only" signs and serve black customers. Change occurred more quickly in Rock Hill, Florence, and Spartanburg, and numerous smaller communities from coast to mountains, although many residents in these towns felt coerced into desegregation by Washington and "outsiders" who had relocated to the state.

Historian Walter Edgar argues that the rate of positive change in race relations in South Carolina was more rapid than in most southern states and offers several explanations. First, state government insisted on maintaining law and order and promised stern punishment to persons of either race who violated state or local law. Stability and order were values long cherished by South Carolinians. They overwhelmingly opposed mob action as a tool to fight racial integration, just as they had condemned Ku Klux Klan violence some 40 years earlier. Second, African Americans in South Carolina were more willing to work within the existing legal system and business community than African Americans in many other states. They were integral members of their towns communities, with much to lose should they advocate or participate in violent demonstrations.

Not specifically noted by Edgar but equally important, much of South Carolina's economic structure required the interaction of whites and blacks; without a cooperative spirit, the already shaky economy might weaken further. It was the salvation of the city's business community and local prosperity that prompted the Greenville's Chamber of Commerce to act favorably on desegregation. They worried that without a peaceful environment economic growth in the county would vanish. Toward that end, textile mills began hiring African-American employees, as did construction companies, restaurants, and most other businesses that had been exclusively white before 1962. In addition, the wartime emigration of African Americans continued, with fully 400,000 blacks exiting the state between 1945 and 1970. Peaceful coexistence was required to retard the out-flow of the state's labor force; if that meant desegregation, then such would have to become state policy.

Universities also began to desegregate at about the same time as the business sector. After winning a favorable decision in the Fourth Circuit Court of Appeals in January 1963, Harvey Gantt was admitted to Clemson University and began his post-secondary academic career that same month. Gantt confronted little overt animosity from his fellow students; he graduated four years later and began a distinguished career in politics that led to his election as mayor of Charlotte, North Carolina in 1984. In September, the University of South Carolina also opened its doors to black students, and by spring 1965 all public colleges and half of the private universities admitted students of all races.

Public schools, however, deliberately moved more slowly toward racial integration. A few black children enrolled in white public schools in 1963, but they faced a far more serious challenge than Gantt at Clemson. Thousands of white parents were so determined not to have their children attend schools with black students that they withdrew their youngsters from public school and enrolled them in private academies. More than 200 private schools, most church-based, were founded between 1964 and 1970, and additional facilities continued to be established well into the 1980s. By 1975, nearly eight percent of all white children in the state attended private school. Parents who could not afford the cost of private school tuition instead battled local public school districts and pursued legal avenues to prevent or minimize desegregation. As late as 1969, only 12 of the state's 93 school districts had integrated. Change came slowly. By the mid-1970s, all school districts in South Carolina were in "legal compliance" with school desegregation laws. Federal court decisions rendered more than ten years after the *Brown* case compelled desegregation, in the 1960s ordering the "busing" of African-American children to white schools to achieve racial balance. This was expanded with the 1972 Supreme Court ruling in *Swann v. the Board of Education* (Charlotte, North Carolina), which ordered the busing of white students into previously all-black schools, and the court's decision was applied across the South. Moreover, federal courts beginning in the mid-1960s also issued rulings that collapsed most Jim Crow statutes, opening previously white neighborhoods to African-American residency. In so doing, communities throughout the South, including those in South Carolina, were desegregated, and this permitted racial integration of neighborhood schools. The few rural schools that remained segregated in the Palmetto State in the 1990s were by decade's end consolidated by order of the state legislature. The long history of schools racially segregated by law ended as the twenty-first century began.

African-American voting opportunities in South Carolina also expanded in the 1960s with passage of the Voting Rights Act of 1965. Protected by federal law, voter registration soared from 58,000 in 1958 to 220,000 in 1970. African Americans were elected from within the Democratic Party to attend the national convention in 1968, and two years later three African Americans were elected to the state's General Assembly, the first African Americans

Must-See Sites: Darlington Raceway

The National Association for Stock Car Auto Racing (NASCAR) was founded in 1949, and on Labor Day 1950 the Darlington Raceway (Darlington, South Carolina) hosted its first stock car race, the "Southern 500." Within ten years, the Southern 500 drew 50,000 spectators annually. "Little Joe" Weatherly emerged as a popular driver among race fans, his antics on and off the track earning him the title "Clown Prince of Stock Car Racing." His victories at Darlington in 1960 and 1963 only endeared him more to South Carolinians, but in 1964 he crashed into the track wall at Riverside, California and died before reaching a hospital. In memory of him, the Darlington Raceway opened the Joe Weatherly Stock Car Museum and Hall of Fame in May 1965. The museum houses the world's largest collection of stock cars and represents 60 years of the sport. Richard Petty's 1967 Plymouth and Darrell Waltrip's 1991 Chevy sit prominently among them. A Hall of Fame is also located in the museum, honoring the drivers and the sport with photos, memorabilia, and exhibits.

The museum and gift shop are open daily. A small admission fee is required. Visit www.darlingtonrace.com/track_info/museum for more information.

to sit in the state legislature in the twentieth century.

South Carolina officially pulled the sheet over Jim Crow and commenced desegregation of all public facilities. The state was changing its position on race segregation and equal rights for African Americans, and in the process South Carolina's Democratic Party was gravitating toward the ideals of the national organization. Moderation within the state's dominant party, however, spawned a political realignment. Democrats in the 1960s increasingly represented a spirit entirely too liberal for many white South Carolinians. President Lyndon Johnson's Great Society funneled billions of dollars into human entitlement programs, public education, medical care, road construction, and a host of other domestic arenas in his bid to raise the standard of living, eradicate poverty, and allow America to bring the blessings of its wealth to all segments of the population. Historians typically ascribe to LBJ a personal desire to "out-Roosevelt Roosevelt," to make the New Deal pale in comparison to the Great Society. To accomplish his goals, Johnson's program erected an extensive and complex web of federal agencies and bureaus, and it infused each state with a mind-numbing body of new laws that touched virtually every thread of the social fabric. For good or for ill, with each Great Society program and with every federal dollar spent, state autonomy withered a little more.

In September 1964 Senator Strom Thurmond appeared on statewide television to announce his intention to switch his party affiliation from Democrat to Republican. He condemned Johnson's open assault on states' rights and blasted Washington's apparent determination to enlarge the authority of the national government at the expense of state sovereignty. Thurmond pointed to Johnson's hand in nationalizing the civil rights issue, but race was only one of many examples of LBJ's efforts to subject the state to the will of Washington. He found in the post–World War II Republican Party what amounted to the values of the old Democratic Party—strict limits on federal authority in the individual states, fiscal conservatism, and local preference. In November, Thurmond led South Carolina into the Republican camp, carrying the state for Barry Goldwater. Only four years earlier South Carolina had supported John F. Kennedy.

Thurmond's abandonment to the Republican Party was the most visible manifestation of South Carolina's disaffection with the Democratic Party since he led the South in the Dixiecrat movement almost twenty years earlier. In 1968, the state solidly backed Richard M. Nixon's bid for the White House, and in 1974 James Edwards of Mount Pleasant became the state's first Republican governor since Reconstruction and the first to be elected in the entire South.

The Palmetto State's Democratic Party continued to place its members in the legislature and in the governor's mansion through the last quarter of the twentieth century, but the Republican Party's hold grew tighter during those 25 years. In presidential elections, the state consistently favored Republican candidates, giving its electoral votes to Ronald Reagan, George Herbert Walker Bush, and George Walker Bush. South Carolina supported the shrinkage of federal programs in the state, reduced federal taxes, extensive reform of federal welfare programs, retrenchment from affirmative action, and less control over public schools. Interestingly, South Carolina's Republicans nonetheless considered sacred many of the federal policies Johnson and his predecessors inaugurated. Numerous human services programs have remained in place, as has the state's willingness to accept federal aid for public schools and universities, highway construction, and civil rights.

Educational Programs Since 1968

In 1968, the legislature approved a one-cent hike in the state sales tax with the revenue earmarked for public school improvement. A chief priority was the establishment of a statewide kindergarten program. Funding, however, aided the wealthier school districts, as appropriations were directly connected to each county's tax base. In short, school districts with small tax bases received very little money from Columbia.

Not until 1977 did the General Assembly pursue a substantive reform agenda. That year, the legislature passed the Education Finance Act (EFA), which allocated more funding for poor districts than for wealthier districts. It also established the Basic Skills Assessment Act (BSA), which identified the essential academic knowledge necessary for graduation and a testing procedure that stretched across a child's twelve years in school to determine periodically the child's progress and areas for remedial training. The state's effort was largely the product of public pressure by South Carolina's citizens, who demanded a more equitable educational program for all residents and an improvement in the quality of instruction for their children. The two programs garnered limited benefit; the state's school systems still lagged far behind the rest of the nation's going into the 1980s, South Carolina typically ranking near the bottom of all 50 states in quality of education, statewide literacy level, and high-school graduation rates.

Crowd standing before the main building of Claflin University, Orangeburg, 1899

The Orangeburg Massacre

Jim Crow race segregation and state restrictions on African-American voting remained in force across most of South Carolina well into the 1960s, contrary to a litany of federal laws and US Supreme Court decisions. On the evening of February 6, 1968, students from the all-black South Carolina State University and Clalfin College, both located in Orangeburg, gathered at the city's All Star Bowling Alley to protest that night spot's preservation of Jim Crow. Tempers rose among the students and among the bowling alley's white staff and patrons, but the local police and highway patrol maintained a tenuous peace. The scene was repeated the following night, again without any serious incident, although fifteen students were arrested in a move to break up the demonstration.

Rather than assemble once more in front of the bowling alley on February 8, approximately 200 students chose to rally on the South Carolina State campus and voice their opposition to race segregation and the racism that pervaded South Carolina society. Given the recent flurry of campus riots nationwide, the state highway patrol was ordered to South Carolina State to ensure order. Students nonetheless ignited a bonfire, and when one highway patrolman moved to put out the fire, he was struck with a board. Pandemonium ensued. A highway patrolman drew his pistol and fired one shot into the air, hoping the sound would grab everyone's attention and return calm to the grounds, but other officers assumed the shot was fired in self-defense. They pulled their weapons and fired indiscriminately into the crowd of students, killing three and wounding twenty-seven.

The Orangeburg Massacre, as it was soon dubbed by African Americans and sympathetic whites, garnered national and international attention. Governor Robert E. McNair held a press conference the next day and said that the event at SC State was "one of the saddest days in the history of South Carolina," but he also ascribed the turmoil on campus and at the nearby bowling alley to "outside agitators." Investigations followed. Nine officers were charged with using excessive force, not murder or manslaughter, and each was ultimately acquitted. Leaders of the demonstrations were also charged with inciting the "riot" that preceded the shootings. One student, Cleveland Sellers, was convicted and imprisoned for seven months. Although he was, indeed, a member of the Student Nonviolent Coordinating Committee (SNCC), he was not an "outside agitator" and no such persons were ever identified by thc state.

Anger simmered for years in the state's African-American community, and South Carolina State University students marked the event annually with rallies on campus. In 1993, an investigation conducted by South Carolina's Probation, Pardon, and Parole Board determined that there was no merit to the charges that earlier led to Sellers's conviction, and board members voted unanimously to pardon him. Cleveland Sellers is now director of African-American studies at the University of South Carolina. Ten years later, in 2003, Governor Mark Sanford issued a formal apology for the state's role in the Orangeburg Massacre, the first governor to do so. In March 2007 the Federal Bureau of Investigation announced that the Orangeburg case would be one of about 100 it intended to re-examine. The matter became one of national interest when South Carolina State University hosted the Democratic Party presidential debate the following month. To the dismay of many in South Carolina and nationally, the FBI in November decided against re-opening the case; doing so, said a spokesman, would most certainly result in double jeopardy for at least one of the nine officers tried and acquitted in 1968.

With such a dismal educational system statewide, the out-migration of South Carolinians continued into the 1980s. In addition, international and national corporations proved hesitant to expand into a state well known throughout America for its poor academic standing. In an attempt to elevate the Palmetto State, Governor Richard Riley in 1984 signed the Education Improvement Act, which once more raised the state's sales tax by one penny but also married state funding to student performance on standardized tests, for the first time holding schools accountable for their students' progress. Appropriations from the General Assembly also provided for classroom computers, expansion of library services, a smaller student-to-teacher ratio, and the construction of additional schools. South Carolina aggressively pursued reform of its public schools and received national acclaim for its commitment to student progress.

Funding was seen as a critical first step toward true reform in the state's educational programs, but Riley, his successors, state legislators, the business community, and parents all wanted more. In the 1990s, the state raised its certification criteria for those who wished to become classroom teachers. Those seeking certification to teach on the secondary level (junior high and senior high) faced a far more demanding training program. In addition to earning a degree in education, prospective teachers were also required to complete a degree program in an academic discipline. Students who planned to become high-school history teachers, for example, had to earn a degree in education and a separate degree in history; before the criteria changed, a student only needed to pass three college history courses to become a certified teacher in the field. The state also opened specialized centers for secondary students, offering vocational programs and in-depth work in the arts. High-school curricula changes were implemented, creating for youngsters programs of study that either prepared them for college or the post-high-school labor market. Statewide, in the 1990s nearly 55 percent of all graduating students enrolled in college, the drop-out rate fell slightly, and standardized test scores rose significantly.

Between 1950 and 1975, the General Assembly also chartered and funded technical colleges statewide. Schools such as Horry-Georgetown and Florence-Darlington Technical Colleges received adequate appropriations to train students in specific career programs and prepare others for transfer to four-year colleges. Students were able to pursue two-year courses of study in the culinary arts, auto mechanics, air conditioning, graphic design, golf-course management, nursing, and a wide range of other career programs. The schools also tended to the needs of adults already in the work force, offering certification programs, skills enhancement, and even high-school diplomas.

But the state's colleges and universities reaped few benefits from education reform efforts and remained woefully underfunded. Salaries for professors were seven to ten percent below the national average and three to five percent below the average for southern universities. Young assistant professors fresh out of their doctoral programs frequently took positions in South Carolina with the intention of getting collegiate-level teaching experience and establishing themselves as published scholars before securing a more permanent teaching assignment at an institution outside of South Carolina where pay was much better. The state found it very difficult to attract and retain faculty from prominent universities outside of South Carolina; those who did stay in the state usually remained for reasons other than pay. Academic programs were also inadequately financed, and as a result the state's universities never claimed high positions on national rankings. Even the "research universities"—Clemson, USC, and the Medical College of South Carolina—faced limited funding from the legislature, generally receiving less than half their budgets from the General Assembly and depending on donations, grants, and business connections for the remainder. Despite the shortfall of funds, the commitment of faculty in many academic disciplines and administrators clever enough to locate supplemental funds together carved out positions of respect for their universities. Clemson's agricultural studies program is today among the best in the South, and the Medical University is respected regionally. Even smaller universities developed regional reputations, among them Coastal Carolina University in Conway–Myrtle Beach, which boasts a regionally respected marine science program and a department of history with a record of publication uncommon for institutions its size. Much work remains, but progress continues. In 2001, voters approved a state lottery with proceeds expressly delegated to public schools and higher education. Lottery proceeds have translated into instate college scholarships for most academically qualified students, and student enrollment is rising. Salaries are slowly rising, and the state's smaller universities attract faculty from nationally prominent graduate schools. Academic programs are expanding, research opportunities increasing, and technological services growing.

Postwar Economic Patterns

World War II stimulated unparalleled economic growth in South Carolina, and much progress continued once peace was restored. Eleven thousand miles of paved roads covered the state in 1950, nearly three times more than had existed just before Pearl Harbor. The expansion of electrical services and telephone lines, construction of new bridges, and port development all proceeded after the war. The state funded the building of hospitals and clinics, technical colleges opened to train workers in modern job skills, radio stations proliferated, and television broadcasting came to South Carolina. Auto sales increased, as did home building. Corporate profits, state revenue, and personal savings that had spiraled upward during the war were now unleashed on the state, creating business growth and raising income.

Agriculture was also changing. Mechanized farming, which had hardly existed in the Palmetto State before 1940, rooted itself during and after the war. Wartime profits allowed farmers to purchase tractors, harvesters, combines, reapers, and other equipment, reducing labor costs and production times and permitting farmers to cultivate greater expanses of land affordably. What appeared to many as a threat to the agrarian base of South Carolina was, in fact, a positive development. The wartime movement of Sandlappers from the land persisted after the war with 150,000 more farmers and farm laborers abandoning farms for the state's leading urban centers, Greenville, Columbia, and Charleston. Sharecroppers, day laborers, and owners of small farms with limited income were essentially "tractored off the land," and those farmers who could afford modern equipment soon purchased the property they had once cultivated. The pattern proved commonplace across the state; by the mid-1970s there were only 32,000 farms in South Carolina in contrast to 148,000 at war's end, but farms were nearly three times larger than they had been in 1945 and more profitable.

Cotton was no longer the principal cash crop. Falling market prices, the development of synthetic fibers, and rising production rates in India, Latin America, and Asia all contributed to cotton's demise not only in South Carolina but across the South following the war. In the Palmetto State alone, cotton production plummeted 75 percent between 1945 and 1975.

In the 1940s, tobacco replaced the one-time white gold as South Carolina's agricultural king. Tobacco production and value rose and fell with the nation's economy between 1920 and 1940, but the war unleashed an almost unquenchable demand for the plant. Most tobacco was manufactured into cigarettes, and by 1944 nearly one-half of all cigarettes were earmarked for shipment to servicemen deployed overseas. Civilians and servicemen on the home front confronted limited wartime rationing and, as a result, had reasonable access to cigarettes. Plentiful and affordable, the product sold quite well. Production soared during the war, South Carolina's yield rising from 92 million pounds in 1942 to 172 million pounds in 1946 with a doubling of market value.

Throughout the 1950s and early 1960s, tobacco reigned supreme in South Carolina's fields. A downward turn, however, appeared in mid-decade. In 1964 the United States Surgeon General's Office issued its first health warning to smokers, stating in no uncertain terms that cigarettes could cause a variety of illnesses, chief among them lung cancer. The federal government ordered manufacturers to print the warning on each pack of cigarettes, and commenced a campaign to encourage Americans to stop consuming tobacco. In addition, a series of lawsuits filed against the major producers of cigarettes in the 1980s and 1990s resulted in hundreds of millions of dollars in cash awards to individual smokers who contracted lung cancer and to state governments to cover their costs in caring for uninsured smokers and in supplementing medical insurance providers. The number of smokers in the United States plummeted, with only 25 percent of all adults continuing the habit in 2008. The sharp decline in demand and the subsequent drop in market values for the crop hit tobacco farmers in the Palmetto State hard. By 1991, only nine percent of South Carolina's croplands were covered in tobacco, and two years later production had fallen to 1937 levels. At present, the state's farmers have not identified another major cash crop. Many have shifted to soybeans, some to wheat, and others to peaches and strawberries; nonetheless, there remains no single plant cultivated in South Carolina that promises the same level of prosperity that tobacco and cotton previously provided.

Image kindly provided by UNC at Chapel Hll

Pat Conroy

Although he was born in Atlanta, Georgia, South Carolina calls Pat Conroy one of its own most brilliant writers of fiction. His stories live in the lush marshlands of the Carolina Lowcountry, where images of modernity are set against the background of the region's natural beauty. His principal characters are "outsiders" living in the midst of a people few understand unless native to the Palmetto State. Indeed, his novels reveal the persistent contradictions of a people and region with one finger hooked on the contemporary world and the other four tenaciously clutching the past.

Born in 1945, Pat Conroy was the oldest of seven children. His father, a career military officer, demanded excellence from all his sons and daughters, but being the eldest child placed additional responsibilities on Pat and shaped much of his perspective toward authority and self. A military family, the Conroys moved frequently; Pat attended eleven schools in twelve years, including several years in the Lowcountry. After graduating high school, Pat attended the Citadel in Charleston, where he was captain of the basketball team and found literature a welcome major. Before graduating, he wrote and published his first book, *The Boo*, which was a personal tribute to one of his instructors.

He taught English in the Beaufort public schools for a short time and married a young widow with two children. Whether he found the school system unsatisfying or the school was displeased with him is unclear, but probably a bit of both caused his departure from Beaufort to teach poor children in a one-room school on Daufuskie Island just off the South Carolina mainland. Although he found the position rewarding and loved working with the youngsters, his views regarding teaching and discipline conflicted sharply with the rigid and traditional perspective of the school's administrator. After one year on the island, Conroy was dismissed. His 1972 novel *The Water is Wide* was largely based on his experiences on Daufuskie Island and won him recognition from the National Educational Association. The book became the film *Conrack*, starring Jon Voight.

Four years later Conroy published his novel *The Great Santini*, a largely autobiographical story inspired by his rollercoaster relationship with his abusive father. Writing the novel nearly devastated him emotionally and directly contributed to his own divorce and that of his parents.

The Lords of Discipline (1980) was set in the halls and barracks of the Citadel. Conroy's years as a student at South Carolina's military college brought him in direct, personal contact with overt, unbridled racism; a level of sexism that exceeded his understanding; and an intensely, brutally abusive system of discipline quietly condoned by school officials despite their public stance against "hazing." *The Lords of Discipline* was an exposé of the Citadel comparable to the works of early twentieth-century muckrakers, whose literature often awakened the general public to inhumanity and compelled a modicum of reform. Much of the sexism Conroy described in his 1980 book remained as virulent as ever and surfaced in the national news media when women first enrolled in the college in the mid-1990s.

Pat remarried and moved to Rome, where he commenced writing *The Prince of Tides* (1986), which would become his most successful published work and bring him international acclaim. *Beach Music* (1996) tracks a young American who relocates to Rome hoping the new surroundings will ease the painful memory of his wife's suicide in South Carolina and be a suitable place to rear his young daughter. It slips back and forth between his life in Italy, memories of the Vietnam War, his years in the Palmetto State, and an understanding of the Nazi Holocaust he acquires while in Europe. The primary character returns to his home in South Carolina to be with his dying mother and there has to deal with the memories of betrayal, parental abuse, and sibling rivalries. It encompasses much of his own life—family conflict, separation, failed relationships, and the inner quest for personal understanding.

Conroy maintains a residence in South Carolina and has a home on the West Coast as well. He continues to write, and the Palmetto State honors him as a "native son."

Textile manufacturing continued to prosper in the postwar years, mills supplying their goods to domestic buyers and to foreign markets in Europe and Asia. By the early 1970s, however, the industry had reached it peak and commenced its decline into near oblivion. New technology replaced much of the workforce, driving unemployed workers into the cities or to other states in search of jobs. As in the displacement of cotton cultivation, the shift to synthetic fibers in the manufacturing of garments also reduced the need for standard milling operations. Perhaps most central in the industry's decline was the concurrent spread of textile production into Asia and Latin America. Labor costs were far lower than in the United States and workers more abundant. Import duties on textile goods entering the United States were also low, a trade-off willingly accepted by Congress in order to stimulate foreign importation of American manufactured products. And in the 1970s, labor unions moved into the larger textile firms and required mill owners to pay higher wages and provide benefits packages, which resulted in a decrease in company profits and increased prices for finished goods, and ultimately provided an additional incentive for companies to outsource to countries without organized workforces. By the 1990s, textile mills that had once dominated the upcountry and supported the state's economy closed their doors.

The failure of cotton, tobacco, and textile manufacturing fractured the state's economy, and in the 1970s South Carolina's future seemed uncertain. Civic and business leaders in the state, however, recognized the pattern early enough to begin cultivating new sources of income for Sandlappers. Together they launched aggressive campaigns to lure business and capital from foreign countries and northern states. In the early 1960s, the largest single recipient of West Germany's overseas investments was South Carolina. Michelin Tire Company, a French corporation, placed its United States headquarters in Greenville. Most European investors, and eventually Asian investors, focused their attention in the upstate region, home to the state's textile industry and wartime manufacturing concerns. Two dozen foreign companies conducted business in Spartanburg alone by the early 1970s, and Greenville and Gaffney also drew significant investments from European corporations. The pattern continued, and in the late 1980s and early 1990s, Honda and BMW both established production plants in South Carolina. In 1995, foreign capital investment in the state totaled $2 billion, nearly one-third of the total investments placed in South Carolina companies.

Northern companies likewise invested in the Palmetto State, opening branch operations, purchasing existing South Carolina corporations, and in some cases actually relocating their firms to the state. Especially aggressive were banks; First Union Bank and Nationsbank, both based in Charlotte, North Carolina, and Wachovia Bank of Winston-Salem, North Carolina incorporated the larger financial institutions of South Carolina into their ranks. Northern newspapers, construction companies, and insurance corporations also acquired financial control over many South Carolina businesses.

Both foreign companies and American corporations recognized certain features conducive to business growth in the state. Corporations were attracted by the fact that wages in South Carolina were among the lowest in the nation, and the General Assembly in the mid-1950s passed a "right-to-work" law that substantially weakened unionization efforts. Antagonism directed against labor unions by state government and management clearly made South Carolina attractive to outside investors and companies contemplating relocation.

Business expansion may have eliminated many longstanding industries in the state, but it also brought thousands of jobs into South Carolina and, in time, higher wages and salaries. Although the corporate tax rate remained low, South Carolina's firms prospered and supplied the state with a revenue windfall necessary for its further modernization. The growth also transformed South Carolina from an agricultural state to an industrial one, a process completed in the 1980s.

Another industry that mushroomed after World War II was tourism. In the late 1950s, Myrtle Beach civic and business leaders were convinced the community's economic survival depended on a lively tourist trade and made a conscious effort to lure visitors to the coast. A pavilion was erected on the beach, replete with a Ferris

Hurricanes Strike the Palmetto State

As storms draw westward from Africa across the Atlantic Ocean in late summer and early autumn, they frequently evolve into tropical depressions and hurricanes. Water current, wind direction, and the movement of weather fronts combine to set a hurricane's course; water warmth determines its strength. Hurricanes were uncommon along the European coast and, consequently, colonists on the North American shore rarely recognized the signs of impending disaster or understood the destruction the storms could bring.

They learned quickly. Two major hurricanes slammed into the South Carolina coast within two weeks in September 1752. These storms proved particularly threatening to Lowcountry rice producers, writes Matthew Mulcahy in "Hurricane Season in the Colonies" (*Business History Review*, 20 June 2005). Indeed, the rice harvest following the 1752 hurricanes was nearly worthless. Rice exports fell more than 50 percent, bottoming out at 37,000 barrels. These same hurricanes also ravaged wharves, warehouses, and the entire commercial district of Charleston and destroyed homes and other structures miles inland.

The destruction caused by these storms and those that smashed into the South Carolina coast well into the twentieth century was made worse because the storms could not be predicted accurately. Technological advances made during World War II, however, gave hope to coastal residents. New meteorological equipment and more powerful aircraft were combined to permit "Hurricane Hunters" to fly into a storm's eye and there measure wind speed, barometric pressure, and water temperature. This information was paired with the movement of known fronts and air masses and other forces that could affect the course and power of a hurricane. Still, much more was needed. On October 15, 1954, Hurricane Hazel crashed onto the South Carolina–North Carolina border, roughly in the area of Little River, South Carolina and only a few miles north of Myrtle Beach. Hazel, a Category 4 storm, generated an 18-foot storm surge that flooded much of the area, and winds that ranged from 130 to 150 miles per hour. Hazel plowed north along the coast, and by the time it dissipated, 95 Americans lay dead and the country had suffered $281 million in damages. In the Caribbean, Hazel had been more costly, taking 1,000 lives and destroying $100 million worth of property.

Although hurricanes routinely hit or darted by the Palmetto State, it was not until 1989 that another monster storm arrived. On September 9, meteorologists and hurricane specialists took note of a storm moving off Africa's west coast into the Atlantic. The National Oceanic and Atmospheric Administration (NOAA) tracked its movement. By September 15, Hurricane Hugo was still hundreds of miles east of the leeward islands and already measured as a Category 5 storm. The very warm waters it was now entering only increased Hugo's speed and aimed it directly for South Carolina. Mandatory evacuations commenced on the 20th, and traffic backed up for dozens of miles leaving Charleston, Georgetown, and Myrtle Beach.

Daybreak on September 21 was absolutely gorgeous on the South Carolina coast—the sky cloudless and blue, the weather warm. On the roads and highways, however, tens of thousands of motorists were still inching westward. That evening, Hugo's strength diminished slightly to a Category 4 before it struck the Palmetto State near Cape Romaine, some 20 to 30 miles north of Charleston. The Francis Marion National Forest was flattened. Houses were washed into the ocean, some still occupied with people who had refused to evacuate. The entire length of the coast was ravaged. In Garden City and Surfside beaches, third-floor hotel rooms were devastated by waves, houses were pushed hundreds of feet from their foundations, fishing peers were crushed, and several inches of sand concealed beachfront roads. Some oceanfront homes were simply gone; some had lost their ocean-side walls, exposing interior rooms with televisions and other items still intact; others were completely unscarred.

Hugo pushed northwest toward Columbia, retracing the march of General Sherman 124 years earlier. It moved north into Charlotte, North Carolina, some 200 miles from the ocean, and from there north-northeast into New England. In all, Hurricane Hugo cost 21 lives and $7 billion in property loss in the US, making it the worst hurricane in American history in terms of property damage until Hurricane Andrew struck south Florida in 1992.

Wheel, a roller coaster, an arcade, and a dance hall. Small shops and restaurants soon opened along narrow Ocean Boulevard, and motels touted air-conditioned rooms. City leaders marketed the community as a family vacation site, and soon the community attracted tens of thousands of guests each summer. Teenagers also descended on Myrtle Beach to celebrate graduation from high school, and college students found it a far more affordable and accessible destination for spring break than Daytona Beach, Florida. By the late 1960s Myrtle Beach emerged as the teenagers' Mecca, as much a resort town as it was an "experience in personal independence." The city, however, never lost its identity as a family vacation community. In the 1980s and 1990s, developers opened numerous music theaters including the Carolina Opry, the Dixie Stampede, the Alabama Theater, and the Palace, all attracting nationally and internationally renowned performers. National franchises such as the House of Blues, Planet Hollywood, and the Hard Rock Café commenced operations in Myrtle Beach, making the city more nationally recognized. Shopping centers such as Waccamaw Outlet, The Factory Stores, and Tanger Outlet attracted thousands of shoppers looking for bargain prices. The Grand Strand by the mid-1990s boasted more than 100 golf courses, many earning national recognition and several hosting professional tournaments yearly. By 1995, the Grand Strand received 12 million vacationers annually, who poured hundreds of millions of dollars each year into the local economy and into the state treasury.

Development stretched the length of the coast between 1965 and 2000. Underpinning much of the development was the 1968 Housing and Urban Development Act that offered federally backed insurance to coastal homeowners and developers. Storms such as Hurricane Hazel that ravaged the coast in the mid-1950s and utterly wiped out the investments of thousands who owned small cottages near the beach no longer carried the same threat. Financial security spawned development. Also, new construction techniques devised in the early 1970s lessened storm damage, expanded drainage systems reduced coastal flooding, and government-financed beach replenishment altogether made waterfront property ownership safer. With these efforts, modern hotels, condominiums, and extravagant houses replaced small, wooden cottages along the waterfront from Little River to Beaufort. Brookgreen Gardens, Huntington Beach State Park, Myrtle Beach State Park, Murrell's Inlet, and Francis Marion Wildlife Preserve all enticed tourists to visit the coast, and Hilton Head Island, Edisto Beach, Kiawah Island, and Pawley's Island all became exclusive resorts.

Following the war, and especially beginning in the 1960s, Charleston also committed itself to the expansion of its tourist trade. Antebellum and colonial plantation homes were refurbished, and magnificent gardens were cultivated, both attracting thousands of visitors each season. Boats began ferrying tourists to Fort Sumter; the aircraft carrier *Yorktown*, a World War II–era submarine, and other vessels

Must-See Sites: Carowinds, Fort Mill

Sponsored by Paramount Entertainment, Carowinds is a 105-acre park featuring more than 50 "world-class" rides, numerous shows, and a popular 13-acre water-park playground. Popular musical artists representing every genre perform at the park's Paladium Amphitheatre throughout the operating season. The park is open March through October. Visit www.carowinds.com or call (800) 888-4386.

were beached at Patriots' Point; colonial and Civil War–era houses inside the city opened to tours; a shopping district was developed at the old slave market; the Isle of Palms and Folly Beach just outside the city lured beachgoers; and the city organized and sponsored an annual Spoleto Festival showcasing the arts.

Inland, Darlington hosted two NASCAR races each year, the larger of them being the Darlington 500 held in September. State parks attracted fishermen and hunters; thousands gravitated to antique stores that littered smaller towns; horse shows in Aiken, plantations, the Andrew Jackson State Park, collegiate sports at Clemson and USC, museums, and professional sporting events have all brought tourists into South Carolina and in so doing generated a level of income the state never imagined before World War II. In 1995, South Carolina attracted 30 million tourists, who spent more than $13 billion in the state.

South Carolina's industrialization and its development of tourism have together resurfaced the state. Income levels have risen over the past thirty years, and increased tax revenues have provided for further expansion of the state's infrastructure, social and cultural programs, and educational services. Economic growth in the Palmetto State since 1970 has been responsible for a significant movement of newcomers into South Carolina as permanent residents. Horry, Beaufort, Berkeley, Dorchester, and Lexington Counties have all witnessed substantial population growth, and nearly half of the residents in each of those counties are not native South Carolinians. Statewide in 1990, fully one-third of South Carolina's 3.5 million residents were born in other states or countries. Prosperity and a more diverse population have combined to remake the state's values, habits, and expectations. South Carolina in 2008 has largely freed itself from its past. To be sure, deep-rooted, traditional values of prewar South Carolina remain and are defended as intensely as they were 50 or 100 years ago, especially in small towns and rural areas, but the removal of the Confederate battle flag from the dome of the state house in 2000 symbolized South Carolina's more recent progressive character and its conscious effort to join fully with the modern South.

Red and white rustic country barn in South Carolina cotton field © Susabell

Chronology of Major Events

13,000BCE Earliest evidence of human activity in present-day South Carolina

1000BCE Evidence of the beginnings of sedentary, agrarian native communities, occupied by peoples commonly referred to as "Mississippians."

1521 Francisco Gordillo and Pedro de Quexos make the first documented Spanish landing on the South Carolina coast, in the vicinity of Beaufort.

1526 Lucas Vasquez de Ayllon establishes Spain's short-lived first settlement in South Carolina at Winyah Bay in Georgetown, naming the community San Miguel de Guadalupe.

1540 Spanish conquistador Hernando de Soto leads his expedition of discovery north through central South Carolina and westward into Tennessee.

1561 Angel de Villefane fails in his effort to establish a permanent and prosperous Spanish colony at Santa Elena in the Port Royal Sound.

1562 French Huguenot Gaspar Coligny leads 150 soldiers to the New World and in late May plants the settlement Charlesfort at Port Royal, hoping to root France in North America. Within months, the outpost is abandoned.

1566 Spain's Pedro Menendez de Aviles, with 150 soldiers, founds Fort San Felipe on present-day Parris Island. Soon afterward, Menendez sends exploratory missions throughout present-day South Carolina, as far west as Spartanburg.

1576 In June, hunger, disease, and warfare with local Indians compel Spanish settlers to abandon Fort San Felipe for the security of Cuba. Spain never again makes a serious effort to implant itself in South Carolina.

1585–90 The Englishman Sir Walter Raleigh attempts the building of a British settlement on Roanoke Island, located in North Carolina's Outer Banks. The colony never succeeds, and more than 100 settlers are pronounced "missing."

1607 In May, three ships and more than 100 settlers under the command of Captain John Smith plant Jamestown Colony in tidewater Virginia. In spite of a staggering death rate, Jamestown survives and becomes England's first permanent colony in the New World.

1620 Nearly 100 settlers, of whom about 35 are Separatists (Pilgrims), make landfall in Massachusetts and establish Plymouth Plantation Colony.

1663	On March 24, King Charles II of England issues a charter authorizing the founding of the Colony of Carolina under the governance of eight Lords Proprietors.
1664	William Hilton, respected adventurer, is hired by investors in the planned Carolina Colony to scout the Carolina coast.
1665	Late in the year, Charles Town is established as the first settlement in Carolina Colony, at the mouth of the Cape Fear River in present-day North Carolina. Within two years, more than 1,000 English citizens reside here, but the hostility of local Indians forces the settlers to abandon the community in 1667.
1669	The Fundamental Constitutions of Carolina, the formal set of laws governing the new colony in Carolina, is completed.
1670	Of three ships to sail from England for Carolina, one makes landfall near present-day Charleston in mid-March, planting a community of 130 Englishmen and women.
1671	The first shipload of African slaves bound for Carolina Colony arrives in Charles Town.
1715	The Yamasee War erupts, pitting English settlers against the local Yamasee Indians. Within two years, the Yamasee are completely defeated, their survivors sold into slavery in the Caribbean.
1718	The pirate Blackbeard plunders British shipping just outside Charleston Harbor; the pirate captain Stede Bonet is captured and in December executed in Charleston.
1720	65 percent of all South Carolina residents are African slaves.
1739	In the Stono Rebellion in September, twenty slaves initiate an escape and, in their southward rush toward Florida, attack white plantations, farmhouses, and shops, destroying much property and killing 25 white South Carolinians.
1760	George III becomes king of England.
1763	The French and Indian War concludes; George III issues a proclamation banning the movement of American colonists across the Appalachian Mountains.
1765	King George III and Parliament issue the Stamp Act, which places a tax on all paper products and government documents. The Stamp Act Congress, with three South Carolina representatives, assembles in New York City and drafts an official letter to the king protesting the act. Violence against tax collectors and

supporters of the Stamp Act sweeps across the South Carolina Lowcountry.

1766 George III repeals the Stamp Act.

1767 Parliament issues the Townshend Acts, a series of taxes on paper, paint, glass, lead, and tea. The Sons of Liberty form in South Carolina to enforce a boycott of all British imports and to punish those who comply with or administer the tax. In Charleston, the Sons of Liberty is most frequently termed the "Charleston Patriots."

1770 The South Carolina General Assembly is dissolved by the colony's royal governor.

1773 Parliament issues the Tea Act, with the approval of King George III. Violent protests erupt across the Lowcountry in response. Governor William Bull orders all tea imports stored securely to protect them from confiscation or destruction by local protestors. In December, the famed Boston Tea Party is carried out by the Sons of Liberty under the direct observation of the Massachusetts governor and the British military commander in the region.

1774 In spring, Parliament crafts and issues the Coercive Acts, intended to punish Boston for its Tea Party and to recoup the cost of all tea destroyed by the Sons of Liberty. In September, the First Continental Congress meets in Philadelphia to discuss methods to resolve the dispute between Crown and colonies. South Carolina sends five representatives.

1775 South Carolina rice exports reach 66 million pounds, the largest shipment to date. In April, the Battles of Lexington and Concord occur in Massachusetts and signal the start of the Revolutionary War. In May, the Second Continental Congress convenes in Philadelphia and assumes the responsibility of a wartime, revolutionary government. In June, South Carolina's Provincial Congress assembles and authorizes the recruitment of three army regiments for South Carolina's defense.

1776 In June, a British fleet and British ground forces try to secure Charleston Harbor and the surrounding islands. The battle at Sullivan's Island prevents a British landing and occupation of Charleston. The defensive structures are soon afterward converted into Fort Moultrie. On July 4, South Carolina's delegates to the Second Continental Congress affix their names to the Declaration of Independence.

1779 After Savannah falls to the British in June, scattered

fighting ranges north to the outskirts of Charleston, the biggest confrontation occurring at Stono Creek near Edisto Island.

1780 In February, the British lay siege to Charleston. On May 7, Fort Moultrie surrenders and on May 14 Charleston itself falls to the British. In July, British General Cornwallis defeats American forces commanded by General Horatio Gates at Camden, a town near Columbia. On October 7, nearly 1,000 American militiamen surround and soundly defeat an equal-sized British and Tory force located on Kings Mountain.

1781 On January 18, after a protracted and purposely designed retreat, American General Dan Morgan positions his forces at Cowpens and there defeats a British force commanded by Banastre Tarleton. American victories at Cowpens and Kings Mountain secured the western Carolinas from British control. In October, British General Cornwallis surrenders his armies to General George Washington at Yorktown, Virginia; although the war would continue until an official peace treaty could be arranged in 1783, for all practical purposes, this ends the Revolutionary War.

1782 On December 16, British forces finally evacuate Charleston.

1785 The College of Charleston is founded.

1786 The General Assembly relocates the state capital from Charleston to Columbia.

1788 South Carolina becomes the sixth state to ratify the US Constitution.

1791 President George Washington travels through coastal South Carolina and spends one week in Charleston.

1793 Connecticut inventor and resident Eli Whitney invents the cotton gin, a machine that revolutionizes South Carolina's agricultural economy.

1795 Beaufort College, today a branch of the University of South Carolina, is founded.

1800 Charleston is the fifth largest city in the United States, behind New York, Philadelphia, Baltimore, and Boston.

1801 South Carolina College, today's University of South Carolina in Columbia, is founded.

1802 The United States' first gold rush is centered in the area of York and Chesterfield, Lancaster Counties.

1811 The General Assembly passes into law the Free School Act, allotting state funds for the construction and maintenance of rural public schools.

1822 Denmark Vesey, an emancipated slave living in Charleston, is accused, convicted, and executed for plotting a slave insurrection in the Lowcountry.

1824 The School of Medicine is founded in Charleston.

1838 Governor John Lyde Wilson publishes *The American Code: Code of Honor, or Rules for the Government of Principals and Seconds in Dueling*.

1842 The South Carolina Military Academy, now known as the Citadel, is founded in Charleston.

1849 The state's first textile mill, Graniteville Mill, is founded by William Gregg in Aiken County.

1850 In December, the General Assembly issues a statement calling on southern states to convene a Southern Convention in Montgomery, Alabama and consider secession as an response to "northern aggression."

1851 Furman College, a Baptist-supported institution, is founded in Greenville.

1860 On November 6, Abraham Lincoln is elected president of the United States; on December 20, South Carolina secedes from the Union, the first state to do so.

1861 The ship *Star of the West* is fired on by cadets from the Citadel on January 9 as it attempts to deliver supplies to federal troops posted at Fort Sumter in Charleston Harbor. On February 4, the Confederate States of America is founded in Montgomery, Alabama. On March 4, Lincoln is inaugurated. On April 12, Confederate batteries open fire on Fort Sumter. The surrender of the federal installation the following day officially signals the start of the Civil War. In early summer, a fleet of Union warships seize Parris Island and convert the rice plantation into a federal naval installation.

1862 The United States establishes the United States Colored Troops, a racially segregated branch of the US Army for African Americans. On November 7, the First Regiment of South Carolina Volunteers is formed and attached to the USCT.

1863 President Lincoln's Emancipation Proclamation, drafted the previous September, becomes an official executive order on January 1 and liberates from bondage slaves in all states presently in rebellion against the US government. In July, Union forces attack the 1,000-man Confederate garrison at Fort Wagner on Morris Island near Charleston. On July 18, the 54th Massachusetts Regiment, part of the United States Colored Troops, launches a frontal assault on Fort Wagner. On September 7, Confederate forces abandon Fort Wagner and Union forces lay siege to the city of Charleston.

1864 The *H. L. Hunley*, a Confederate submarine, conducts a successful attack against the Union ship USS *Housatonic* in Charleston Harbor on February 17; the submarine never returned to port and was presumed lost.

1865 Units of General William Tecumseh Sherman's Union Army enter Columbia on February 17, and by mid-evening the city is ablaze. On April 9, Confederate forces under General Robert E. Lee surrender, unofficially ending the Civil War. In October, South Carolina ratifies the Thirteenth Amendment to the US Constitution, which officially ends slavery in the United States.

1868 A new constitution is drafted and approved for South Carolina at the constitutional convention held in Charleston; of 124 delegates in attendance, 73 are African American. The University of South Carolina hires African-American professors and enrolls African-American students, who comprise 90 percent of the student body by 1875.

1871 The post–Civil War state militia is approximately 97 percent African American. President Ulysses S. Grant imposes martial law in upstate counties.

1876 Wade Hampton is elected governor of South Carolina, the first postwar Democrat to hold the office.

1886 "Pitchfork" Ben Tillman establishes the Farmers' Association, which effectively becomes the state's branch of the National Farmers' Alliance, an agrarian-based reform movement and sponsor of the Populist Party.

1889 Clemson College is founded in Clemson, South Carolina. Its doors open to students five years later.

1896 The US Supreme Court ruling in *Plessy v. Ferguson* gives constitutional sanction to South Carolina's laws requiring race segregation in public facilities.

1900 25 percent of all textile employees in South Carolina are children under the age of sixteen.

1910 Coleman Blease of Newberry is elected the state's first Progressive governor, championing the working class, regardless of race.

1914 To reduce child labor, South Carolina raises the minimum age for full-time employment to fourteen. The state ranks 47th among 48 states in its rate of illiteracy. World War I begins in August.

1917 The United States enters World War I in April. The State Highway Commission and State Highway

	Department are created to oversee road expansion and maintenance.
1918	Two South Carolinians earn the Congressional Medal of Honor while fighting German forces in France—James Dozier (30th Infantry Division), who became the state's adjutant general, and Fred Stowers (93rd Infantry Regiment), who was the only African American honored with the medal. In November, an armistice brings the Great War to its conclusion.
1923	Governor Thomas McLeod organizes a "Boost South Carolina" convention to promote the tourist industry statewide.
1929	On October 29, the collapse of the stock market signals the official beginning of the Great Depression.
1933	President Franklin Delano Roosevelt is inaugurated into his first term as president. The Works Progress Administration, Civilian Conservation Corps, Agricultural Adjustment Act, and other New Deal programs commence operation in South Carolina.
1935	The Santee Cooper Hydroelectric Power Project is approved by and receives funding from the federal government; construction begins in 1939.
1939	World War II begins in Europe on September 1.
1941	On December 7, Japanese naval forces strike America's Pacific Fleet Headquarters at Pearl Harbor, Hawaii. The United States enters World War II.
1942	The Santee Cooper Hydroelectric Power Plant "goes on line," providing electric service throughout the Lowcountry and Midlands region. By 1985 it would supply fully half of South Carolina's energy needs. In August and again in September, German submarines (U-boats) deposit sea mines in Charleston Harbor.
1944	Congress passes into law the Servicemen's Readjustment Act, or G. I. Bill, providing financial support for post-secondary education, home purchases, and small-business startup expenses for veterans. The measure will have a profound imprint on South Carolina.
1945	World War II ends in Europe in May and in the Far East in September.
1946	Strom Thurmond, a veteran of World War II, is elected governor and begins a 55-year career in state and national government.
1948	The southern conservative wing of the Democratic Party assembles in Birmingham, Alabama and forms the States' Rights Democratic Party, or Dixiecrats, and selects Governor Strom Thurmond as its presidential contender.

1954 In May, the US Supreme Court issues its ruling in *Brown v. the Board of Education of Topeka, Kansas*, declaring racially segregated schools unconstitutional.

1963 Harvey Gantt becomes the first African-American student at Clemson University.

1964 The University of South Carolina enrolls its first African-American student since Reconstruction.

1968 In the town of Orangeburg and on the campus of South Carolina State University in February, African-American students demonstrations against race segregation result in the death of three students and the wounding of many more by highway patrolmen.

1972 A team of archaeologists and historians begin to search for the *H. L. Hunley*.

1977 The General Assembly passes into law the Education Finance Act, which allocated more additional funding for poor districts than for wealthier districts.

1989 Hurricane Hugo makes landfall near Charleston and moves northwest across South Carolina and into the North Carolina piedmont region, the greatest natural disaster in state history.

1990 Fully one-third of all residents statewide were born outside of South Carolina.

1995 In May, wreckage of the *H. L. Hunley* is located near Sullivan's Island.

2000 The *H. L. Hunley* is successfully raised from the ocean floor on August 8 and placed at Charleston Naval Base. George W. Bush wins South Carolina in the presidential race.

2001 Voters approve a state lottery with proceeds earmarked for public education. Al-Qaeda terrorists attack the United States on September 11.

2003 The United States invades Iraq.

2004 South Carolina once more votes for George W. Bush, helping him secure his second term as US president.

2007 The 218th Infantry Brigade of the South Carolina Army National Guard deploys in force to the war in Afghanistan. Construction begins on the Hard Rock Park in Myrtle Beach, a theme park planned to be second only to Disney World on the East Coast.

2008 On January 26, US Senator Barack Obama from Illinois, an African American, wins the South Carolina Democratic Party primary.

Characteristics of South Carolina's Population, 2006

Category	*South Carolina*	*United States*
Population, 2006 estimate	4,321,249	299,398,484
Population % Change, 2000–2006	7.7	6.4
Population, 2000	4,012,012	281,421,906
Population % Change, 1990–2000	15.1	13.1
White, non Hispanic, % in 2006	65.4	66.4
African American, % in 2006	29	12.8
American Indian, % in 2006	0.4	1.0
Asian Persons, % in 2006	1.1	4.4
Persons of Other Race, % in 2006	1.0	1.8
Hispanic-Latino, % in 2006	3.5	14.8
Foreign Born, % in 2000	2.9	11.1
Language Other than English, %	5.2	17.9
High School Graduates, % in 2000	76.3	80.4
College Graduates, % in 2000	20.4	24.4
Home Ownership rate, % in 2000	72.2	66.2
Median Value of Housing, 2000	$94,900	$119,600
Number Households, 2000	1,533,854	105,480,101
Persons Per Household, 2000	2.53	2.59
Median Household Income, 2004	$39,454	$44,334
Per Capita Income, 1999	$18,795	$21,587
Persons Below Poverty, % in 2004	15	12.7
Persons Per Square Mile, 2000	133.2	79.6

Source: U.S. Census Bureau: State and County QuickFacts.

Famous Sons and Daughters

ARTISTS

Washington Allston (1779–1843)

Washington Allston was born in 1779 in Georgetown. He traveled extensively, studying at Harvard College, at the Royal Academy in London, and with various painters in France and Italy. Artists widely consider him the founding painter of the American Romanticism movement, known for its representation of man's insignificance in Nature and the all-pervading presence of God in the universe.

William H. Johnson (1901–1970)

Born in 1901, Johnson was reared in abject poverty in a small African-American community within the city of Florence. As a child he copied comic strips and displayed an unusual talent for art. Encouraged by his teachers, he traveled to New York in 1919 where he eventually studied at the National Academy of Design and in 1926 relocated to Paris to escape the racial discrimination he constantly encountered in the United States. Johnson painted in the Expressionist style, but in the 1930s he adopted what he termed a "primitive style" that used bright, contrasting colors and two-dimensional figures and focused on the African-American experience. Johnson never received much recognition of his work while alive; however, following his death in 1970 critics "discovered" the soul of Johnson's art and now consider him one of the most important African-American artists of the twentieth century.

EDUCATION

James Mark Baldwin (1862–1932)

James Mark Baldwin received his academic training in psychology at Princeton in New Jersey and at several institutions in Germany. He taught at the university level for many years, co-founded the journal *Psychology Review*, and published several important books, among them *Mental Developments in the Child and the Race*, *Social and Ethnic Interpretations*, and *History of Psychology*. His career coincided with that of internationally recognized Sigmund Freud, and Baldwin directed the course of the International

Congress of Psychology as its president from 1909 to 1913. Baldwin was born in Columbia.

Mary McLeod Bethune (1875–1955)
Mary McLeod Bethune was born on July 10, 1875 in Mayesville, the fifteenth of seventeen children. Her parents and several of her older siblings had lived as slaves before 1865. Mary received her education at a school established by the Mission Board of the Presbyterian Church and became a teacher at several small, racially segregated institutions throughout the Southeast. She was active in the women's suffrage movement, championed women's rights, served on the National Urban League Executive Board, and founded a home for delinquent black girls. Her work won her the attention of President Calvin Coolidge and President Herbert Hoover, and she held appointive positions in each administration. She also served as President Franklin D. Roosevelt's special advisor on minority affairs. For more on Bethune, see pages 240–241.

MILITARY

James Longstreet (1821–1903)
Born in Edgefield on January 8, 1821, James Longstreet was the son of a wealthy planter. He attended the United States Military Academy at West Point, was commissioned as a second lieutenant in the US Army, and served in the Mexican–American War. When the American Civil War erupted in April 1861, Longstreet resigned his commission and accepted the rank of general in the Confederate Army, where he earned the admiration of the men he commanded and the respect of soldiers who confronted him on the battlefield. He served with General Robert E. Lee at Gettysburg. Following the war, he abandoned the Democratic Party for the Republican Party and was appointed minister to Britain in 1880. He died at age 82.

Francis Marion (1732–1795)
Marion is remembered as one of the state's first military heroes, beginning his service in the state militia in 1761 in warfare against Cherokee Indians. During the Revolutionary War, he was promoted to lieutenant colonel and conducted guerilla warfare against British troops in

South Carolina, earning the nickname the "Swamp Fox." Following the war, he was elected to the state senate.

William Westmoreland (1914–2005)
Born in Spartanburg in 1914, William Westmoreland began his military career as a student at the United States Military Academy at West Point, graduating in 1936. He served in the army during World War II and in 1960 returned to West Point as superintendent. In June 1964, Westmoreland was appointed commander of US forces in Vietnam and was responsible for raising troop strength to 500,000 men. Following the Tet Offensive in 1968, Westmoreland was relieved of his command and appointed chief of staff of the US Army. General Westmoreland retired from service in 1972.

MUSIC

Alabama
Although the members of the popular county music band Alabama are not by birth Sandlappers, they are nonetheless considered South Carolinians within the Palmetto State. Alabama rose to popularity in the 1980s, getting their musical start at Myrtle Beach's nightclub "The Bowery," located on the oceanfront next to the Pavilion. They currently sponsor the Alabama Music Theater in Myrtle Beach and appear there frequently.

James Brown (1933–2006)
"The Godfather of Soul" was born in Barnwell. His childhood was one of intense poverty, his family home having no plumbing or electricity. The Brown family was a "colorful" one, known for their many brushes with local law enforcement, and James himself was frequently in trouble as a teenager. He swept floors for the Trinity Baptist Church to earn a little money, and he developed a passion for music. Brown cofounded the Famous Flames in the early 1960s and earned quick recognition for the group's hit song "Please, Please, Please." As an individual performer, he brought soul music into widespread popularity among white listeners with songs such as "Papa's Got a Brand New Bag," and his "Say It Loud, I'm Black and I'm Proud" became something akin to an anthem for the Civil Rights Movement.

Dizzy Gillespie (1917–1993)
John Birks "Dizzy" Gillespie was born in Cheraw in 1917. Early in his distinguished musical career, he performed with Cab Calloway and Earl Hines and instantly gained a reputation as a free-spirited jazz trumpeter. His distinctive bent horn, puffed cheeks, and almost spiritual relationship with the trumpet placed him among the most renowned musicians in American history.

Eartha Kitt (1927–)
Eartha Kitt was born on a poor cotton farm in the community of North. She and her family frequently moved, and as a small child she was left with a neighboring family where she was mistreated. At eight years of age, she moved to Harlem to live with an aunt. There she was encouraged to play the piano and sing, although her relationship with her aunt was never good. She worked several odd jobs before earning a scholarship to Katherine Dunham Dance School, through which she began to travel as a singer and actress. From this she entered a professional acting career, appearing in numerous movies beginning in 1950 and continuing in the profession to the present.

PROMINENT POLITICAL AND LEGAL FIGURES

Bernard Baruch (1870–1965)
Baruch, known as the "Park Bench Statesman," made his personal fortune on Wall Street at the turn of the nineteenth century. Born in Camden on August 19, 1870, Baruch and his family moved to New York ten years later and he attended college there. He became a broker for A. A. Housman and Company, earned his first million dollars by age thirty, and took a seat on the New York Stock Exchange. During World War I, he served as President Woodrow Wilson's economic advisor, chaired the War Industries Board, and participated in treaty negotiations in Versailles. Baruch owned a 17,000-acre plantation in Georgetown County, the Hobcaw Barony, where he entertained Franklin Roosevelt during World War II. Baruch died on June 10, 1965 in New York, following a one-month stay at his South Carolina estate.

Harold R. Boulware, Sr. (1913–1983)
A pioneer in civil rights litigation, Boulware was born in Irmo in 1913. He attended Johnson C. Smith University in Charlotte, North Carolina and Howard University Law School in Washington, D.C. In 1941, Boulware became the chief counsel for the South Carolina NAACP and campaigned for equal pay for African-American schoolteachers. He served as lead attorney in the Clarendon County schools desegregation case, *Briggs v. Elliot*, which was joined into the landmark 1954 US Supreme Court case *Brown v. the Board of Education of Topeka, Kansas*, in which the court ruled against the segregation of public schools. In 1969 he was appointed as associate judge for the Columbia Municipal Court.

James F. Byrnes (1879–1972)
James Byrnes was born in Charleston. As a public servant, he served in all three branches of the federal government. He sat in both the US House of Representatives and Senate, served as secretary of state and director of war mobilization, and was a Supreme Court justice. He was considered seriously by Franklin Roosevelt as a potential vice presidential candidate in 1944, and from 1951 to 1955 served South Carolina as governor.

John C. Calhoun (1782–1850)
John Caldwell Calhoun was born into a slaveholding plantation family on March 18, 1782 near Abbeville. As a young man he graduated from Yale University and was admitted to the South Carolina bar in 1807. He served in the state legislature, held a seat in the US Senate, served as secretary of war in 1817 under President James Monroe, and was elected vice president of the United States in 1825. A staunch advocate of states' rights, Calhoun attained his greatest fame in 1828 with his assertion that a state had the authority to nullify any federal law within its borders that it considered unconstitutional. In the 1840s he fully defended the institution of slavery and its expansion into the West and predicted civil war more than twelve years before it erupted. For more on Calhoun, see pages 134–135.

Andrew Jackson (1767–1845)
The seventh president of the United States, Andrew Jackson, was born on March 15, 1767 in the frontier community of Waxhaw, and later moved to Tennessee, where as an adult he built the plantation "Hermitage." Jackson was the only president to fight in both the Revolutionary War and the War of 1812, serving in the former at thirteen years of age with the South Carolina Militia. He was the first president born in a log cabin, the first reared in a frontier setting, and the first to ride on a train. Andrew Jackson State Park is located nine miles north of Lancaster, on Highway 521. For more on Jackson, see pages see pages 102–103.

Jesse Louis Jackson (1941–)
Born in Greenville on October 8, 1941, Jesse Jackson has emerged as one of America's most prominent civil rights leaders. He commenced his career with the Southern Leadership Conference founded by Martin Luther King, Jr., founded Operation PUSH (People United to Save Humanity), formed the Rainbow Coalition, and competed for the Democratic Party presidential nomination in 1984 and 1988. Throughout his career, Jackson has traveled the nation and globe promoting the fair and equitable treatment of all people regardless of race.

James Strom Thurmond (1902–2003)
Thurmond was born on December 5, 1902 in Edgefield, earned his degree from Clemson College, and held several local offices until 1933 when he was elected to the South Carolina Senate. He sat on the bench of the Eleventh Circuit Court, served with the 82nd Airborne Division in World War II, and was elected governor in 1946. From 1954 to 2002 Thurmond represented South Carolina in the US Senate.

SCIENCE AND TECHNOLOGY

Joseph H. Burckhalter (1912–2004)
Joseph H. Burckhalter was born in Columbia on October 9, 1912. In 1934 he received his Bachelor of Science degree in chemistry from the University of South Carolina, a Master of Science in 1938 from the University of Illinois, and the

coveted Ph.D. in medicinal chemistry in 1942 at the University of Michigan. After nearly twenty years with Parke-Davis, he returned to academia as a professor of medicinal chemistry at the University of Michigan (1960–1983) and at Florida Institute of Technology (1983–). He and a colleague jointly developed the synthesis of fluorescein isothiocyanate (FITC), which is currently used in the detection and diagnoses of AIDS, leukemia, and lymphoma. In 1995, Burckhalter was inducted into the National Inventors' Hall of Fame.

Ernest Everett Just (1883–1941)

Termed by his biographer the "Black Apollo of Science," Ernest Just attended the Colored Normal Industrial Agricultural and Mechanics College at Orangeburg (now South Carolina State College) at the age of thirteen and later studied biology at Dartmouth College and earned a Ph.D. from the University of Chicago. He worked as a pioneer researcher in the fertilization of marine invertebrates and the role of the cell in those organisms. Opportunities were limited because of the extent of racial discrimination he encountered, and in 1931 Just relocated to Europe, where he spent the rest of his career and published *The Biology of the Cell Surface*.

Ronald McNair (1950–1986)

Ronald McNair was a crewmember of the ill-fated *Challenger* space shuttle that exploded shortly after liftoff from Cape Canaveral in January 1986; all astronauts on board perished in the accident. He was born October 21, 1950 in Lake City, attended North Carolina A&T University, from which he graduated in 1971 with a degree in physics, and earned Ph.D. in physics from the Massachusetts Institute of Technology in 1976. Before his death in 1986, McNair was a mission specialist on a 1984 *Challenger* flight.

Charles H. Townes (1915–)

Born in Greenville on July 28, 1915, Townes graduated summa cum laude in 1935 from Furman University with a degree in physics. He earned a masters degree from Duke University and the Ph.D. from the California Institute of

Technology in 1939. In his career, Townes held positions on college faculty, in corporations such as Bell Laboratories, and in nonprofit organizations, such as serving as the director of research for the Institute of Defense Analyses. In 1951, Townes specialized in microwave physics and conceived the idea of the maser (microwave amplification by stimulated emission of radiation) and helped develop the laser by decade's end.

WRITERS

Pat Conroy (1945–)

Perhaps the most prolific writer of novels set in South Carolina, Conroy is not a native of South Carolina but a man whose life has been shaped in the state. Born in Atlanta, Georgia on October 26, 1945, he was the oldest of seven children and son of a career military officer stationed in South Carolina. Conroy was a student at the Citadel in Charleston when he wrote and published his first book, *The Boo*. *The Water is Wide* (1972) was based on his short-lived teaching experience on Daufuskie Island and made into the movie *Conrack*. Conroy also published *The Great Santini*, *The Lords of Discipline*, *The Prince of Tides*, and *Beach Music*. For more on Conroy, see pages 298–299.

William Gibson (1948–)

Born in Conway, near Myrtle Beach, William Gibson is a contemporary author of science fiction novels and short stories. Generally, Gibson's plots center on an individual's loss of personal identity in a dark, depressive society set in a not-too-distant future in which technology governs humanity. Perhaps his most popular novel is *Neuromancer*, in which computers regulate human emotion and behavior. Gibson is credited with having coined the term "cyberspace" in this novel.

Edwin DeBose Heyward (1885–1940)

Born in Charleston, DeBose Heyward worked on the waterfront as a teenager, where he observed the variety of cultures that dwelled and worked in the coastal port city. From his experiences, he published a collection of poems titled *Carolina Chansons* (1922) and his first novel, *Porgy* (1925), which became the literary base for a successful play, opera, and motion picture. With George Gershwin, Heyward scripted the novel into *Porgy and Bess*, long since considered a classic, although it didn't play in South Carolina until 1970.

Annie Green Nelson (1902–)
South Carolina's first known female African-American author, Annie Green was born on December 5, 1902 in Darlington County, the oldest of fourteen children. She spent much of her life seeking knowledge, beginning with a five-month school-year program in her hometown, continuing at Benedict College as a young adult, and at the age of 80 studying drama at the University of South Carolina. She is known for her poetry and her plays, which were performed off-Broadway.

Julia Mood Peterkin (1880–1961)
Julia Peterkin is the only South Carolinian author ever awarded the Pulitzer Prize in literature, the honor bestowed on her in 1929 for her novel *Scarlet Sister Mary*. Peterkin was born in Laurens County on October 31, 1880 and attended Converse College in Spartanburg. Her stories avoid the stereotypes of African Americans common in southern literature of the pre–World War II era, show an understanding of and a respect for African Americans, and her characters are fully developed and credible regardless of gender or race. Among her greatest works are *Green Thursday* (1924), *Black April* (1927), and *Roll, Jordan, Roll* (1933).

Garden and stairway of historic Charleston mansion. Image © Appleman52

Special Events

JANUARY

Carolina Marathon **(statewide)**

Throughout the months of January and February, individual cities and towns host a variety of races, among them a 10k run, a 10k wheelchair event, an 8k walk, a 6k run, and special contests for children. For specific dates and locations, see www.carolinamarathon.org.

FEBRUARY

Carolina Marathon **(statewide)**

See preceding description.

MARCH

Atalaya's Special Day **(Murrells Inlet)**

Celebrate the wedding anniversary and birthdays of Anna and Archer Huntington, founders of Brookgreen Gardens. Visit the castle and relax in the courtyard. Refreshments provided. Date: March 10. Cost: $10 per visitor. Contact (843) 235-8755 or visit www.hungtingtonbeachsc.org.

Can-Am Days Festival **(Myrtle Beach)**

The Canadian-American Festival is held the entire month of March annually to welcome Canadians on "spring break." Activities vary and are sponsored by both the city and local businesses, but historical tours, musical concerts, and sporting events are common. For information, call (843) 626-7444 or visit www.discovermyrtlebeach.com/canamdays.

Carolina Cup Races **(Camden)**

50,000 spectators gather each year for this steeplechase race of thoroughbreds, one of South Carolina's oldest annual events. The race is held on the last Saturday of March. Call (803) 432-6513 for details or visit www.carolina-cup.org.

APRIL

Azalea Festival **(Pickens)**

Usually in April, the myriad colors of the towns' azalea gardens are celebrated. Live entertainment, arts and crafts, and food vendors participate. All profits go to local charities. Contact (864) 878-7145 or visit www.pickenschamber.org.

World Grits Festival **(St. George)**
On the second weekend of April, the town of St. George celebrates grits, a dish unique to the South. A grits eating contest and a beauty pageant that crowns the Miss World Grits Queen are the highlights, but the town also holds a parade and offers gospel singing and band performances, along with booths offering crafts and food. For additional information, call (843) 563-7943.

Three Rivers Music Festival **(Columbia)**
More than 100 musical acts perform on eight separate stages on the first weekend of April each year. Musical varieties include gospel, country, jazz, alternative rock, classical, bluegrass, cajun, and southern beach music. Activities are available to entertain guests of all ages. Contact (803) 401-8990.

MAY

Abbeville Spring Festival on the Square **(Abbeville)**
Tours of homes, a town parade, art show, antique car show, crafts on display, children's events, street dance, live entertainment, and food vendors. Generally held the first weekend of May. Free admission. For more information, call (864) 459-1433 or visit www.discoversouthcarolina.com.

Pontiac GMC Freedom Weekend Aloft **(Greenville)**
Greenville hosts Freedom Weekend Aloft on the last weekend of May. It features 100 hot-air balloons, games, crafts, food, and nationally recognized entertainers. Call (864) 232-3700 for details or visit www.freedom weekend.org.

Rivertown Jazz Festival **(Conway)**
The Rivertown Jazz Festival is held the first weekend of May on the banks of the Waccamaw River that runs through Conway. Stages situated throughout the town and along the river walk feature jazz performances, and vendors offer a variety of local foods. Entertainment for children is available. Admission is free. Call (843) 248-6260 for more details or visit www.rivertownjazzandarts.com or www.conwaysc chamber.com.

***Canoeing Workshop & Trip on the South Edisto* (Windsor)**
In mid-month and again on the last weekend of May, a special course is offered for beginner canoeists. The class teaches basic skills of paddling followed by a guided two-mile canoe trip on the South Edisto River. Cost is $20 per person, and interested visitors must book reservations three days in advance. For more information, call (803) 649-2857.

***Spoleto Festival, USA* (Charleston)**
Charleston's celebration of the fine arts, which extends from the third weekend of May to the first weekend of June, showcases world-renowned artists and performers in theater, music, and dance. The festival is one of South Carolina's largest and most popular. Call (843) 722-2764 for additional information or visit www.spoletousa.org.

***Gullah Festival* (Beaufort)**
Held on the fourth weekend of the month, the annual festival celebrates Lowcountry African-American culture with exhibits in the Black Inventions Museum, local music and dance performances, unique foods, and craft booths. Call (843) 525-0628 for details or visit www.gullah festival.org.

***Hell Hole Swamp Festival* (Jamestown)**
On the first Saturday of the month, Jamestown residents and their guests enjoy a day filled with attractions for all ages, including a tobacco-spitting contest, a greased pole climb, softball games, horseshoe games, arm wrestling, a beauty pageant, talent shows, and exhibits of crafts and local foods. For details, call (843) 257-2233.

JUNE

***Harborwalk Festival* (Georgetown)**
The last weekend of June marks the annual Harborwalk Festival in the historic district of Georgetown, nestled along the harbor. A boat show, tours of historic sailing ships, five stages of live musical performances, an antique car show, boat tours of the harbor, a street dance, and booths with crafts and food are available to guests. Admission is free. Call (843) 546-1511 for additional information or visit www.georgetown-sc.com/events.

Sun Fun Festival **(Myrtle Beach)**
This festival runs the entire first week of the month annually and includes numerous events scattered along the Grand Strand. Among them are the Miss Sun Fun Beauty Pageant, the Sun Fun Parade, golf tournaments, fishing tournaments, beach games, sand-castle building contests, Jazz in the Park, and special live performances at local musical theaters. The festival has been held since 1951. For additional information, call (843) 626-7444 or visit www.sunfunfestival.com

South Carolina Festival of Flowers **(Greenwood)**
On the fourth weekend of June, visitors to Greenwood are invited to tour the George W. Park Seed Company's Trail of Gardens, which includes more than 1,500 varieties of flowering plants. The town also offers art and photo shows, beach music dancing, square dancing, and activities for children. Call (864) 223-8411 or visit www.scfestivalof flowers.org.

JULY

Pageland Watermelon Festival **(Pageland)**
This festival celebrates the local crop, the watermelon. Events include a parade, concerts, crafts booths, an antique car show, a beauty pageant, helicopter rides, a petting zoo, watermelon eating and seed spitting contests, gospel music, and lawnmower tractor races. The festival is held on the third weekend of the month. Call (843) 672-5257 or visit www.pagelandcham.net.

South Carolina Peach Festival **(Gaffney)**
This eight-day festival in mid-July honors one of the state's principal crops. Included in the festival are country music performances featuring nationally recognized musicians, sporting events, parades, and "tractor pulls." Of course, numerous desserts made with peaches are available. For details, contact (864) 489-9066 or visit www.scpeachfestival.org or www.gaffney-sc.com.

An Evening at Prospect Hill **(Edisto Island)**
This local historic antebellum-era plantation hosts a shrimp Creole dinner for guests and provides a storytelling hour,

pottery-making demonstrations, and gospel singing. Call (843) 869-1954 for reservations.

AUGUST

Summerfest (York)

This one-day event is held on the forth Saturday of August annually. Admission is free. The day features a 5k run, a "fun run," a softball tournament, crafts, food vendors, a parade, live entertainment, and activities for children. Call (803) 684-2590 or visit www.greateryorkchamber.com/summerfest.

SEPTEMBER

Aynor Harvest Hoe-Down Festival (Aynor)

Held on the third weekend of the month in Aynor, ten miles west of Conway, the hoe-down is a Saturday celebration for the family. More than 200 booths featuring local crafts as well as foods such as "chicken bog." A parade and street dance highlight the day. Contact (843) 365-9154 visit www.aynorscchamber.org/harvesthoedown.

South Carolina Tobacco Festival (Lake City)

Lake City hosts the annual state festival celebrating the year's tobacco harvest. Several stages present live entertainment throughout the weekend, and guests can enjoy radio-controlled airplane demonstrations, a pet parade, a street dance, a motorcycle rally, gospel singing, and a tobacco tying and stringing contest. For more information, call (843) 374-8611 or visit www.discoversouthcarolina.com.

OCTOBER

Apple Harvest Festival (Windy Hill Orchard and Cider Mill, York)

This festival, generally held in mid-month, features apple picking, hay rides, pumpkin picking, cider making and baked apple goods. Admission is free. Call (803) 684-0690 for more information or visit www.discoversouthcarolina.com.

Autumn Candlelight Tour (Ninety-Six)

Usually held in mid-month, this evening includes guided tours on a one-mile length of historic trail, illuminated by candles and torches. Volunteers dressed in civilian and military clothing of the Revolutionary Era describe life and war in colonial America. Contact (864) 543-4068 or visit www.nps.gov/nisi/planyourvisit/candlelight-tour.htm or www.discoversouthcarolina.com.

Pawley's Island Tour of Homes **(Pawley's Island)**
In mid-month, visitors to the island are invited to tour both historic and contemporary homes. Admission is $20 per person. For details, call (843) 546-5685.

South Carolina State Fair **(Columbia)**
The state fair stretches over eleven days, beginning the first weekend of the month. It includes exhibits of flowers, canned foods, quilting, artwork, baked goods, and livestock. Stage acts throughout the fair feature comedians, instrumental bands, singers, dancers, and varied local entertainers from public schools and colleges. Visitors can also enjoy a number of popular rides and games. Call (803) 799-3387 for more information or visit www.scstatefair.org.

Carolina Downhome Blues Festival **(Camden)**
The Fine Arts Center of Kershaw County presents a variety of performers, generally on the first weekend of October, and local bars and restaurants in Camden provide nightly blues performances in intimate settings. Call (803) 425-7676 or visit www.camden.bluesbash.com

South Carolina Sweet Potato Festival **(Darlington)**
The Sweet Potato Festival attracts approximately 10,000 guests annually. Clowns and mimes provide street entertainment, and stages located throughout the community offer live entertainment. In addition to the extensive display of sweet potato dishes, other booths feature international foods. Admission is free. For details, call (843) 395-2940 or visit www.discoversouthcarolina.com.

Beaufort Shrimp Festival **(Beaufort)**
Held on the second weekend of the month, the Shrimp Festival celebrates the foods peculiar to South Carolina's Lowcountry. A shrimp cooking contest awards prizes for best recipe and most creative recipe. On the waterfront on Friday evening is a picnic, with lighted shrimp boats providing illumination. A 5k run and a 5k walk are held on

Saturday, and live entertainment and locally made crafts are highlights of the day. Food is ever present. Visitors are encouraged to tour local homes and historic buildings. Call (843) 986-5400 for additional information or visit www.beaufortsc.org or www.cityofbeaufort.org.

NOVEMBER

Celebrate Freedom (Columbia)

Held at Owens Field Airport, the event features an air and ground show of World War II history. Restored aircraft from the period perform aerial demonstrations, and visitors may get a close-up view of the planes throughout the day. On display, too, is a replica of an army field hospital, memorabilia of and representatives from the 82nd Airborne Division, the 30th Infantry Division, and anti-aircraft weaponry. The event is generally held on the first weekend of November. For details, contact (803) 772-2945 visit www.discoversouthcarolina.com.

Colonial Cup (Camden)

Long noted for its horseshows, Camden sponsors the Colonial Cup in mid-November each year. The one-day event includes six races of thoroughbreds and culminates in the Colonial Cup steeplechase event that determines the year's national champion. In addition to the races, there are specialty shops and booths for shopping and numerous children's activities. Tailgating parties are permitted. Call (803) 432-6513 for additional information or visit www.camden-sc.org and www.carolina-cup.org.

DECEMBER

Dickens Christmas Show and Festival (Myrtle Beach)

The Dickens Christmas Show is held yearly at the Myrtle Beach Convention Center and features nearly 500 booths of arts and crafts along with a variety of Christmas decorations. A Victorian theme prevails, with vendors attired in clothing in the style of the period. The show runs Thursday through Sunday. For additional information, call (843) 448-9483 or visit www.dickenschristmasshow.com and www.myrtlebeachinfo.com/holiday/events.

Colonial Christmas in Camden **(Camden)**
This celebration includes a parade through the town, fireworks, and a candlelight tour of selected private homes and local buildings all in seasonal décor. Service personnel from local restaurants wear Victorian-era clothing, shops in the business district extend their hours, and live music groups perform on town streets. The event is generally held in mid-month. Call (803) 432-9841 for more details or visit www.camden-sc.org.

Family Yuletide at Middleton Place **(Charleston)**
A variety of Christmas-themed activities are provided to guests of all ages at the Middleton Plantation. Christmas caroling, craft demonstrations, wreath-making, and a bonfire are all features of this celebration. This is an evening event, generally in mid-month. For details, contact (843) 556-6020 or (800) 786-3608 or visit www.middletonplace.org.

A closeup of a ripe cotton boll in a Southern cotton field © Jay Waldron

Contact Information

State Tourism Agencies
South Carolina Department of Parks, Recreation, and Tourism
1205 Pendleton Street
Columbia, SC 29201-0071
(803) 734-1700 or (800) 346-3634
ccorning@scprt.com
www.discoversouthcarolina.com

Visitors' Bureaus

Charleston
Charleston-Trident, SC Convention/Visitors' Bureau
PO Box 975
Charleston, SC 29402
(843) 853-8000 or (800) 868-0444
www.charlestoncvb.com

Columbia
Columbia, South Carolina Metropolitan Convention and Visitors' Bureau
1276 Assembly Street
PO Box 15
Columbian, SC 29202
(803) 254-0479
www.columbiasc.net

Georgetown
Georgetown County Convention and Visitors' Center
PO Box 2068
Pawleys Island, SC 29585
(866) 368-TOUR or (800) 777-7705
www.visitgeorgetownsc.com

Greenville
Greenville Convention and Visitors' Bureau
PO Box 10527
Greenville, SC 29603
(864) 421-0000 or (800) 351-7180
www.greatergreenville.com

Hilton Head Island
Hilton Head Tourist, Visitor, and Convention Bureau
PO Box 5647
Hilton Head Island, SC 29938
(843) 785-3673
www.hiltonheadchamber.org

Myrtle Beach
Myrtle Beach Area Visitors' Bureau
PO Box 2115
Myrtle Beach, SC 29578
(843) 448-1629 or (800) 356-3016
www.myrtlebeachlive.com

Rock Hill
York County Convention and Visitors' Bureau
130 E. Main Street
PO Box 11377
Rock Hill, SC 29730
(803) 329-5200, or (800) 866-5200
www.yccvb.com

Spartanburg
Spartanburg Convention and Visitors' Bureau
298 Magnolia Street
Spartanburg, SC 29303
(863) 594-5050 or (800) 374-8326
www.spartanburgsc.org

Websites

www.discoversouthcarolina.com

Widely recognized as the best internet site for those planning a visit to South Carolina. It details every state and national park in the Palmetto State, the hundreds of permanent attractions by region and city, annual events and programs, and standard tourist sites as well as those out-of-the-way but equally distinctive points of interest. Each attraction and event listed includes hours of operation, costs, restrictions on use, local weather, driving directions, and contact information.

www.sciway.net

The official state site for a wealth of diverse information, Sciway (South Carolina Information Highway) provides dozens of government links covering the state's history, vital statistics, entertainment, tourism, calendar of events, maps, churches, economic development, libraries and museums, and weather. Of particular interest, Sciway provides "WebCams" that offer live video feeds from the cities most frequently visited by tourists. The site also includes state-sponsored links regarding African-American history in South Carolina, current employment opportunities, government information, city and county histories, and general facts about the Palmetto State.

www.sc-heritagecorridor.org

This site is sponsored by the state of South Carolina and was developed by private citizens' groups, conservation organizations, businesses, and individual communities to promote visitation to sites central in the state's history. The heritage corridor extends from Oconee County in the northwestern corner of the state and runs along the Savannah River to Edisto Island and north to Charleston. The website highlights nature paths, mountain lakes, small but historic river communities, railway lines, and two-lane backroads through less visited towns. It includes a "photo album" and links to other internet sites.

www.50states.com

This site is similar to Sciway but not as extensive or complete. Nonetheless, it is quite valuable and recommended.

www.beentheresawthat.com/sc/south_carolina/pages/guide.htm

This website offers photos of the principal tourist destinations along with links to key attractions, travel books, tourist offices, maps, places to stay, restaurants, and travel packages.

www.southcarolinabedandbreakfast.com
The South Carolina Bed and Breakfast Association site lists B&Bs scattered from the coast to the mountains.

www.state.sc.us/scsl
Site of the South Carolina State Library in Columbia.

www.museum.state.sc.us
The South Carolina State Museum. The site includes summaries of permanent and special exhibits, tour information, and archival materials. The museum is located in Columbia.

The following websites are grouped according to principal tourist destinations:

Aiken
www.aiken.net

Beaufort
www.beaufort.com
www.beaufortcitysc.com

Charleston
local.msc.com/Charleston
www.charleston.net
www.charleston-us.com

Conway
www.cityofconway.com

Florence
www.cityofflorence.com
www.florencechamber.com/area

Greenville
www.downtowngreenville.com

Hilton Head Island
www.hhisland.com
www.hiltonheadisland.org

Myrtle Beach/Grand Strand:
www.welcomecenters.com/PPF/MyrtleBeach/SouthCarolina
www.myrtlebeachgolf.com
www.myrtlebeach-info.com
www.welcomecenters.com/myrtlebeach
www.discovermyrtlebeach.com

Sources and Further Reading

General Histories

Belcher, Ray. *Greenville County, South Carolina: From Cotton Fields to Textile Center of the World.* Charleston: The History Press, 2006.

Coclanis, Peter. *The Shadow of a Dream: Economic Life and Death in the South Carolina Low Country, 1670–1920.* New York: Oxford University Press, 1991.

Edgar, Walter. *South Carolina: A History.* Columbia: University of South Carolina Press, 1998.

Fraser, Walter J. *Charleston! Charleston!: The History of a Southern City.* Columbia: University of South Carolina Press, 1991.

Lewis, Catherine Heniford. *Horry County, South Carolina, 1730–1993.* Columbia: University of South Carolina Press, 1998.

Moore, John Hammond. *Columbia and Richland County: A South Carolina Community, 1740–1990.* Columbia: University of South Carolina Press, 1992.

Specialized Works

Bartlett, Irving, H. *John C. Calhoun: A Biography.* New York: W. W. Norton, 1994.

Blumer, Thomas. *The Catawba Indian Nation of the Carolinas*. Mt. Pleasant, South Carolina: Arcadia Publishing, 2004.

Borick, Carl. *A Gallant Defense: The Siege of Charleston, 1780.* Columbia: University of South Carolina Press, 2003.

Brown, Douglas Summers. *The Catawba Indians: The People of the River.* Columbia: University of South Carolina Press, 1966.

Chepesiuk, Ron, and Edward J. Lee. *South Carolina in the Civil War: The Confederate Experience in Letters and Diaries.* Jefferson, North Carolina: McFarland and Co., 2004.

Cisco, Walter Brian. *Wade Hampton: Confederate Warrior, Conservative Statesman.* Herndon, Virginia: Potomac Books, 2006.

Cohodas, Nadine. *Strom Thurmond and the Politics of Southern Change.* Atlanta: Mercer University Press, 1995.

Detzer, David. *Allegiance: Fort Sumter, Charleston, and the Beginning of the Civil War.* New York: Harcourt, 2001.

Dusinberre, William. *Them Dark Days: Slavery in the American Rice Swamps*. Athens: University of Georgia Press, 2000.

Edelson, S. Max. *Plantation Enterprise in Colonial South Carolina.* Boston: Harvard University Press, 2006.

Edgar, Walter B. *Partisans and Redcoats: The Southern Conflict that Turned the Tide of the American Revolution.* New York: William Morrow, 2001.

Federal Writers' Project of the WPA. *South Carolina Slave Narratives.* Carlisle, Massachusetts: Applewood Books, 2006.

Frederickson, Kari. *The Dixiecrat Revolt and the End of the Solid South, 1932–1968.* Chapel Hill: University of North Carolina Press, 2000.

Freehling, William. *Prelude to War: The Nullification Controversy in South Carolina, 1816–1836.* New York: Oxford University Press, 1992.

Grose, Philip G. *South Carolina at the Brink: Robert McNair and the Politics of Civil Rights.* Columbia: University of South Carolina Press, 2006.

Hayes, Jr., Jack Irby. *South Carolina and the New Deal.* Columbia: University of South Carolina Press, 2001.

Heidler, David S. and Jeanne T. Heidler. *Old Hickory's War: Andrew Jackson and the Quest for Empire.* Baton Rouge: Louisiana State University Press, 2003.

Helsley, Alexia Jones. *Beaufort, South Carolina: A History.* Charleston: The History Press, 2005.

Hirsch, Arthur. *Huguenots of Colonial South Carolina.* Columbia: University of South Carolina Press, 1999.

Holden, Charles. *In the Great Maelstrom: Conservatives in Post Civil War South Carolina.* Columbia: University of South Carolina Press, 2002.

Kantrowitz, Stephen. *Ben Tillman and the Reconstruction of White Supremacy.* Chapel Hill: University of North Carolina Press, 2000.

Krech, Shepard. *The Ecological Indian: Myth and History.* New York: W. W. Norton, 2000.

Lau, Peter F. *Democracy Rising: South Carolina and the Fight for Black Equality since 1865.* Lexington: University of Kentucky Press, 2006.

Lerch, Patricia. *Waccamaw Legacy: Contemporary Indians Fight for Survival.* Birmingham: University of Alabama Press, 2004.

Lerner, Gerda. *The Grimke Sisters from South Carolina: Pioneers for Women's Rights.* Chapel Hill: University of North Carolina Press, 2007.

Lesesne, Henry H. *A History of the University of South Carolina, 1940–2000.* Columbia: University of South Carolina Press, 2002.

Littlefield, Daniel. *Rice and Slaves: Ethnicity and the Slave Trade in Colonial South Carolina.* Urbana: University of Illinois Press, 1991.

McCaig, Donald. *Rhett Butler's People.* New York: St. Martin's Press, 2007.

Merrell, James. *The Indians of the New World: Catawbas and Their Neighbors from European Contact through the Era of Removal.* Chapel Hill: University of North Carolina Press, 1989.

Mooney, James and George Ellison. *James Mooney's History, Myths, and Sacred Formulas of the Cherokees.* Fairview, North Carolina: Bright Mountain Books,1992.

Myers, Andrew H. *Black, White, and Olive Drab: Racial Integration at Fort Jackson, South Carolina and the Civil Rights Movement.* Charlottesville: University of Virginia Press, 2006.

Poole, W. Scott. *South Carolina's Civil War: A Narrative History.* Atlanta: Mercer University Press, 2005.

Prince, Jr., Eldred E. *Long Green: The Rise and Fall of Tobacco in South Carolina.* Athens: University of Georgia Press, 2000.

Pritzger, Barry M. *A Native American Encyclopedia: History, Cultures, and Peoples.* New York: Oxford University Press, 2000.

Remini, Robert V. *Andrew Jackson: The Course of American Democracy, 1833–1845.* Baltimore: Johns Hopkins University Press, 1998.

Robertson, David. *Sly and Able: A Political Biography of James F. Byrnes.* New York: W. W. Norton, 1994.

Ruymbeke, Bertrand Van. *From New Babylon to Eden: The Huguenots and Their Migration to Colonial South Carolina.* Columbia: University of South Carolina Press, 2006.

Simms, William Gilmore. *The Life of Francis Marion.* Charleston: The History Press, 2007.

Sinha, Manisha. *The Counterrevolution of Slavery: Politics and Ideology in Antebellum South Carolina.* Chapel Hill: University of North Carolina Press, 2002.

Stannard, David E. *American Holocaust: The Conquest of the New World.* New York: Oxford University Press, 1992.

Thomas, John Peyre. *History of the South Carolina Military Academy.* Lexington, South Carolina: Palmetto Bookworks, 1991.

Washington-Williams, Essie Mae. *Dear Senator: A Memoir by the Daughter of Strom Thurmond.* New York: Regan Books, 2005.

Weiner, Marli. *Mistresses and Slaves: Plantation Women in South Carolina, 1830–1880.* Urbana: University of Illinois Press, 1997.

Weir, Robert M. *Colonial South Carolina: A History.* Columbia: University of South Carolina Press, 1997.

Wilson, David K. *The Southern Strategy: Britain's Conquest of South Carolina and Georgia, 1775–1780.* Columbia: University of South Carolina Press, 2005.

Index of Place Names

Must-See Sites are highlighted in bold.